DILEMMAS OF
ECONOMIC COERCION

DILEMMAS OF ECONOMIC COERCION

Sanctions in World Politics

Edited by
Miroslav Nincic
and
Peter Wallensteen

PRAEGER SPECIAL STUDIES • PRAEGER SCIENTIFIC

New York • Philadelphia • Eastbourne, UK
Toronto • Hong Kong • Tokyo • Sydney

Library of Congress Cataloging in Publication Data

Main entry under title:

Dilemmas of economic coercion.
    Includes index.
    1. Sanctions (International law) 2. International
economic relations. I. Nincic, Miroslav.
II. Wallensteen, Peter, 1945–
JX1246.D54 1983   341.5′8   83-21191
ISBN 0-03-064236-1

Published in 1983 by Praeger Publishers
CBS Educational and Professional Publishing
a Division of CBS Inc.
521 Fifth Avenue, New York, NY 10175 USA
© 1983 by Praeger Publishers
All rights reserved
3456789   052   987654321
Printed in the United States of America
on acid-free paper

TABLE OF CONTENTS

1

ECONOMIC COERCION AND FOREIGN POLICY

Miroslav Nincic
and
Peter Wallensteen

THE GROWTH OF ECONOMIC COERCION

Economic sanctions are increasingly central to the foreign policy of those nations that can credibly resort to such instruments of external coercion. Whether or not one regards them as a welcome tool of coercion in international affairs, their importance cannot be slighted nor their foundations overlooked. Currently, the United States is applying economic pressure against the Soviet Union and, following the repression of the Solidarity movement, against Poland too. Nicaragua is the victim of an economic boycott instigated by Washington, as are Cuba and, to a certain extent, Vietnam, Angola, Mozambique, Iran, Iraq, and Libya. The United States has sought to influence *specific* policies by such means as well: as when economic aid has been made contingent upon attainments in human rights or on measures of nuclear nonproliferation by the recipient. The U.S. has not been alone in its readiness to pursue foreign policy ends through economic coercion.

Arab nations opposed to the Camp David agreements have sought to punish Cairo's adherence to the accord by curtailing economic cooperation with Egypt. The European Economic Community responded to Argentina's invasion of the Falkland Islands with economic sanctions. When relations between Moscow and Peking deteriorated, the Soviet Union withdrew the substantial assistance it had provided its ideological rival. The Russians also mustered all their capacity for economic retaliation against Yugoslavia when that nation embarked on an independent path, as well as against Albania when Tirana sided with China in the Sino–Soviet rivalry. More recently, China curtailed its own economic relations with Albania when the latter refused to support its invasion of Vietnam.

Economic pressure has become a particularly frequent foreign policy tool since 1945. There had been earlier instances of economic coercion (e.g., the Continental Blockade), but they were not very frequent—the tariff wars of the late 19th century or the beggar–my–neighbor policies of the interwar years had a different character and involved the use of economic means for economic ends. The recent emergence of this instrument of foreign policy can be traced to two major circumstances: the first involving principally the superpowers, the second concerning the nature of the international economy.

As the Cold War locked its protagonists into two rival military blocs, and as the potential costs of their confrontation grew, economic coercion became a less perilous manner of fighting the East–West conflict. A comprehensive strategic embargo was initiated by the United States in the late 1940s and was targeted directly against the Soviet Union and its Warsaw Pact allies. Curtailments of grain deliveries, of oil and pipeline equipment, of air traffic, and of movements of people were associated with this embargo. Apart from direct economic pressure against the Soviet bloc, each superpower has extended the use of economic pressure to Third World nations whenever this has been deemed a suitable tool for East–West confrontation.

Growing international economic interdependence has been a second circumstance encouraging the resort to external economic coercion. Foreign trade and the flow of capital among nations have expanded significantly in the post–war period and have generated vulnerabilities that would have been absent in a world of greater autarky. This has led, in part, to increased leverage among like–minded nations with similar economies, but it has been most relevant to relations between less compatible states. Still, interdependence is a knife that cuts two ways, for it means that any disruption of an economic relationship may ramify further than intended and, in particular, that it will create costs for the initiator as well as the target. At a minimum, economic coercion seems to require that the latter should suffer more than the former (or than the former's friends) which, in turn, implies *uneven* levels of mutual vulnerability. Interdependence might therefore not have been a major source of external economic pressure had it not been sufficiently *asymmetrical*. Networks of international economic relationships associated with significant inequality and asymmetric levels of dependence, of the sort identified and dissected by a recent and vast body of literature[1] were necessary to the surge in economic pressure. This has been as true of East–West relations as of those between developed and developing nations.

Some conceptual clarifications are called for at this point. Economic coercion will be defined as the imposition of economic pain by one government on another in order to attain some political goal. It is implemented, or at least initiated, by political authorities who thus intervene in the "normal" operation of economic relations (whether these involve market, centrally planned, or mixed economies). Interventions undertaken for economic ends (e.g., "trigger" prices designed to protect steel producers) obviously do not come under this heading, only those related to political goals. The nature of these goals will be discussed later but it will be useful, at the outset, to distinguish economic coercion (as defined here) from *economic warfare*. Although the boundary between the two is admittedly fluid, in the latter case economic privations are imposed with a military objective, i.e., to weaken the target's capacity to wage war. The bombing of an enemy's industrial installations could be a valid example but, in most cases, economic warfare would involve purely economic actions directed to a military objective. Cutting vital exports to the adversary is probably the major form of economic warfare. Shutting out the other side's imports or, for example, preemptive buying on world markets of goods needed for his war effort,[2] are other methods. Since Napoleon's Continental Blockade, economic war has generally occurred in tandem with acute military rivalries.

Often, however, it is difficult to distinguish such measures from economic sanctions since the line between political and military goals is evanescent and, even when adequate distinctions can be made, both objectives may be pursued by the same means. For example, the purpose of U.S. controls of its exports (and those of its allies) to the Soviet Union has been to undermine Russia's military capacity by depriving it of relevant technology; controls, however, have also been designed to demonstrate distaste for Soviet communism, to punish specific policies, to display toughness in Cold War sparring, and so forth. Still, the distinction can be made, and it is useful to locate economic sanctions on a continuum of foreign policy instruments distinguished by their coerciveness. At its least coercive end, such a continuum would be anchored by *diplomatic bargaining* by which external objectives are pursued by exchanges founded on reciprocity and often coupled with persuasion. At the opposite end, adjustments in other nations' policies can be pursued by *military force*, by the direct destruction of life and property. Economic sanctions occupy a middle ground between the two extremes. They are coercive but not directly destructive. This middle ground is also shared by most forms of covert intervention in the affairs of other countries. But, whereas infiltration, propaganda, and the clandestine support of opposition groups are within the purview of many nations, effective economic coercion is the practical prerogative of a bare handful of members of the international community.

SANCTIONS AND FOREIGN POLICY GOALS

It is generally assumed that the principal purpose of economic sanctions is to influence the policies of the nation to which the policy is directed. To force it, by the imposition of economic pain, to act in a manner that conforms more closely to the initiator's preferences and interests. In turn, this can be achieved by forcing the target's political authorities to alter their policies or, failing that, by causing their removal as a result of the economic dislocation produced by the sanctions.

In the first case, it is assumed that the economic costs would induce the victim nation's decision makers, out of concern for the national welfare and their own incumbency, to abandon the course that provoked the economic retribution. A loss of external markets, of needed goods and capital, would lead them to reason that the costs of the controversial policy outweigh its benefits. For example, the sanctions imposed by 17 Arab nations against Egypt because of Camp David were mainly intended to force the Egyptian leadership to renege on its accommodationist policy. The apparent intent of

Washington's sanctions against Nicaragua is to pressure the Sandinistas to withdraw their military support of El Salvador's leftist rebels and to loosen Managua's ties to Castro.

Although this may be the main function that is popularly attributed to sanctions, instances of major policy changes under economic pressure are quite rare, as the studies in this volume demonstrate. Usually, in fact, the target government will adhere steadfastly to its chosen policy, and it may even be that the initiators doubt their own ability to force governments, via sanctions, to abandon policies to which they are firmly committed. Official declamations notwithstanding, it may be that the real intent is to engineer the ousting of the recalcitrant government and to replace it with a more compliant set of leaders. The idea is that other politically potent actors, as well as the nation's public, will blame the incumbents for bringing the economic difficulties upon them, resist their clinging to such costly policies, and ultimately remove them from power by any means necessary. This is what Galtung, in his contribution to this volume, terms the "naive" theory of economic sanctions. (Its foundations are further challenged in Wallensteen's own piece.)

When, following Belgrade's apostasy, Stalin recalled Russian technical advisors, cut off trade with Yugoslavia, canceled promised loans, and forced Soviet allies to follow his example, the expectation was not that the Yugoslav leaders would repent but that they would be overthrown by groups loyal to Moscow. Indeed, when contemplating these measures the Soviet dictator boasted, "As soon as I move my little finger, Tito will be thrown out."[3]

Similarly, U.S. actions against Cuba seem to have been motivated more by the hope of causing Castro's downfall rather than by the expectation that he could be forced to reform: "to make it plain," as George Ball indicated at the time, "to the people of Cuba and to elements of the power structure of the regime that the present regime cannot serve their interests."[4]

Although neither of the two regimes has fallen as a result of the sanctions, it may be that governmental instability can indeed be increased by externally created economic dislocations. The ouster of Chile's President Allende was, for example, encouraged by the problems resulting from American efforts to promote economic disruption by blocking credits to Chile and by other forms of economic pressure. Still, such sanctions are rarely the main cause of a government's overthrow. In the Chilean case, it was principally the consequence of the opposition of the country's upper and middle classes, as well as of right–wing military officers, to the redistributive policies promoted by the regime. Also, whereas economic pressures may hasten political decay in a highly polarized society, it may produce the opposite effect in a nation where cleavages run less deep. Numerous examples testify to this possibility. The sanctions directed against Sadat by the hard–line nations may, for instance, have strengthened domestic support for the Egyptian government (a tendency encouraged by Mr. Sadat's suggestions that other Arab states grew rich while Egypt bore the brunt of the conflict with Israel). Tito's internal popularity was also enhanced by Russian belligerence and a similar conclusion might apply to Castro's position in the face of U.S. pressure.

None of this is surprising. The spectacle of an implacably hostile superpower wielding its economic might against a weak and beleaguered nation will usually rouse the patriotic indignation of its population and generate a "rally–round–the–flag" effect to the government's benefit (as discussed in Galtung's, Wallensteen's, and Green's contributions).

On the whole then, the effectiveness of economic sanctions seems rather doubtful—at least if the purpose is to force a significant policy change or to cause the removal of an unpalatable government. Their overall usefulness has not, however, been refuted since these objectives do not exhaust the functions that can be served by economic coercion. Sometimes, political elites probably do understand the limited ability of sanctions to induce immediate political compliance, but this may not be their intent. Frequently, in fact, the purpose is to *deter* objectionable *future* policies by demonstrating an ability to retaliate rather than to modify extant behavior. If the undesirable behavior is punished with sufficient severity it may not be repeated by the target country. In addition, the example of the chastisement may discourage *other* countries from engaging in the unacceptable activities. The interests of the sanctioning country can thus be promoted although the initial offense has not been undone. For example, another purpose of the measures against Cuba was, according to George Ball, to discourage other Latin American nations from emulating Castro's policies.[5] It is unlikely, in retrospect, that the Carter Administration really believed that a Russian withdrawal from Afghanistan could be forced through economic pressure. The more plausible intention was to deter further instances of Soviet aggression. Although Stalin probably hoped to cause the disintegration of Tito's regime, the wish to discourage similar displays of independence on the part of other communist countries (some of which were of greater strategic importance to the Soviet Union) may have been a more potent motive for the economic retaliation.

Although deterrence may often motivate external sanctions, it is also in the nature of deterrence that their success in this respect cannot be confidently assessed. An absence of further instances of the undesirable behavior cannot be taken as definitive proof of the sanctions' effectiveness since it cannot be known for certain whether, without the sanctions, the target nation would have acted differently. Nevertheless, the effectiveness of the sanction can at least be plausibly inferred from what is known of the needs and motivations of the governments to which the dissuasion is directed. With this caveat, it does seem that economic coercion, particularly when coupled with political pressure, may often perform a useful deterrent function. Although other concerns presumably affected Soviet caution in the decision not to intervene militarily in Poland to quell the Solidarity movement, the memory of the sanctions that attended the invasion of Afghanistan might help explain why Poland was spared the fate that befell Czechoslovakia in 1968. Similarly, the economic coercion to which Yugoslavia was once subjected may have played some part in discouraging emulation of Tito's independent path elsewhere in the Soviet bloc.

Thus, sanctions may produce a learning effect, either for the target over the longer term or for other putative transgressors. At the same time, the initiator too may learn from the effects of his own actions, and a failure of the sanction may induce a reluctance to attempt this form of coercion again. (The failure of Soviet economic pressure against Yugoslavia in 1948 may have led Moscow to opt for military action against Hungary in 1956.)

On the whole then, there is less reason to dismiss the utility of sanctions if deterrence is their goal than if their aim is to alter current policies of the target state. Yet, even this typically may not be their major purpose and it may be that they are usually meant to produce a *domestic*, rather than external, effect. Changing the behavior of other nations may be less important to the initiator's government than addressing the desires of domestic political groups and tending to the incumbents' own political interests. For example, it could be argued that the principal objective of the Carter Administration's retaliation against the Soviet Union was to demonstrate to the American public that aggression in Afghanistan would not be met by passive acquiescence. Forceful action typically produces a surge of domestic support for U.S. presidents. This is a benefit which, in the case of sanctions, does not involve the risks that would be associated with military measures. Similarly, the support of many governments for the economic boycott of Ian Smith's Rhodesia was apparently intended as a display of opposition to racist policies and meant for domestic consumption within the initiator nations. Indeed, from the initiator's perspective, sanctions may be most valuable for the symbolic content they convey domestically and the added support that this may mean for the political elite. As *The New York Times* observed, following the U.S. ban on imports of Iranian oil in 1980: "The decisions . . . appeared to many to be more effective in bolstering the President than in bringing the release of the hostages."[6]

It is a matter of realism rather than cynicism to understand that, typically, the major objective of external economic coercion is to advance the interests of the government applying it. In any case, of all the ends that sanctions can plausibly be intended to promote, it is here that such policies may be most effective. Not all of the effects of sanctions can be anticipated, however, and many of those that should be expected may actually be counterproductive to the initiator's interests.

DILEMMAS OF ECONOMIC SANCTIONS

Although the professed purpose of the sanctions is often to weaken the position of the foreign government pursuing the objectionable policy, the opposite effect is frequently produced. For, as we have pointed out, domestic support that might otherwise have been denied the government may be readily granted when it is suffering an external assault. Paradoxically, and in the short run at least, the major beneficiaries of the economic measures could be its targets.

Just as counterproductively, the sanctions may drive a nation into the arms of the initiator's adversaries—weakening the international position of the country that is applying the pressures. Clearly, the other benefits of the sanction must be weighed against this danger. A major consequence of Soviet attempts to jeopardize Yugoslavia's economy was to drive that country into much closer commercial ties with the capitalist world and toward a nonaligned foreign policy that has often tilted toward the West. Although Castro had been moving into the Soviet orbit before American sanctions were applied, the sustained pressure to which the Cuban economy was subjected further strengthened its links to the Eastern bloc—a conclusion also reached by a study of the Commerce Department's International Trade Administration.[7] Much the same could be said of recent U.S. policy toward Nicaragua. Similarly, it seems evident that the U.N. sponsored economic boycott of Rhodesia (porous though it was) reinforced the commercial bonds between Salisbury and Pretoria.

Occasionally, desired effects may be produced over the long term: U.S. sanctions forced the close ties between the Soviet Union and China which demonstrated to Peking how unsatisfactory relations with the Soviet Union could be. Ultimately, this produced a wider rift between the two than might otherwise have occurred—an unanticipated, but from Washington's perspective nevertheless welcome, consequence of the United States' attempts to isolate the People's Republic in the 1950s. More frequently, however, the effect of sanctions is to provide one's rival with a new partner and ally. To this should be added the danger that the economic coercion might, directly or indirectly, injure the commercial interests of the initiator's own friends and weaken the solidarity of his own camp. Recent attempts by the Reagan Administration to increase the Soviet Union's economic difficulties by pressuring a number of West European countries to downgrade their economic relations with the Soviets met with substantial resistance and did not advance the cause of Western unity.

The economic partners of the actual target will, as a rule, also suffer some indirect effects of the sanctions and, if the aim is to weaken the rival groupings' overall economic capacity, this may be to the initiator's benefit. Still, the situation is rarely that simple, and, while the initiator's adversaries may bear some economic costs, their solidarity may actually be reinforced in the face of the hostile external pressure. Heightened intrabloc solidarity could stem from a bolstered sense of common purpose and destiny; the foreign threat might also make it easier for the group's leader to assert his authority and control. On the other hand, it is conceivable that the hostility of the member nations could be directed toward the country whose behavior brought on the sanctions, rather than the nation imposing them. This will presumably be determined by the extent to which the other members of the group identify with the policies that provoked the external retaliations. For example, other Latin American nations may have suffered the indirect consequences of the U.S. and European attempts to apply economic punishment to Argentina for its invasion of the Falkland Islands. But most of these countries viewed the Argentine action as an instance of the struggle against the vestiges of colonialism and granted it their political support. Overall then, the manner in which such policies can backfire should be considered when evaluating their net benefits. It should also be recognized that current economic sanctions may jeopardize the initiator's *subsequent* ability to pursue foreign policy goals via economic pressure (this point is further discussed in Paarlberg's contribution). The more total is the present punishment, the more one's future capacity to apply such measures may be undermined. Partly, this is because the target is forced to find other economic partners or to enhance its self-sufficiency—we have already alluded to this and the point is developed by other authors in this volume—but this is also so because the initiator's means of economic coercion may be exhausted as it curtails its trade and investment relations with the target (even if the target made few adaptive responses). Quite simply, if almost all links are cut, there is little left with which to inflict *additional* economic pain. Total denial can, of course, be translated into *incentives* for good behavior since the beneficial relations can be restored in response to a change of policy or an abstention from future misconduct. But this could be precluded in a number of ways. The mobilization of domestic hostility toward the target, which typically accompanies the government's use of economic sanctions, may yield a more lasting effect than had been anticipated, and a relaxation of the pressure may be considered unacceptable by an aroused public. This could be true even if the initiator also suffered from the sanction since it could be feared that a retrenchment would signal an inability to absorb costs and hence weaken the credibility of future threats. Thus, there may be an element of incompatibility between short–term and long–term interests and this too should be taken into account.

A contradiction of another sort should also be considered. We suggested above that a major objective of sanctions might be to create a favorable domestic impact benefiting the government's image and incumbency. To achieve this aim, it is evident that the sanction should be overtly applied and well-advertised. But the more conspicuous it is, the more difficult it may be for the target government to capitulate in terms of its own internal politics. Although it may be more important for the initiator to bolster its internal position than to force compliance on another nation, the two goals could be mutually inconsistent. One author has, in fact, argued that the most effective (from a foreign policy perspective) U.S. sanctions were those which were most discreetly applied.[8]

THE LEVERS OF ECONOMIC COERCION

We have discussed the reasons for the increased interest in economic sanctions as instruments of foreign policy, and we have examined the intents and dilemmas associated with such sanctions. It is now useful to ask also whether certain aspects of external economic relations are most likely to be put to political use. The question can be formulated from several standpoints. One can inquire whether economic pressure is more likely to operate through restriction of *imports* from the target or of *exports* to that nation. It is also worth asking whether certain *types* of *goods* are more apt to be the object of sanctions than others.

Exports are most frequently the chosen tool, as exemplified by U.S. attempts to block grain shipments to the Soviet Union following the invasion of Afghanistan, or by the more recent efforts to restrict transfers of advanced technology to the Soviets. Imports too are sometimes used as instruments of economic pressure. Thus, Britain's sanctions against Rhodesia relied heavily on depriving that country's tobacco industry of British and other foreign markets.

Similarly, U.S. sugar imports from Cuba were barred in 1960. Yet it is unlikely that sanctions could selectively involve only imports or exports: counter-sanctions by the target state will typically lead to a reduction in both, independently of the initiator's own emphasis. Even without explicit counter-sanctions, it would be difficult for the target to keep importing from a country when its export earnings have been significantly reduced.

Let us, however, examine the attractiveness of various goods as objects of economic sanctions. An obvious observation is that a good (or service) will not be very valuable from the perspective of economic coercion if it is easily available from a source other than the initiator. Thus, supply must be concentrated and accounted for primarily by the initiator or by nations over whose policies the initiator exercises sufficient control. The greater the number of suppliers of a commodity, the more difficult it is to politicize its availability. On the other hand, a credible sanction should hurt the target more than the initiator, and this may not be the case if the former represents the latter's principal market. From the initiator's point of view, the ideal situation is thus one of near monopoly coupled with a very marginal dependence on the target as an outlet for the good. From the reverse perspective, a high level of supply dispersion, associated with a very concentrated demand, puts the potential target in the least vulnerable position. This is the idea behind consumer cooperatives within many nations or, for example, of the International Energy Agency (which strives to coordinate the oil needs of rich industrial nations in order to avoid consumer competition and unnecessary concessions to oil producing countries).

Not only should supply be concentrated, but the good in question should have no obvious substitutes. Even a monopoly over some commodity will yield little political leverage if the need that it satisfies can be adequately met by another good. Tea and coffee are clearly mutual substitutes and to a certain extent so are iron and tin, or copper and aluminum. On the other hand, there are few obvious substitutes for petroleum or advanced microchips.

Finally, the need associated with the good in question should be experienced as vital by the target. Although the notion of what is vital may depend on social and cultural considerations, as well as on a nation's level of economic development, neither of the previous conditions will have any practical meaning if the good addresses a need that is irrelevant or redundant.

These points are illustrated by some of the sanctions we have described in this chapter. In the U.S.–Cuban case, the target's position was further weakened by the ready availability of sugar from non–Cuban sources. The United States could, at minimal cost to itself, inflict considerable economic damage on Cuba by shifting its imports to other Caribbean and Central American countries. In another vein, American use of grain as a political weapon has suffered from the ability of other nations (e.g., Argentina) to replace it as supplier to the Soviet Union and from the fact that the Soviet market is clearly a major outlet for American grain. It has benefited, on the other hand, from the vital need that grain satisfies (especially given the nature of the Soviet diet).

Let us examine the goods that are frequently used for economic coercion. We have already noted the use of food, as well as of oil, raw materials, or agricultural products other than food (tobacco, for instance). Here, the source of the good is easily identifiable and usually involves rather asymmetric trade relations. However, the more advanced the goods exchanged, the more symmetrically integrated are the relations involved. Indeed, the more advanced the product, the more difficult it is to determine its origin: it may be designed in one country, require the raw materials of another, the labor of a third, and the finance of a fourth. Although this is part of international divisions of labor associated with multinational corporations, it makes it more difficult to define a discrete target and decreases the political feasibility of the sanction.

Thus, in U.S.–Japanese commerce, we encounter embargoes on soybeans but not on cars. As studies in this volume indicate, American efforts to get Western European countries to withhold technologically advanced pipeline equipment from the Soviet Union threaten an entire international economic network.[9]

Military transfers represent a particular case of highly sophisticated goods that are, nevertheless, often the object of economic sanctions. Unlike many other modern industrial goods, weapons production follows national boundaries rather closely. At the same time, supply is relatively concentrated, while demand is dispersed. The fact that the security needs that military goods supposedly meet are deemed vital (and that there is often much urgency involved) makes the manipulation of supply an attractive tool of political influence.

But there are other sides to this kind of good as well. Given the intense demand for arms, a target will try very hard to circumvent sanctions. Although supply of the most sophisticated military equipment is quite concentrated, this is less true at slightly lesser levels of technological complexity. Thus, other suppliers may seek to supplant the initiator either in search of economic gain or of political influence.

Denial of access to capital is a newer form of sanction. Capital is the fuel of all economies and it tends to follow political boundaries very imperfectly. Measures to control private credits to the Soviet Union are an example of the foreign policy uses of economic capital. The decision to freeze Iranian financial assets in the United States, in response to the taking of American hostages, is an example of another sort.

The international mobility of people, rather than of capital, can also be manipulated for purposes of diplomatic coercion. Indeed, for many years U.S. citizens were prohibited from traveling to certain Communist countries, presumably as part of a comprehensive embargo effort. The same has applied to the travel of citizens of a number of Arab nations to Israel.

Finally, the curtailment of communications and transportation can also be used as part of campaigns of economic coercion. For example, trade can be affected by withdrawing transit privileges or by revoking docking and landing rights. The visibility of this form of retribution has made it a popular component of sanctions designed for demonstrative purposes.

Each form of sanction is likely to be part of future patterns of international influence and coercion. The circumstances that have made sanctions increasingly used tools of foreign policy in the postwar period are likely to exist during coming decades. There is, indeed, little indication that economic interdependence will be reduced in the foreseeable future; on the contrary, the multinationalization of industrial production, the reliance on external sources of raw materials, and the transnational integration of financial markets is likely to grow. Also, there is little indication that this interdependence will assume a more symmetric nature, maintaining at least the possibility of unilateral pressures. Moreover, the reticence of the major powers, and the superpowers in particular, to use military force will probably not diminish: the seemingly inexorable nuclear proliferation, as well as the spread of highly sophisticated conventional arms, will make the consequences of even limited conflicts increasingly unpalatable. Some of these trends may make certain types of goods, such as industrial products created through a multinational effort, less appropriate as instruments of economic pressure. Others, such as controls of capital flows, may be experimented with more frequently.

Sanctions will continue to be associated with many of the dilemmas outlined in the previous section. Normal learning patterns suggest that they may be used in a more carefully calculated manner, but many of their problems and counterproductive effects are simply inherent in the nature of economic tools of external pressure. Whether one regards sanctions with equanimity or misgivings will depend upon how one assesses the options. A new form of coercion is only as attractive or unattractive as are its alternatives.

NOTES

1. Representative literature includes: Samir Amin, *Accumulation on a World Scale* (New York: Monthly Review Press, 1974); Arghiri Emmanuel, *Unequal Exchange: A Study of the Imperialism of Trade* (New York: Monthly Review Press, 1972); André Gunder Frank, *Capitalism and Underdevelopment in Latin America* (New York: Monthly Review Press, 1969); Johan Galtung, "A Structural Theory of Imperialism," *Journal of Peace Research*, 8 (1971), pp. 81–117.

2. For example, during World War II, both the United States and Great Britain purchased large amounts of Turkish chrome as well as Spanish and Portuguese wolfram with the purpose of depriving Germany of these raw materials.

3. Vladimir Dedijer, *The Battle Stalin Lost* (New York: Viking, 1970), p. 35.

4. Quoted in Margaret P. Doxey, *Economic Sanctions and International Enforcement* (Oxford: Oxford University Press, 1971), p. 41.

5. *Ibid.*, p. 41.

6. Steven Ratner, "The Economic Warfare was also Psychological," *The New York Times*, November 18, 1979, p. 32.

7. Barbara Crossette, "Study Says Trade Ban Is Driving Cuba Closer to Soviet," *The New York Times*, April 4, 1982, p. 1.

8. Richard S. Olson, "Economic Coercion in World Politics," *World Politics* (July, 1979), pp. 471–94.

9. Here, however, the line between economic sanction and economic warfare (above, end of first section) is blurred.

2

ON THE EFFECTS OF
INTERNATIONAL ECONOMIC SANCTIONS

By Johan Galtung*

I. INTRODUCTION

It may seem preposterous to write about the effects of the economic sanctions currently in effect against Rhodesia since the process is not yet completed: we do not know how it will all end, and primary source material of a crucial nature is not yet available.[1] But the purpose of this chapter is more in the direction of a general the-

* This chapter is a revised version of a lecture given at the Department of Political Science, Makerere College, Kampala, Uganda, January 14, 1966; at Folkuniversitetet, Uppsala, Sweden, January 21, 1966; at a seminar organized by the Swedish International Development Authority and the Scandinavian Institute of African Studies, Gothenburg, Sweden, January 22, 1966; and at the Foreign Policy Association of the Swedish M.P.'s, Riksdagen, Stockholm, Sweden, March 10, 1966. The author wants to express his gratitude to the Scandinavian Institute of African Studies, Uppsala, Sweden, for a travel grant that made the research possible; to a large number of informants in Rhodesia and other African countries for their comments; and to colleagues at the International Peace Research Institute, Oslo, Norway. The responsibility for the conclusions drawn or indicated rests entirely with the author. The article may be identified as PRIO Publication 20-3, International Peace Research Institute, Oslo.

ory, using the case of Rhodesia as a source of examples and illustrations. The material on Rhodesia included here consists of some secondary sources, such as books and articles, and some primary sources, such as documents and other printed material; but the basic sources are mainly personal observation and a number of informal interviews with Rhodesian citizens (mostly businessmen) and with citizens of other African countries (mostly politicians), all dating from January 1966, about two months after UDI.[2] The purpose of such an exploratory study is obvious: to get some impressions about the psychological and social mechanisms of economic boycott when they are operating, instead of having to rely on retrospection. Besides, such an exploration can serve as a pilot study for a more thorough investigation both of the general theory of economic sanctions and other sanctions in the international system based on historical cases mainly in this century, and of the Rhodesian case in particular.[3] It is as such that this article must be interpreted, not as anything more pretentious. Thus, although it is our impression that the interview excerpts presented are typical of attitudes of the majority of whites in Rhodesia and that the phenomena reported are significant, we have no formal way of proving this contention—for instance, by representative sampling.

Another warning may also be in order: the reader who looks for anything like a complete account of the antecedents and present circumstances of the entire complex of problems referred to today as "Rhodesia" will have to look elsewhere; in the present article only the bare minimum of background data and hypotheses is included, mainly in footnotes.[4]

This being said, the virtues of studying Rhodesia in order to understand better the local impact of international economic sanctions should be stressed. Rhodesia is in no sense a simple case but offers all the complexities of the modern world: racial strife, struggle for independence, complex relationships between national (UK), regional (OAU, Commonwealth), and universal (UN) sources of power, and the ingredient of North–South and East–West conflict. Thus, even though no one would generalize from the case of Rhodesia to other cases, an understanding of the Rhodesian case will serve as a basis for understanding other cases better.

II. THE GENERAL THEORY OF ECONOMIC SANCTIONS

We shall define sanctions as actions initiated by one or more international actors (the "senders") against one or more others (the "receivers") with either or both of two purposes: to punish the receivers by depriving them of some value and/or to make the receivers comply with certain norms the senders deem important. This definition at once raises an interesting question. It is not obvious that the same action or sanction can serve both purposes; in fact, modern penology does not seem to warrant much belief in punishment as a *general* method for making people comply.[5] Punishment may have other effects, as when criminals are kept off the streets and isolated in prisons where their deviant actions are hidden from the general view and thus are less consequential to the outside world, but this is not the same as making them comply.

Thus, when sanctions are discussed it makes good sense to ask which purpose is dominant. Imagine, in the Rhodesian case, that another policy had been enacted: that of rewarding the Smith government for any positive step toward majority rule, instead of punishing it for any step interpreted as a negative relative to the goal of majority rule. Expressed concretely, this would have meant a policy of increased trade, or increasingly favorable trade conditions, and more contact and more diplomatic cooperation as less discriminatory practices were introduced in Rhodesia, with a well–thought–out and well–communicated pattern of action: so much reward for so much compliance. Even a positive escalation process might be envisaged. Imagine that arguments in favor of such a policy as a method of bringing about compliance were in fact quite convincing. Nevertheless there would probably be counter–arguments to the effect that "This is selling out to the enemy," "This is rewarding sinfulness," "This means that any rascal can come around and do something nasty and then extort a reward for undoing the harm he has done—which is tantamount to blackmail," "There will be inflationary effects and we shall soon run out of rewards," and "Who will pay for all this, anyhow?"

Without belittling the significance of any one of these arguments, it makes good sense to ask a politician engaged in sanction policies, "If you cannot have both, which outcome would you prefer, punishment without compliance or compliance without punishment?" If he insists that punishment is a sufficient condition for compliance, then he is simply naive; if he insists that punishment is a necessary condition for compliance, then he is probably in addition highly punishment–oriented in the sense that punishment has become an automatic and probably also cherished goal in itself. This punishment–oriented attitude is probably fairly widespread, particularly as applied to the international system, and serves to maintain negative sanctions.[6] If compliance is not obtained, there is at least the gratification that derives from knowing (or believing) that the sinner gets his due, that the criminal has been punished. In this sense negative sanctions are safer than positive sanctions. And when hatred is strong, positive sanctions would probably be out of the question anyway.

In this chapter we shall disregard the punishment aspect and be interested in sanctions only as a way of making other international actors comply, and we shall concentrate on negative sanctions. As a reference for a more complete discussion, however, the following dimensions for classifying sanctions may be useful:

1. Are the sanctions *negative* (punishment for deviance) or *positive* (reward for compliance)?
2. Are the sanctions aimed at responsible *individuals* in a receiving nation, or are they *collective* (hitting the nation as a whole, including individuals and groups that are not particularly responsible)?
3. Are the sanctions *internal* (a result of changes arising inside the receiving nation) or are they *external* (having to do with the interaction pattern with other nations)?
4. Are the sanctions *unilateral* (only one sending nation) or *multilateral* (several sending nations, with regional sanctions being a special case) or *universal* (with all or almost all other nations participating)?
5. Are the sanctions *general* or *selective* (involving all possible measures or only some special measures)?
6. Are the sanctions *total* or *partial* (involving all or only some measures of a special kind)?
7. Types of sanctions (types of values of which the receiving nation is deprived):[7]

    a) diplomatic sanctions
       (1) nonrecognition
       (2) rupture of diplomatic relations
       (3) no direct contact with political leaders
       (4) no cooperation by international organizations
    b) communication sanctions
       (1) rupture of telecommunications
       (2) rupture of mail contact
       (3) rupture of transportation (ship, rail, road, air)
       (4) rupture of news communication (radio, newspapers, press agencies)
       (5) rupture of personal contacts (tourism, family visits)
    c) economic sanctions
       (1) internal destruction (economic sabotage, strikes)
       (2) rupture of trade relations (economic boycott)
          (a) hitting imports to receiving nation (import boycott)
          (b) hitting exports from receiving nation (export boycott)

       Economic boycott can comprise *goods, capital, services.* If passage of goods, capital, and/or services to or from the receiving country is reported, the boycott is *supervised*; if in addition passage is impeded, the boycott may be referred to as a *blockade.*

For simplicity we may disregard the cases of internal sanctions and sanctions directed at individuals: with the present structure of the international system, territorial integrity makes such actions—unilateral, multilateral, or universal—impossible unless they are combined with a military presence. In a future world, the supranational structure might include permanent enforcement machinery stationed in all nations—like local police stations in the nations of today—but this is for the future.[8] Thus, our discussion here is limited to *negative, collective,* and *external* sanctions, and like most other analysts we shall concentrate on the theory of *economic* sanctions.

The theory is simple. The input–output matrix of the economy of the receiving nation is inspected. The impact of partial or total boycott of selected imports or exports is calculated. As a matter of rational politics, maximum effect with minimum boycott is sought; in the case of a receiving nation for which there are accessible data on the economic system, this is a problem that might be left to computers. The ideal case would be that of a system in which total boycott of one product alone would be sufficient, and oil is often held to be this product.[9]

If the goal is to damage the economic system of the receiving nation without similarly damaging the sending nation, this can obviously be attained if a number of conditions that we can refer to as "the ideal case for an economic boycott" are fulfilled. The ideal conditions would be more or less as follows:

1. that imports have a very high loading on important sectors of the economy of the receiving nation;
2. that there is no internal substitute for the imports;
3. that a high loading of the important imports comes from the sending nation(s);
4. that there is no external substitute for these imports, so that the receiving nation cannot threaten to change trade–partners;
5. that the imports make up a very small part of the exports of the sending nation(s), and/or that the products can be exported to other nations;
6. that the exports from the receiving nation are sent mainly to the sending nation(s), and that there are no easy substitutes for them, so that the receiving nation cannot obtain income easily;
7. that these exports from the receiving nation can easily be obtained elsewhere by the sending nation(s) so that the sending nation(s) are not hurt economically and can threaten to change trade–partners, *or* that the exports cannot be obtained elsewhere by the sending nation(s) so that the sending nation(s) can demonstrate that they would rather suffer deprivation than touch products from the receiving nation; and
8. that trade relations are easily supervised and even controlled (as when the receiving nation is an island or is surrounded either by impenetrable terrain, such as swamps or deserts, or by nations that participate in the boycott).

It is easily seen that the case in which these conditions are met is that of a small economic satellite of a major economic power. In such a case, perhaps seventy-five percent, or perhaps even ninety percent, of both exports and imports of the small country may be with the big country, yet this trade volume may still be less than one percent of the big country's total trade. This trade structure occurs not infrequently in the present world, and it gives a major potential for control by the big nations of those small nations in their "sphere of interest," particularly since the power of any weapon lies more in its potential than in its actual use.

One could use this kind of situation as a point of departure for a complete theory of economic sanctions. The crucial concept here is *vulnerability*, which has an external and an internal component. The key to the understanding of vulnerability seems to be *concentration*: the more a country's economy depends on one product, and the more its exports consist of one product, and the more its exports and imports are concentrated on one trade–partner, the more vulnerable is the country. To launch economic sanctions without a careful examination of all these factors would be like launching a military campaign without military analysis.

Without going into a great many details, it is interesting to determine which countries rank highest in external vulnerability. As a first approximation, information about the percentage of the GNP comprising foreign trade (exports plus imports) is useful. Among the first ten ranks in the list given in the *World Handbook of Political and Social Indicators*[10] are four islands (Barbados, Mauritius, Cyprus, and Malta), and among the first ten ranks in a similar list in the UN's *Yearbook of National Accounts Statistics 1964* are three islands (Mauritius, Trinidad, Iceland) and Hong Kong, which for all practical purposes is an island. The two ranking lists are not identical, which reflects problems in connection with national accounts statistics more than changes between the periods of time the two lists cover. However, it is interesting to note that six of the first seven countries on the UN list are or have been under British rule. Also, the superpowers, the United States and the Soviet Union, rank eightieth and eighty–first on the *World Handbook* list (with foreign–trade percentages of seven and five), which marks them as particularly invulnerable. The People's Republic of China ranks seventy–ninth, France ranks sixty–seventh, and the United Kingdom, fifty–first. Clearly, the big powers are very different from the smaller powers in external vulnerability. On the other hand, the rank order correlation between the foreign–trade variable and GNP per capita is less than .10, so vulnerability should be seen more as a property of the small power than as a property of the poor nation. Thus, the general picture is that economic sanctions as a source of power tend to preserve existing power structures.

This becomes even more evident when we examine the extent

to which exports are limited to a few commodities and their markets to a few countries. The rank order correlation of .606 between Michael Michaely's indices of these two types of concentration suggests that these two aspects of external vulnerability tend to co-vary.[11] Most vulnerable on both counts (if we also take into consideration the percentage of the GNP comprising foreign trade) are Hong Kong, Trinidad, and Mauritius; least vulnerable are big countries such as the U.S., Brazil, Mexico, India, Argentina, and Colombia. Bigger countries of course have in general more diversity in raw materials and bigger domestic markets; hence they have more potential for diversified domestic industries, which can be converted to export industries. On the other hand, the rank order correlation between the *coefficient of commodity concentration* and the percentage of the GNP made up of trade is only .108, and the corresponding correlation for the *coefficient of geographic concentration* is only .098. Hence, even if there is concentration of exports in terms of commodities and trade–partners it does not follow that exports are very important for the GNP.

Let us then imagine that the three factors of concentration we have discussed (concentration in the economy, concentration in commodities, concentration in trade-partners) are of equal weight in determining external vulnerability. Of course, if sanctions were universal (and not unilateral) geographic concentration would not count; if sanctions were general (and not highly selective) commodity concentration would not count; and if sanctions were both universal and general (and total) then only the trade percentage of the GNP would count. But *a priori* it may be as difficult to make sanctions universal and general as it is to make them "bite." Hence, we have added the ranks for each country reported in Michaely's data on commodity concentration and geographic concentration[12] to its rank for the trade percentage of the GNP. The distribution is interesting, but it should be noticed that the socialist countries are not included in Michaely's lists, which comprise only forty countries. A high score on this index means low vulnerability and a low score means high vulnerability.

The least vulnerable countries are the United States (109 of 120 possible points), France (108), Italy and Japan (104), the Federal Republic of Germany (100), and the United Kingdom (99)—as one would expect. Most vulnerable is Mauritius with 9 points (3 is the minimum); then follow Trinidad and Panama (20) and Rhodesia which ranks high on both kinds of concentration (ninth and tenth) and on the trade percentage of its GNP (27 points, giving a rank of four on this composite vulnerability list; it ranks eighth on the list in the *World Handbook*). All countries with point scores lower than 50 are or have recently been colonies, which means that they are vulnerable relative to their former mother countries.

For our purpose it is significant that Rhodesia (here including Zambia and Malawi) ranks fourth on the score of external vulnerability, since what we say would apply *a fortiori* to less vulnerable countries. (This rank is based on combined data for the Federation of Rhodesia and Nyasaland for 1959, showing trade to be sixty–six percent of GNP, about half of that percentage comprising exports. Exports of Rhodesia alone, excluding Zambia and Malawi, constitute about forty–three percent of its GNP, according to the Supplement to the *Standard Bank Review*, indicating that Rhodesia's position on that variable is not lower than that of the former Federation, so that Rhodesia alone would not rank lower on the index of external vulnerability.) Most of the countries scored fall between Rhodesia and the United Kingdom, indicating that if they are vulnerable according to one of the variables, then they compensate for it on either or both of the remaining variables.

The determination of a nation's external vulnerability reflects only some of the ideal conditions for economic boycott described earlier. There are still the problems of how important the imports actually are, how easily internal or external substitutes can be found, and so on. Imagine then that all external conditions listed above (conditions 3-8) are obtained by extending the boycott from a unilateral through a regional to a universal action. Then the receiving nation is left with only three counterstrategies:

1. to train itself in sacrifice by doing without certain commodities, and preferably even liking it;
2. to restructure the national economy so as to absorb the shock of the boycott, by producing locally the imported commodities denied it or by making some substitutes for them, by finding alternative employment for people made jobless, and so forth; and
3. to organize changes of trade *with* third parties, or *via* third par-

ties,[13] or, if the boycott is truly universal, to engage in smuggling.

To what extent these counterstrategies are sufficient as defense will be discussed below; here it will be noted only that this repertory of defense measures is already quite limited. On the other hand, the world has yet to see a universal boycott.

The theory of the effects of economic warfare is now fairly similar to the theory of the effects of military warfare. Both kinds of warfare are means toward the same end: political disintegration of the enemy so that he gives up the pursuit of his goals. The method used is value–deprivation, which may or may not increase with time according to how the action proceeds and what countermeasures are enacted. Countermeasures may take the form of offensive measures (value–deprivation from the attacker) or defensive measures (reducing the value–deprivation inflicted upon oneself) of active or passive varieties.

We shall now distinguish between a naive and a revised theory of the effects of economic warfare. The *naive* theory of the relation between economic warfare (and also military warfare) and political disintegration sees some kind of roughly proportionate relation: the more value–deprivation, the more political disintegration.[14] The idea is that there is a limit to how much value–deprivation the system can stand and that once this limit is reached (resulting in a split in leadership or between leadership and people), then political disintegration will proceed very rapidly and will lead to surrender or willingness to negotiate. The theory can be illustrated as in Figure 2.1.

However, this theory disregards the simple principle of *adaptation*: that which seems unacceptable at the beginning of the conflict becomes acceptable as one gets used to life under hardship. Thus, the "upper limit" of what can be tolerated recedes as the value–deprivation progresses, and political disintegration becomes less easily obtainable. However, there remains an upper limit of value–deprivation, short of total destruction, that presents difficulties for the attacker. Even if we exclude moral problems, the attacker must recognize that he may have to restore the attacked nation and have to coexist with its new leadership, not to mention its future and possibly revanchist generations. Thus, an important de-

FIGURE 2.1

The Naive Theory of Economic Warfare

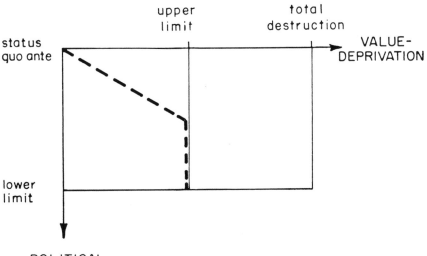

fense strategy is to indicate that one will hold out at least until the attacker's upper limit is reached.

But we refer to this theory as "naive" also because it does not take into account the possibility that value-deprivation may initially lead to political *integration* and only later—perhaps much later, or even never—to political disintegration. The basic point here is that value–deprivation creates the social conditions under which much more sacrifice is possible so that the limit for political disintegration will be reached much later. The theory can be illustrated as in Figure 2.2.

The problem is now under which conditions the revised theory is the more valid and under which conditions the naive theory is less naive. A short list of such conditions includes these:

1. The attack from the outside is seen as an attack on the group as a whole, not on only a fraction of it;
2. There is very weak identification with the attacker, preferably even negative identification; and

FIGURE 2.2

The Revised Theory of Economic Warfare

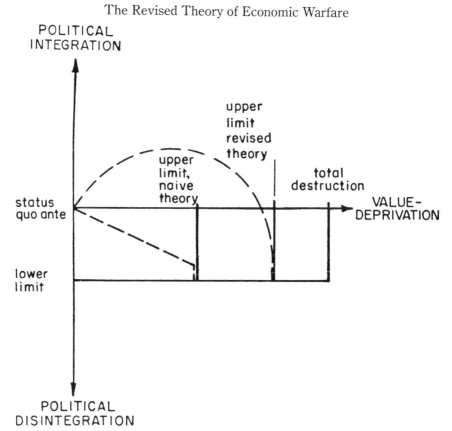

3. There is belief in the value of one's own goals in the sense that no alternative is seen as better.

The interesting thing is that in economic warfare, often even more than in military warfare, the first condition is almost immediately and automatically satisfied. The collective nature of economic sanctions makes them hit the innocent along with the guilty. They are in practice, if not in theory, an application of the principle of collective guilt. However, if the other two conditions are not satisfied, then this *may* turn to the benefit of the attacker. Internal dissension in the receiving nation may result when the people feel harassed.

The people may then bring pressure upon the leaders to change their policy—in other words, political disintegration.

Thus, the recipes for economic sanctions of various types are fairly obvious. Like a military operation, the logistics of sanctions can be worked out in great detail, and this can even have its bureaucratic appeal since there is an element of administrative challenge, as well as neatness, about the operation when modern, well-organized societies with good national bookkeeping are involved. At the same time it is obvious where the weaknesses of the theory of economic warfare lie. There are two weak points: (1) the idea that political disintegration is more or less proportionate to economic disintegration, and (2) the idea that economic disintegration cannot be counteracted. Of course, no politician of any standing would be so naive as to subscribe to the idea that economic sanctions—once they are effective, economically speaking—will automatically cause either partial or complete surrender. But the politician who is sophisticated at the verbal level may still be naive at the level of actions: he may simply be at a loss as to what to do when faced with the complexities of the effects of economic sanctions—or of other sanctions, for that matter. We shall try to describe systematically some hypotheses about such effects that are negative from the point of view of the sending nation(s), but before we do that, let us look more closely at the kind of theory the sending nation(s) (in this case, the United Kingdom) may have as to how the sanctions will eventually work.

Prime Minister Wilson's methodology and theory of economic sanctions have been set forth in some detail in speeches given in Parliament on December 10, 1965, and January 25, 1966.[15] First of all, there has been a policy of graduated escalation along two dimensions: starting with the United Kingdom, measures have proceeded from selective and partial sanctions toward practically general and total economic sanctions; they have proceeded from relatively unilateral action by the United Kingdom toward the universal action envisaged and hoped for. Some of this gradualism has been deliberate (to permit the threat of worse measures to be invoked at any time, as well as to prevent too much damage to Rhodesia, which will have to function in the future) and some of it has been a virtue of necessity. On the day of UDI, a number of financial measures excluding Rhodesia from the sterling area and from the preference

status enjoyed by Commonwealth members were introduced, together with a ban on Rhodesian tobacco imports to the United Kingdom and on weapons exports from the United Kingdom to
Rhodesia. Then, in the three months that followed UDI, most
moves toward complete boycott were made.

Incidentally, communications restrictions were remarkably
underutilized, particularly considering how tempting it must have
been to use them since white Rhodesians are heavily dependent on
such communications for maintaining their identity as an outpost of
British (if not Labour) civilization. The United Kingdom has, however, tried to control access to Rhodesia, probably partly to symbolize its sovereignty over the "runaway colony," partly to control the
information flow.[16]

The Wilson theory as to exactly how political disintegration will
take place within the very short time spans he announced in the first
weeks and months after UDI contains such elements as increasing
unrest among the whites due to unemployment and material depri-
vations resulting from reduced exports and imports. According to
this theory, either development may be used by the existing opposition elements in Rhodesia or may lead to the formation of new cen-
ters of opposition; in either case the opposition may make an appeal
to the governor, and a solution will be found through him. Thus, the
governor may symbolize a return to "law and order," and the troops
stationed in Zambia may be recalled at the governor's request. Exactly what may happen to Smith and his numerous followers in this
context is not clear, but then Wilson is speaking as a politician, not
as a social scientist.

Clearly, if political disintegration should take place it would happen through the dual effect of sanctions, which weakens the people
in power and strengthens those in opposition. For this to happen, as
Wallensteen points out, it is not sufficient that the sanctions are perceived as an evil; alternative courses of action must also be perceived as lesser evils.[17] Thus, it is Wilson's task not only to escalate
into a sanction pattern as harsh as possible, but also to present alternatives as acceptable as possible. To achieve the latter aim, a vision
of the near future that does not contain majority rule must be presented to the white Rhodesians—and the famous six points were designed to do this. What was held out to them was legal rule, not
majority rule.[18]

Equally clear is Smith's counterstrategy: to reverse the order of utilities. For that purpose, sanctions must appear as manageable, even slightly ridiculous, and the alternatives must be defined not merely as a return to the pre-UDI situation but as alternatives that will of necessity have even more negative implications for the white Rhodesians. There are many ways of achieving this purpose. One of them is to maneuver Wilson into a position in which, because of the African Commonwealth members, he is unable to offer an alternative that does not contain majority rule. Another method is censorship, so that information about attractive alternatives (as well as information about serious effects of the sanctions) does not reach the Rhodesian reader. To the extent that the reader is in general agreement with Smith, this method will work, because there will be no demand for these two types of news; they will both cause severe cognitive dissonance. But the major counterstrategy will always be to channel the effects of the sanctions themselves in the best possible directions—and this is the topic to which we now turn.

III. THE DEFENSE AGAINST ECONOMIC SANCTIONS

Two principles for discussing counterstrategies against economic sanctions have here been presented. One of them follows from the logic of the attacker. There are three holes in this system, however, even when the sanctions are universal (adaptation to sacrifice, restructuring the economy to absorb the shock, and smuggling). The other principle follows from the logic behind what we have called the revised theory (that the collectivity is threatened, that there is no identification with the attacker, and that there is firm belief in one's own values).

The details about how the first three counterstrategies work out in the Rhodesian case are in a sense obvious aspects of the total situation. More important is the question the social scientist observing the situation will immediately ask: Are these strategies *self-reinforcing*, so that some immediate benefit or reward can be derived from engaging in them, and so that one does not have to rely on belief in ultimate victory or loyalty to the regime alone? The following accounts seem to indicate that this is the case for all three.

Q. How do you manage with so little petrol?

A. Oh, that is easy enough. You know, if a family has two cars and receives some petrol for both, to put one car in the garage is not very much of a sacrifice. Besides, some of us who live in the countryside and have offices in Salisbury join our rations and form a car pool and go in together. It is strange to see how much better friends one becomes with one's neighbors in such situations—we really did not know them before. And if even this should not work, this may be the great impetus that forces the city to develop adequate collective transportation, and if even that does not work, doctors are almost unanimous that walking is good for you.[19]

Thus, an important mechanism increasing group solidarity is revealed: the car pool seems to have some of the same functions as the bomb shelter during an air raid.[20] *Adaptive measures* have become goals in themselves.

Q. But what about all kinds of luxury goods, or household appliances?

A. You must remember that very many families here are quite well off. They have a refrigerator, maybe even two. They work. If refrigerators cannot be bought, well, some will be without and others will not have the latest models. But most will have refrigerators, and they will last—our technicians are not so bad that they cannot improvise some spare parts. And as to luxury goods—we have been without them during two world wars when we helped Britain, the same Britain that attacks us today, and we can do without them again. Besides, one family has some and another family will borrow from it. That was also the pattern during the war.

Again, there is the possibility of improvisation and of mutual aid, with the well-known social implications of both. Hence, there is immediate reward in the process, and this reward may be particularly attractive as more people are deprived of this kind of experience in their daily life. (Thus, in a more traditional and poorer society there would be only marginal reward to derive from this sort of experience, since it is not scarce.)

However, *sacrifice* also has its immediate, built-in reward. *Conspicuous sacrifice*, when indulged in by the leaders of a society, may have its obvious propaganda effect: the sanctions themselves may give the leaders pretexts to demonstrate their ability to share the plight of the people. Under normal conditions such occasions are denied them and such demonstrations would in fact make them appear ridiculous; under moderate hardship they can act out a carefully balanced amount of heroism and sacrifice. And this signal is communicated not only to their own believers and disbelievers, but also to the sending nation(s), conveying to them the message "We would rather suffer at your hands than give in."[21] Thus, the situation opens possibilities for the use of symbols out of which strong ideological sentiments can be made, and this is another self-reinforcing ingredient.[22] It should be noted in passing that this advantage does not apply equally to the case of military action, since there heroism may be too risky: the leaders may be captured or simply perish if they carry it too far.

Let us then turn to the possible consequences of *restructuring the economy*. People in key economic positions are also usually people with political influence. An economic boycott may reshuffle the relative importance of economic sectors so that new economic elites emerge. The question is, Will the new elites be more or less willing to comply with the norms of the sending nations? Since economic boycott in general implies a rapid decrease of import–export business and a change toward home–based production, the question is whether the cosmopolitan layer of the tertiary sector (engaged in trade), which stands to lose some of its significance, is more or less amenable to compliance than are the emerging leaders of home-based industry or agriculture (or other primary activities).

In the Rhodesian case, the farmers are seen as the group most solidly behind Smith.[23] In addition to the simple structural reasons that are conducive to making farmers nationalists in most nations,[24] and in favor of cheap labor, there is also the element of isolation from world trends and consequently a solid measure of conservatism, a kind of asynchrony relative to the second half of the twentieth century. For the cosmopolitan business men nothing of this applies, or it applies much less. Businessmen are more likely to have connections abroad—or money. They depend for their personal needs less on development in Rhodesia, whereas the farmers have no or few alternatives. But for this same reason the farmers might also feel that the policies of the Smith government are rather hazardous, and one day the farmers could turn against him. In our view, however, this is unlikely precisely because of the way in which economy and sociology here seem to go hand in hand: changes in the economy put power more and more into the hands of the farmers; they increasingly become the symbol of national survival. Moreover, when an import–export firm has to close down there is little alternative use to which it can be put, whereas it makes a great deal of sense for the government to subsidize the conversion of tobacco land to grain fields or pasture.[25]

Thus, there is a built–in and ever more powerful mechanism of reinforcement here, and the same effect seems to apply to efforts to make substitute products. If such efforts fail, then Britain is to blame; if they succeed, then it is a proof of local ingenuity and justifies the claim to independence. To make automobile fuel out of sugarcane—or even out of coal, which is also a surplus product—would be the ideal.[26] To assume that the nation receiving sanctions will never be able to do such things because it never did them before is a little bit like trusting that children will never grow up when left alone. At any rate, the self–reinforcing power of such inventiveness will probably lead to a chain reaction both in inventiveness and in feelings of autonomy. Thus, it is almost certain that regardless of the political outcome, Rhodesian industry will come out of the crisis with a greater share of the home markets—and this possibility probably serves as an extra incentive.

In the pattern of employment, however, it is difficult to discover anything self-reinforcing. The governmental policy of letting imported labor from neighboring countries to be the first to absorb the shock so as to deflect the effects of sanctions and even turn them toward friends of the enemy (except for the case of Africans from Mozambique and South Africa) is probably clearer, but it is not internally stimulating. The next in line to absorb the shock would be, or could be, native Africans. A cleverer policy would be to distribute the impact more evenly and to display some cases of conspicuous sacrifice by the white community.

But very strong reinforcement, as far as we can judge, comes from the third strategy, that of *smuggling*:

Q. But haven't you all become so well adjusted to rather regular business patterns that it is difficult to do more irregular types of business?

A. As to the moral aspect, No—if we have to do something irregular, Britain is to blame, not we. And as to habits, I'll tell you how it is. Look at Salisbury; see how beautiful and perfect everything is. Look at the surroundings; see what a good life we have. My wife and I used to go to garden parties and give garden parties perhaps three times a week; there were shows and exhibitions; the weekend trip to Beira for a good swim, an occasional hunt—we had and still have everything except, I have to admit, life had a tendency to be somewhat boring. And then these blessed sanctions came into our existence and we had to get out of our smug practices and use all our talents again. I have never had so much fun since I came here—years ago! You have to figure out how products can be brought in by middlemen, how you can threaten that firms we used to import from will lose their markets here forever if they do not help us, how goods can eventually be smuggled into the country if that is necessary, how to get petrol more cheaply than from the Portuguese merchants who set up filling stations across the border from Umtali and charge exorbitant prices for the gallon. You really get a chance to show what you are worth.

At this point it must be added that the challenge of smuggling is not enough; one also has to be at least moderately successful in order to be rewarded in the process. Thus, if the sending nations are able to ensure that regardless of how much talent is invested in smuggling very few goods will in fact materialize, the rewards from this defense mechanism will dwindle away. But in Rhodesia, with its extensive borders adjoining friendly territories, even moderate talent should be able to bring about major success.[27]

Thus, in general the thesis that economic sanctions, at least to start with, will have a tendency to create social and political integration rather than disintegration seems to be a relatively strong one.[28] But this thesis is not unconditional. Thus, it will probably not hold in traditional societies based more on primary relationships, but then such societies are less likely to depend on trade for their continued existence. The theory also presupposes that there is strong support among the sectors that become dominant in a crisis economy, and it presupposes that smuggling is not entirely impossible. Under these conditions the short-term impact of economic sanctions will be negligible.

However, it can be argued that even if the *economic* effect of sanctions is negligible, or at least manageable, there will always remain a *moral* element. Other nations have by their action declared themselves against the receiving nation and have tied their action to moral depreciation, even condemnation. What are the effects of such moral disapproval?

These effects may lead to surrender—for instance, under the conditions mentioned above of strong latent identification with sending nation(s) and severe doubts as to the propriety of one's own actions. However, both of these conditions can be manipulated by means of modern propaganda, for the government in the receiving nation will legitimize its control of the machinery of news communication with reference to the crisis and will probably gain acceptance for its claim. The obvious techniques are to keep public expressions of approval of the motives of the sending nations below a certain threshold, perhaps even down to zero percent, and approval of one's own motives above a certain threshold, perhaps even up to a hundred percent. Only a very unrefined government will aim for the extreme thresholds here—the more sophisticated will stay away from the extremes to satisfy the more sophisticated members of the population. What matters is not so much what people think as whether they think there are many who share their treacherous thoughts—in other words, what matters to the government is the creation and maintenance of "pluralistic ignorance."[29] And complete censorship will only lead to suspicion.

Much more complicated is the case, as in Rhodesia, where there is at the same time very strong identification with the sending nation and strong disapproval of its sanctions. In other words, there is cognitive dissonance, as illustrated in Figure. 2-3.[30] The simplest way of solving these dissonances would be either to accept the sanctions and become, in fact, an adherent of Wilson's policies or to reject Britain and become an anti–British Rhodesian. No doubt both these factions exist, but they are not majority factions. In fact, there are

FIGURE 2.3

A Simple, Unbalanced Configuration
WORLD POLITICS

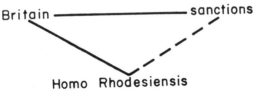

strong formal and informal pressures against either position; against the former for obvious reasons and against the latter because so much of the local ideology is based on the idea of loyalty to British symbols. Hence, the technique for resolving the dissonance is to split the cognitive elements, and since attitudes toward sanctions are homogeneously negative, "Britain" will have to be split. Some interview excerpts give insights into the mechanisms:

Q. But Queen Elizabeth, whom you say you greatly admire, and pay allegiance to, declared herself in favor of the sanctions. . . .

A. Do you really believe that? Oh no, that was because she was *forced* to do so, and by whom do you think, by that same Wilson. He told her to do so. But you know what, some of us who watched television very closely saw a twinkle in her eye; that was a secret signal to us that she is really in favor of us, she is with us.

The structure of this cognitive configuration, shown in Figure 2.4, is obtained by introducing "Wilson" and splitting "Queen Elizabeth" into the apparent and the real one. There is not only one cycle but sixteen (one with five, five with four, and ten with three elements), all of them balanced. The structure has several advantages. It preserves the basic attitudes, and at the same time it has a measure of sophistication that can serve as a good basis for speeches, editorials, and such. The ability to distinguish between the apparent and the real is usually highly thought of, and much involved conversation is possible on the basis of Figure 2.4, with Wilson pictured as a crook and Queen Elizabeth as schizophrenic.

FIGURE 2.4

A Revised, Balanced Configuration

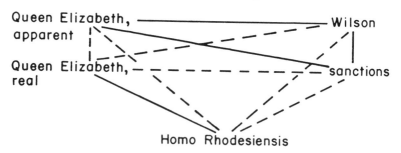

Another example, based on the Rhodesians' intense dislike of Harold Wilson, is presented in Figure 2.5.

Q. You love Britain and want to remain within the Commonwealth, and you dislike Wilson. But you cannot deny that
Wilson is a part of Britain, and even a rather important one,
the country's Prime Minister. . . .

A. Oh yes, he is. By a rather slim majority, though.[31] But that
does not prove that Wilson is a true Briton. It only proves how
clever he is, and how effective international communism is.

Q. How so?

A. Well, it is well known here that Wilson is really a Communist;
you see it quite clearly in his earliest writings. In later years he
has disguised it, or tried to do so. But we believe there is some
kind of link between him and Peking. For how could you otherwise explain all these things that happen? That we, the
best–run colony in Africa and the most truly anti–Communist
of them all should be the last ones to gain independence, that
everything should be turned against us when we want what
was due to us rightfully after our partners in the Federation,
Northern Rhodesia and Nyasaland, or Zambia and Malawi as
they like to call themselves now, gained independence?

Again, there is the same technique. "Wilson" is split into two, the
position as prime minister and the person Wilson—and just as the
apparent Queen Elizabeth should be dissociated from the real one,
so should the person Wilson be dissociated from the prime minis-

FIGURE 2.5

A Simple, Unbalanced Configuration

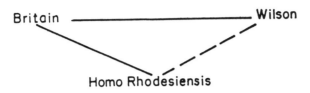

ter's office, which he holds unrightfully, not because of any electoral fraud, but because he has not revealed his true intentions. Moreover, "international communism" is brought into the picture, as in Figure 2.6. Again there is an extension from one unbalanced cycle to sixteen balanced ones, and again, an increase not only in balance, but also in sophistication of the structure of argumentation. The evils are now brought back to "international communism," which offers an extensive basis of explanation since there is a great deal of tradition, even literature, that the theories can be hooked on to.

Q. But how does international communism operate here?

A. Well, you know the hold they have on Tanzania, with that Peking Communist Nyerere. You also know that Peking wants copper. So what would be better than to create the conditions under which better land transport would have to be built from Tanzania right into the copper belt, under the pretext of helping Zambia with oil and petrol, and then the Chinese can sit on it? Also, conditions are created whereby the moderate Kaunda regime may have to yield to extreme leftists, and Zambia is also theirs. Kenya can fall any moment—so isn't it rather strange that Britain should attack the only real friends they have down here in the fight against international communism? And how do you account for that, except by admitting that communism has crept into Britain itself—or rather, at its very head, in that Mr. Wilson? And that he was able to persuade the others, playing on their fear of losing the votes of the Afro-Asian nations in the United Nations?

Expressions like these are so frequent that they seem to be a rather accepted ideology. There is no sign of the Rhodesians' underesti-

FIGURE 2.6

A Revised, Balanced Configuration
WORLD POLITICS

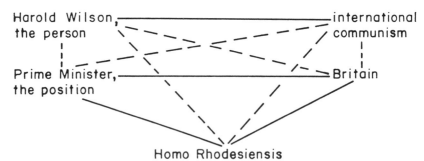

Homo Rhodesiensis

mating the enemy: to them he is both strong and extremely intelligent in his machinations. However, he does make a mistake; he underestimates the dormant power of Britain, and fails to foresee that one day the British people will awake and see the spell that has been cast over them. And in the meantime it is up to Rhodesia to keep vigil, to be on guard and tell the truth to the world. This duty also gives an international role to the Rhodesians, a deeper meaning to their existence and to their fight. The parallel with Cuba in the Western hemisphere is immediate.

Thus, the world is dichotomized into one good and one bad part, as it usually is in times of crisis. But, one may ask, what has happened to the basic issues, majority rule and UDI? And this is precisely the point: the basic issues have in a sense disappeared; a reinterpretation has taken place, giving the sanctions a new meaning. Not that Rhodesians are not able at any moment to argue about these issues, but the third issue of communism is always there as an even more dominant theme. Whether it is called a smoke screen or not, its role in the cognitive system is considerable.

The insertion of "majority rule" and "British rule" in the cognitive system presented above is simple: both kinds of rule are possible agents of communism. "British rule" is seen as such only as long as it means Wilson or Labour rule (for which reason the Rhodesians paid enormous attention to all British by–elections that might have upset Wilson's precarious majority in early 1966 and to all signs of a split in the Conservative party, which they analyzed as they did

Queen Elizabeth) and alignment with Afro–Asian nations in the UN. And "majority rule" is seen as the agent of communism only as long as it means government dominated by "all these Communist-trained Africans, coming out of Dar es Salaam, aligning themselves with Nkrumah, Touré, and others" and "so-called Pan–Africanism." Thus, the final goal is arrived at: the portrayal of independent Rhodesia as one of the few remaining bastions of the free world, misunderstood and betrayed by people who would do well to put their own house in order before they criticize white Rhodesians.[32]

> Here are we in little Rhodesia trying to form a bastion of democracy against the shaky black states to the north of us only to find the formidable might of the good old U. S. A. pitted against us. Why?
>
> Have we ever asked you for anything in the way of foreign–aid handouts or squandered your gifts on graft, personal gain, or flashy cars, like so many of the black despots in Africa and Asia? One day you are going to need a trustworthy and staunch ally in this part of Africa and, apart from the Republic of South Africa, which is likely to be your next target for destruction, on which other country in the whole of this continent you can honestly rely with confidence?
>
> Where is your much-vaunted sense of fair play? Where were your sanctions and embargoes when Hungary was crushed or when India seized Goa? Perhaps the nations involved were a little too powerful for your might, and it is only the smaller, comparatively defenseless countries like ours that you are prepared to tackle.
>
> Well, good luck to you—you go right on trying to placate and pander to the petty little tyrants on this continent and see what you get by way of thanks for it in the end.
>
> As for criticism and your holier–than–thou attitude in the United Nations and elsewhere regarding our relationship with the Africans, may I suggest that you put your own house in order and start treating your own Negroes and Red Indians (especially the latter—they have more right to the country than the European "settlers") fairly before throwing stones in our direction.
>
> You had better snap out of your fawning terror of the Afro-Asian bloc and give us a chance before you lose yet another of the few friends left to you in this sorry world.

However, consistent ideologies are not enough. They may appeal to the intellectual and be useful in discussions, but in an atmosphere where political discussion is discouraged and contact with foreigners is seriously reduced, they are of limited value except as a ritual, not unlike religious liturgies. People cannot repeat these arguments in their daily conversations; in such contexts other symbols and forms of expression appealing more directly to the emotions are needed. And they have not been wanting in Salisbury after UDI.

First of all, there are the *jokes* ridiculing the sanctions. An advertisement in the *Rhodesia Herald* announced the New Year's Eve party in a certain restaurant with an admonition to "order tables now," some alluring comments on the culinary pleasures to be expected, and the assurance that "there will be no sanctions against drinks." The point about this jocular remark is not that it is particularly good—much better jokes were heard in everyday conversation—but that it appeared in an advertisement for everyone to see. Thus, the people became familiarized with the sanctions, and the sanctions became more manageable, just as "doodlebugs" were more manageable than V-weapons. At the same time, jokes heard by the present observer were never directed against Britain as such, but rather against Wilson; never against Commonwealth symbols, but rather against policies and some member nations of the Commonwealth.

Second, there is the element of superstition, even *mysticism*, dear to anyone exposed to a crisis. Thus, the word "Rhodesian" was held to carry a secret message, revealed when a line is drawn between the *s* and the *i*—Rhodes/ian—or Cecil *Rhodes* and *Ian* Smith:

> So, you see, it is already in the word! Rhodes founded the colony;
> Ian is giving us independence!

It was also reported that the Friends of Rhodesia Association went out of their way to get their offices in Durban set up in Salisbury House, Smith Street, but were unable to get them on the eleventh floor to symbolize the date of UDI(11/11/65).[33] This kind of magic is probably linked to right–wing extremism in somewhat the same way as dogmatism and quasi-scientism are tied in with left–wing extremism.

Third, there is an element of *style* in the Smith regime that may appear spurious to its style-conscious antagonists in the mother country, but not necessarily to the Rhodesians themselves. A great proportion of the customary rigamarole of British democracy is carried over, and the solemn phraseology remains intact.[34] However, Smith himself is as an orator considerably closer to the style of the Rhodesian farmer than is, for instance, Wilson. Symbols associated with Smith, such as the RAF, "wounded in the war," "a farmer himself," a certain lean handsomeness, and the idea that he is not so much a professional politician as a solid Rhodesian who has taken on himself the responsibility for a job to be done, must contribute to identification. Above all this distinctly Rhodesian style underlines the justification of UDI and the idea that Rhodesians are different from and yet of the same blood as the British.

In a sanction process a receiving nation is greatly aided by a general tendency to *underestimate* it. It is customary in human affairs to underestimate one's opponent, under a relatively wide variety of conditions. There is a particularly simple reason why this is *a fortiori* true for the case of economic sanctions. A nation about to be punished is a nation that has done something wrong; it is morally inferior in one way or another. To attribute to it intelligence, tactical ability, moral strength, tenaciousness, or other properties valued highly by the punishing nation(s) can easily lead to serious cognitive dissonance. The more such virtues sending nation(s) admit the receiving nation has, the less justified do the former's own actions appear and the less probable their chances of victory, for the properties mentioned are precisely among the ones needed to counteract the effect of sanctions.

Thus, one can predict easy acceptance of ideas to the effect that the population of the receiving nation is inferior where intelligence and morality are concerned. Varieties of this theme—for instance, that this inferiority applies "only to the leaders and not to the people" or "only to the people and not to the leaders" (who control the people in an authoritarian or totalitarian manner)—will also in all probability appear, just as theories about gray eminences.[35] Obviously, such theories may often have a nucleus of truth or may even be quite adequate descriptions of objective reality—but this is not the reason that they are held to be true. When pressed for data, people in the sending nation(s) will usually quickly reveal a nonempirical attitude, a lack of data, and a lack of ability to revise their judgment when new data that point toward revisions of the prejudices appear.

In the Rhodesian case the most common themes are expressed in these excerpts:

> The white population in Rhodesia is, in fact, so uneducated that they say about ninety-seven percent of them are illiterate. The reason why they are there is that they cannot compete with West Indian labor (Nigerian politican).

> The white population is about the size of the population of Chelsea. Now, imagine you asked the city council in that city to take care of the affairs of a nation. They would simply not be able to do so; more talent and training are required (British politician).

> Most of the settlers are there to seek comfort alone; that is all they care for; they have no higher ideals than their own well-being. Deprive them of some of their material comfort, deny them some of their imported stuff, and they will ask for fair weather very quickly (countless informants, rank–and–file and politicians).

> One reason why the Wilson team could not negotiate with Smith's people was that they were so silly that they did not even understand the proposals put forward to them (British informants).

> Smith is not able even to write his own speeches, not to mention formulate governmental policies—but there are men behind him who are the real rulers and who do all the brain work. Smith is only a front figure (Opposition member, Rhodesia).

> They have poorer brains down there, and they are shut out from the general trends. They used to say that "Kenya was for officers, Rhodesia was for other ranks." And these poor whites have of course much more to lose (white newspaperman, Kenya).

What all such statements do not take into account is above all the same factor: that human beings and social systems change when exposed to crisis. The city council of X–town, when given the responsibility of heading a nation, may develop abilities not expected by either itself or others; and a society, when worked upon by the forces of cohesion, may draw on reservoirs of strength and ability not only to resist stress but also to act creatively—qualities that lie latent in quieter periods. This is in a sense a truism—anyone who lived through the occupation of, say, a European nation during World War II will know by his own experience that there is a great deal of truth to this.

More important is the advantage of being underestimated. First of all, it makes the sending nation(s) overestimate the probable effect of the sanctions they initiate, and that gives the receiving nation a better chance to counteract the effects. Moreover, if the receiving nation is clever enough, it will conceal some of its unrecognized strength and conform to its image as inferior and may be able to extend the fight on this basis. Besides, to appear stupid in a conference may be a very clever tactic since it impedes communication and makes it easier afterward to claim that there were misunderstandings. In more formal terms: one can retain the pretense of willingness to negotiate and yet make negotiation impossible. At any rate, to have hidden resources is always an asset.[36]

We know of no better way to summarize all this discussion of the defense against sanctions than by quoting the following lines from Ian Smith's "Three Months of Independence" broadcast to his nation:

> The thought of operations carried out by British troops based in a Commonwealth country—which is now a republic and no longer acknowledges the Queen or flies the Union Jack—against a fellow-member of the Commonwealth which has no wish to become a republic, unless the Commonwealth abandons the ideals upon which it was built, still shows loyalty to the Queen and is proud to fly the Union Jack, is to me incomprehensible. . . . Is it not appropriate to ask Mr. Wilson a direct question: Is he a fellow traveler?
>
> If not, why does he allow British ships to pour British provisions into the Viet Cong, thus assisting them to wage their deadly war against Americans, Australians and New Zealanders?
>
> If not, why is he aiding and abetting the Communist forces in their march down the American continent?
>
> If not, why does he continue to supply and assist the Communist revolutionaries in Cuba?
>
> If not, why does he continue to aid and finance, with British taxpayers' money, the openly Communistic countries of Ghana and Tanzania, in spite of their withdrawal from the Commonwealth, accompanied as it was by the hurling of vile insults at Britain?

If not, why—when Rhodesia is holding the front line against the Communist forces in Africa—is Mr. Wilson boasting and bragging about his efforts which are calculated to bring us to our knees?

If he is not a Communist, perhaps he could tell us precisely what he is doing to combat the spread of communism in the world today, on the one hand, and on the other hand, what he is doing to promote democracy and democratic institutions in the world, and particularly in Africa?[37]

IV. CONCLUSIONS

In this chapter the conclusion about the probable effectiveness of economic sanctions is, generally, negative. To arrive at this conclusion the target society has been analyzed as an organism with a certain self–maintaining potential. When hit and hurt it reacts—like most organisms—in such a way as to try to undo the damage and to restore the *status quo ante*. In so doing, the target society may even be partially strengthened because of the hidden forces that are activated. The goals of the system may not only be maintained but even be reinforced; the sending nation(s) not only may fail to achieve their goals, but may even contribute to exactly the opposite of what they hoped for.

Sanctions against collectivities will always affect the just together with the unjust, since collective sanctions correspond to a philosophy of collective guilt. From the outside, where nations as such (Germany, Rhodesia) appear as the wrong–doers, sanctions are just another way of acting out the billiard–ball image of nations— that is, nations as undifferentiated wholes. From the inside, collective sanctions seem unreasonable to both the just and the unjust, with the consequences we have tried to describe.

To many, these effects will serve as an example of the lack of isomorphism between interpersonal and international relations: what works at the individual level does not necessarily work at the level of interaction between nations. However true this may often be, it is not a good example. Prisoners will often feel precisely that "only a part of me did wrong, and only a short time—and here all of me is imprisoned, and for a long time." Even if great care is taken, verbally, to draw a line between the *peccatum* and the *peccator* and not generalize from the sinful act to definitions of the whole person as a sinner, imprisonment is nevertheless a way of putting all parts of the person, sinful or not, in prison. Thus, there is in practice also a billiard–ball conception of man as an undifferentiated whole. Biology protects this billiard ball from differentiated imprisonment, much as norms of national integrity protect the nation billiard ball. In both cases imagination must be exercised to find more differentiated forms of punishment.[38]

But nothing of what has been said should be taken to imply that there are no conditions under which economic sanctions will work. For reasons due to the structure of the internal economy of the target nation as well as to its trade structure, the damage wrought or anticipated may appear so much more frightening than the renunciation of its goals that capitulation or compromise may be the result. Also, although there may be short–term adaptation, the long–term effect may nevertheless be capitulation or compromise out of boredom, fatigue, and desire to return to more normal conditions and ways of life.

Then there is another, and much more important, class of conditions under which sanctions may work and often do work. In fact, sanctions are used continuously, in everyday social interaction, at the individual and at the national levels of interaction. But characteristic of this use of sanctions is a communality of interest in which rupture of generally smooth relations is perceived as a worse threat than some short–run lack of gratification. Hence, sanctions not only "bite," they also "work" in the sense that compliance is obtained. This is the case within primary relations, as within a family or a peer group, and is also the case within secondary relations based on contractual or normative situations. But when this sense of communality of interest is lost, i.e., when there is conflict and patterns of influence become predominantly coercive, then sanctions seem to function in a completely different manner. This does not mean that they cannot both bite and work in this case, too, but there are indeed many conditions that must be fulfilled, as has been indicated in this chapter.

The condition for sanctions to be effective that is most often referred to in more or less scholarly analyses is the problem of *universality*. The argument is that economic sanctions have failed because they were not universal; some countries did not participate, or some other way of circumventing the sanctions was found (smuggling, use of third parties, and so on). Only detailed analysis of individual cases can do justice to this argument. But even though the argument no doubt has some validity, there are also important reasons to believe that this validity is limited.

First of all, even under a totally effective blockade a country may continue to run on its internal resources, and these resources (economic, social, moral, political) may be strengthened rather than weakened by the sanctions. The question is whether these resources are sufficient to maintain a society and a political community—and this question cannot be answered in general and *a priori*.

Second, although the economic effect of sanctions by definition increases with the increasing participation of the senders, it is not obvious that the moral effect increases. On the contrary, to feel that the rest of the world is "ganging up" on one may serve as a very effective and hardening stimulus, supporting paranoid and psychopathic tendencies as well as more salutary forces.[39] However, we know very little about this.

But even if the direct and intended consequences of sanctions are unlikely to obtain, there may be other effects. When analyzing political actions in terms of their consequences, and particularly in terms of whether the actions serve the purposes intended for them, less rational purposes are often forgotten. If economic sanctions do not make a receiving nation comply, they may nevertheless serve functions that are useful in the eyes of the sending nation(s). There is, for example, the punishment aspect referred to earlier. There is the value of at least doing something, of having the illusion of being instrumental, of being busy in time of crisis. When military action is impossible for one reason or another, and when doing nothing is seen as tantamount to complicity, then *something has to be done to express morality*, something that at least serves as a clear signal to everyone that what the receiving nation has done is disapproved of. If the sanctions do not serve instrumental purposes they can at least have *expressive* functions. Thus, as a highly dramatic (and costly) way of reinforcing international morality, economic sanctions may be useful, although it would be interesting to compare their effects with those of much cheaper means, such as declarations, resolutions, or demonstrations.

This judgment leads to the suspicion that economic sanctions may serve the purpose of expressing moral disapproval best when they are of a symbolic nature and value–deprivation is kept low. Moreover, we believe that this purpose is served still better if the senders deprive themselves of as much or even more value as the receivers are deprived of. Thus, a boycott of South African oranges may by itself be a meaningful demonstration of an attitude, an act of communication so to speak. But which case is more effective: when there is no other way for the boycotters to obtain oranges, whereas South Africa easily finds other markets, or when South Africa finds no substitute market, whereas the boycotters indulge in oranges from Israel, Cyprus, or Spain?—in other words, when only the senders are hurt, or when only the receivers are hurt? The dilemma may serve well as an illustration of the difference between nonviolent and violent reasoning, but where the resolution of the dilemma is concerned we simply do not know the answer.[40]

Let us now turn the argument around and imagine that experiences with economic sanctions in this century had been more positive. Let us imagine that economic sanctions as a coercive measure have become a permanent and frequent aspect of international interaction. What changes does this imply in the structure of the system? And, to what extent are these changes cherished results and to what extent less-applauded consequences?

First of all, if economic sanctions have come to stay, it would be unwise of realistic and clever governments not to think about countermeasures. Some governments will even today define themselves as belonging to minority groups in the international system against whom such sanctions might be wielded; others are foresighted enough to appreciate that the world structure may change and that they may one day become the victims of such policies, however improbable that might seem today.[41]

The first and most obvious countermeasure would be to do what many nations do today as a part of their program of total defense: broaden their basis of production for exports so that their economy cannot be destroyed by actions pertaining to one or a few products only. One–crop countries are vulnerable because of the greater ease with which an economic boycott can be supervised.[42] This, then, leads to *diversification of the national economy.*

Second, nations will try to increase the number of recipients of their exports and suppliers of their imports in order to be less dependent on a single nation that might engage in unilateral boycott actions against them. This will also make boycott actions less easy to carry out since there will be fewer relationships like the one between Britain and Rhodesia. One may refer to this as the *defeudalization of international trade*.

Both of these strategies will be applauded by many today since they are compatible with general moves toward political and economic independence. This approval also applies partly, but only partly, to the third countermeasure: the tendency toward *economic self-sufficiency*, which has been a classical component of defense against military warfare and is an equally obvious component of defense against economic warfare. This tendency is also consistent with the almost universal need for economic structures that can save a nation from expenses in foreign currencies. But the consequence of self–sufficiency is decreased world interdependence; and to the extent that a high level of interdependence, economic and otherwise, between the nations of the world is seen as a way of strengthening the capacity of the international system to resist war, this is a rather negative consequence.

Thus, the countermeasures consequent to a declared policy in favor of the application of economic sanctions are consistent with economic policies pursued by many nations today, but are based on other reasons. This consistency will facilitate their implementation, and, since there will then be less to fear, their implementation will probably also further the acceptance of economic sanctions. But these consequences do not appear to be consistent with a view of the interdependent international structure as more resistant against violent conflict than a structure very low in interdependence. Thus, one may run the risk of buying a (dubious) nonmilitary coercive measure at the expense of an even more dangerous international structure than that we already have.

In conclusion, although this is outside the general scope of this chapter, let us indicate some classes of answers to the obvious and highly legitimate question, *What, then, can be done?* If we exclude military actions on moral grounds and economic sanctions on pragmatic grounds, what is left? This question can be discussed by reference to the survey given in Section II, with special attention to the dimensions of positive versus negative, individual versus collective, and external versus internal sanctions. This article has dealt with sanctions that are negative, collective, and external—and of a further special type, economic. Answers to the question may, however, possibly be found among the other combinations.

But first of all, there are all the other *negative, collective, and external sanctions*. We have indicated above some reasons why communications sanctions may be effective, but in general we feel that very much of what we have said in this article about economic sanctions would apply *a fortiori* to these other types of sanctions. More particularly, it does not seem that the "nonrecognition games" often indulged in by governments are very instrumental, although they may serve a number of expressive functions. The same probably applies to diplomatic ruptures. But many detailed studies are needed to know more about this.

Second, there is the possibility of *positive, collective, and external sanctions*—in other words, of indicating the conditions under which sending nations will offer *rewards* rather than conditions under which they will try to administer punishment. In the Rhodesia case this would mean outlining a policy of (even escalating) rewards for every step toward majority rule and social integration. It may be argued that this was tried and failed; we shall not enter that debate. The important fact from our point of view is only that we know very little about how such positive sanctions would actually operate. Thus, would none, some, most, or all of the mechanisms we have described for negative sanctions be operative, only in reverse? Would sending nations be willing to renounce the punishment element of negative sanctions? Would there be more or less opportunity to express morality when right rather than wrong actions were singled out for attention through the system of sanctions? Could positive sanctions and negative sanctions be combined?

Third, there is the possibility of *negative, external, but individual sanctions*. These are impossible under present conditions of international law, which reserves the right of jurisdiction over individuals to nationals and/or individuals on national territory. Nevertheless, let us imagine for a moment that international society was structured in such a way that sanctions could be *aimed at responsible individuals*, like federal police actions in some cases in the United States. In that case, almost none of the processes we have indicated would be operative. It is the collective nature of economic sanctions that sets in motion processes that counteract the impact and have the additional quality of being almost automatic. Thus, the skilled politician in the receiving nation who knows or senses these processes has at his disposal a force that he can amplify if he has the necessary talent. He can ride a wave, so to speak, and his major temptation will probably be to overdo the amplification, to emphasize too much the spirit of sacrifice, to use too vivid colors in the way he presents the picture of the situation to his followers, and so on. But, if key individuals in the nation had already been arrested through quick action (perhaps parachutists?), there would be fewer to rally around—and if, in addition, there was a certain level of identification with the world police, this might solve the whole problem.

Fourth, there is the possibility of *external and individual, but positive, sanctions*. This would mean that the sending nations would single out for attention particularly valuable individuals in the receiving nation and would reward them. This is already being done to a considerable extent, through prizes, awards, invitations to lecture, and so forth, but it could be done more systematically and on a grander scale. It would encourage individuals, reduce pluralistic ignorance, serve as a reinforcement of morality, and emphasize the brotherhood of mankind—but it could also open the way to all kinds of retaliation against the rewarded individuals by the authorities to be influenced. It would effectively change loyalty patterns of some people more in the direction of the sending nation(s), but what the short–term and long–term effects of that would be is difficult to tell.

Finally, there is the possibility of *internal sanctions*. In the case of Rhodesia, this would mean the whole repertory of Gandhian techniques, from general strikes to parallel rule—if we exclude direct violence against people or against objects (sabotage). The virtues of internal action are many: it would provide training in political action and organization (but would also presuppose it); it would increase self–reliance instead of strengthening the pattern of reliance on outsiders; it could be much more effective than external sanctions since most of a nation's economy is internal—but it would also set in motion many of the same counteracting processes. White Rhodesia would still feel persecuted and would be able to play on the David and Goliath theme—and there will always be many on the side of a David.

In short, it is difficult to tell, but the *a priori* value of these alternative techniques is at least as positive as that of economic sanctions, the world's experiences in this century considered. Thus, the field is open for both research and new policy measures—and it seems safe to predict that the rest of this century will witness much experimentation in this field. It is only to be hoped that such experimentation will be not completely unguided by good theory and good data—as well as by a constructive and positive orientation in international affairs.

NOTES

1. Using the term "Rhodesia" rather than "Southern Rhodesia" or "Zimbabwe" has no political implications; this usage is simply shorter and more frequently found.
2. UDI is used as the common abbreviation for the Unilateral Declaration of Independence by the Smith government on November 11, 1965.
3. A study of this kind is currently under way at the International Peace Research Institute, Oslo, under the direction of Frederik Hoffmann.
4. There are, of course, many works available giving various accounts of the background of UDI. Scandinavian readers will find Holger Benettsson, *Problemet Rhodesia* (Stockholm 1966) elucidative. Very valuable information, as well as attempts at analysis, can be found in two papers by Peter Wallensteen, *Den rhodesiska självständighetsfrågan efter december 1962,* mimeographed (Uppsala 1965) and *Aspekter på Rhodesiakrisen efter självständighetsförklaringen,* mimeographed (Uppsala 1966). Non-Scandinavian readers will find Philip Mason, *The Birth of a Dilemma* (London 1958), Patrick Keatley, *The Politics of Partnership* (London 1963), and Nathan Shamuyarira, *Crisis in Rhodesia* (London 1965), valuable. However, apart from Wallensteen, *Aspekter,* these publications do not deal with the sanctions. A recent and relevant work on sanctions is Ronald Segal, ed., *Sanctions Against South Africa* (London 1964), presenting the papers and the recommendations of the International Conference on Economic Sanctions Against South Africa, London, April 14–17, 1964. For Scandinavian readers, Kaj Björk, *Sydafrika och vi* (Jönköping 1965), gives some of the arguments in connection with sanctions against South Africa.
5. For a general discussion of the problem of compliance, see Galtung, "On the Meaning of Nonviolence," *Journal of Peace Research,* No. 3 (1965), 228–57.
6. The best treatment of this theme is probably found in Bjørn Christiansen, *Attitudes to Foreign Affairs as a Function of Personality* (Oslo 1959).
7. Many of these sanctions are mentioned in the relevant Article 41 of the Charter of the United Nations:
"The Security Council may decide what measures not involving the use of armed force are to be employed to give effect to its decisions and may call upon the Members of the United Nations to apply such measures. These may include com-

plete or partial interruption of economic relations and of rail, sea, air, postal, telegraphic, radio and other means of communication, and the severance of diplomatic relations.''

These provisions, of course, also apply to the United Nations itself. According to information given by Mr. David Owen to the meeting of the Technical Assistance Committee on November 24, 1965, the United Nations withdrew its experts from Rhodesia almost immediately after adoption of the Security Council resolution condemning developments there.

To give some impression of how the measures suggested in Article 41 of the Charter have in fact been used by the member nations, we have used the UN Press Services Reference Paper No. 4 (March 23, 1966) to study how the sanctions employed by four major groupings among the sixty nations that had reported to the Security Council were distributed.

Table 2.1

Sanctions Against Rhodesia, By Type of Sanction and Country Grouping (Percent)[a]

	No recognition	Dipl. rel. restricted	Dipl. rel. not estab.	Telecomm.	Passport	Part. econ.	Compl. econ.	(N)
Socialist	84	0	17	25	0	0	33	(12)
Commonwealth	23	13	15	8	23	38	46	(13)
African, not Commonwealth	0	11	11	0	44	11	33	(9)
All other	46	12	23	0	15	50	27	(26)
(N)	(25)	(9)	(8)	(4)	(11)	(19)	(20)	(60)

[a] The figures do not add up horizontally to 100% since one nation may employ several types of sanctions.

The table should be read with utmost caution since it is based on a press release, not on primary sources, and since one does not know to what extent the UN asked for information. However, the differences are nevertheless quite remarkable. The focus is on sanctions of the verbal, expressive type (such as nonrecognition) and on economic sanctions, with the socialist countries specializing in the former and Commonwealth and African countries in the latter. Telecommunication and travel sanctions have been remarkably underutilized, as have diplomatic sanctions. In December 1965, twenty nations had consulates general or high commissions in Salisbury. Only six of these—Denmark, the Federal Republic of Germany, Italy, Japan, Sweden, and the United States—were affected as of March 25, 1966. The table seems to indicate that the more remote a nation is from Rhodesia, the more it uses nonrecognition; the closer the nation is, the more it uses economic sanctions.

On the other hand, the less the trade with Rhodesia, the more complete the boycott; here the nations that are big traders have the most difficulties.

Also, there are very important exceptions to the relatively comprehensive sanctions called for by the UN in the resolution of November 20, 1966, in which the Security Council (with France abstaining) called upon "all states not to recognize this illegal authority and not to entertain any diplomatic or other relations with this illegal authority." Thus the information given by the Commonwealth Relations Office on January 31, 1966, is interesting in showing the loopholes in the sanctions system. Briefly stated, they are as follows, using the calculations made by Wallensteen (*Aspekter*, 29–32):

1. Zambia (export sanctions 30% effective)
2. South Africa (export sanctions 0% effective)
3. West Germany (export sanctions 70% effective)
4. Malawi (export sanctions 0% effective)
5. U.S. (export sanctions 45% effective)
6. Congo (L) (export sanctions 0% effective)
7. Portuguese territories (export sanctions 0% effective)
8. France (export sanctions 60% effective)

The loopholes have a clear structure. First of all, there are Rhodesia's ideological allies, South Africa and Portugal, who have a vested interest. They can hardly afford to have Rhodesia lose, since this might encourage similar processes directed against themselves. Second, there are Rhodesia's African neighbors, Zambia, Malawi, and the Congo, who are evidently more concerned with the impact of sanctions on their own vulnerable economies than with the use of sanctions as weapons against an ideological enemy. Third, there are the three biggest Western powers (the United Kingdom excepted): the United States, West Germany, and France, all with their vested interests. The diversity of motives for not making sanctions complete is impressive. Such diversity is a factor on which a skillful government in a receiving nation can base policies designed to demoralize the sending nation.

8. For an excellent study, see Louis B. Sohn, "Responses to Violation: A General Survey," in Richard A. Falk and Richard J. Barnet, eds., *Security in Disarmament* (Princeton 1965), 178–203.

9. The basic facts about the structure of the Rhodesian economy seen from this point of view can be found in the survey reported in a Supplement to the *Standard Bank Review* (November 19, 1965), according to which a boycott of the major product for export, tobacco, should affect Rhodesia more than the United Kingdom if the latter were to stop importing it from Rhodesia.

10. Bruce M. Russett and others (New Haven 1964). The data are from Table 46.

11. *Concentration in International Trade* (Amsterdam 1962), esp. chap. 2.

12. *Ibid.*, 22.

13. An excellent account of how South Africa was able to get around the Indian boycott launched against it in July 1946 by means of trade via third parties is given in K. N. Raj, "Sanctions and the Indian Experience," in Segal, *Sanctions Against South Africa*, 197–203.

14. This must, by and large, have been a major theory behind many efforts in recent history to bomb an adversary into submission. For an interpretative analysis of the effects of bombing in World War II on the United Kingdom, Germany, and Japan, see Galtung, "On the Effects of Bombing Civilians" (forthcoming). The line of argument is very much as for the effects of economic sanctions in the present article.

15. See the *Official Report* for these two days. For another and very similar example of a theory as to how sanctions might work, let us quote from the article "Can Smith be brought down?" *Peace News* (November 19, 1965), 1, 4. Six factors are mentioned: white supporters will desert Smith (1) "as the economic life of the country becomes more unmanageable"; (2) because of the staunch attitude of the governor and the symbolism of some people's indication of their support for him; (3) because of the blank spaces in the newspapers, indicating censorship; (4) because of "unrest among members of the civil service, police and army"; (5) because of "unrest among the African population"; and (6) because of "South Africa's refusal to deal in Rhodesian currency." This list shows a clear overestimation of the organizational power of the African population and an equally clear overestimation of the force and legitimacy of British symbols far from home. Moreover, there is always the question of how many people really worry about censorship, particularly when it is directed against opinions and writers they dislike themselves.

16. This control of access to Rhodesia dates from November 1965 when "Great Britain established a general requirement for visas for travel to Rhodesia, and stated, on this occasion, that the sole legal authorities outside Great Britain having the right to issue such visas are the British embassies and consulates." Later on, sanctions were added to this rule: "The British authorities . . . reserve the right to refuse entry into Great Britain to persons who have sought visas for entry into Rhodesia from the representatives of Ian Smith's regime" (quoted from Royal Norwegian Ministry of Foreign Affairs, Circular No. 27, March 11, 1966).

17. *Aspekter*, 25–26.

18. Wilson's thinking about how Rhodesia should be made to comply can be interestingly contrasted with the thinking of one Conservative M. P., Mr. G. Lloyd, who "suggested that Britain should look back and consider what might have been done and how much money could have been spent in the past to bring Rhodesia to a position today where it was felt independence could be granted. Britain could then get the Commonwealth together and raise, say £200 million to bring Rhodesia to such a position by possibly 1980. Of this, possibly £50 million could be spent on education, £50 million on boosting the economy, £50 million on communications and £50 million on other projects" (the Salisbury correspondent in *The Star* [Johannesburg], January 12, 1966, 21). Although this suggestion reflects the paternalist position of "education for maturity," it also reflects the approach of the positive reward, provided there is a way of tying the transfer of £200 million to the steps toward majority rule.

19. Thus, there were stories in the press about the Masais, who are able to keep fit and healthy because they walk to work (hunting) over long distances every day.

20. A good account of the effects of air raids on Britain is found in R. M. Tit-

muss, "Argument of Strain," in Eric and Mary Josephson, eds., *Man Alone* (New York 1962), 505–15.

21. After UDI, shops in Salisbury displayed posters with drawings of Rhodesians in uniform, with rather determined faces, tightening their belts. The general idea was that of serving the country again, of "the men being called up," something of the prewar atmosphere described by Doris Lessing in her novel *A Proper Marriage*.

22. Thus, the idea of the prime minister bicycling to his office might appeal to many. (Incidentally, the photograph of Smith on a bicycle that figured in many newspapers implied no permanent change in his means of transportation.) But just as important might be the idea of symbolizing "everything normal"; the receiving nation can make political gains on this as well as on conspicuous sacrifice.

23. According to observers, the opposition in the white Rhodesian population amounts to around 20,000 and consists mainly of the press, the bankers, the industrialists, the lawyers, the teachers, and people in their primary circles. We know of no solid data to support this contention.

24. One very simple reason is that the ownership of farms is usually hereditary, which ties farmers to the territory for generations ahead. A professional's job is not hereditary; he can afford to be nonnationalist or even antinationalist since his position will not similarly affect his offspring.

25. Of course, the list of people belonging to the opposition according to observers (footnote 23) is impressive, and these people could be most dangerous to the regime. However, they have lost much of their prestige simply from being less functional than the farmers, who will always have the important task of keeping the population alive during a period of crisis. Thus, our argument is in terms of transfer of legitimacy due to a dislocation of the center of gravity in being functional to the community at large. The result may be more legitimacy to sectors favoring more apartheid.

26. Thus, in South Africa, the technology of extracting oil from coal is already quite advanced. According to the *Times Review of Industry* (December 1963), about ten percent of the country's needs are taken care of that way (the state-owned plant SASOL produces about forty million gallons of gasoline annually).

27. According to the report on the fuel situation in Rhodesia circulated to member states by the UN Secretary–General, the oil expert Walter J. Levy states that "oil shortages are already the cause, and will increasingly be so, of the major and most overt upset in the Rhodesian economy and society." The statement is interesting since it is not phrased in absolute terms; all it says is that the oil embargo causes more economic difficulties than the other embargoes. And Levy also adds, ". . . If the question were one of survival the availability of oil, in itself, would certainly not be the decisive consideration during the next few months." This sounds reasonable, since only twenty-seven percent of the energy needs are covered by means of oil, whereas sixty-three percent are met by coal from the Wankie coal belt and ten percent of the needs are covered by hydroelectric power from the Kariba Dam. Since the Wankie coal belt is in Rhodesia and "to blow up the Kariba Dam would mean to flood Beira" (according to a Rhodesian informant), this means that about three–quarters of the energy needs are under control. And where oil is

concerned, the railroads have been switching from diesel engines back to steam engines and the forty-three percent of the oil that went into ordinary gasoline for cars covers a substantial fraction of luxury consumption. It is worse with the ten percent that was used for airplanes, but this is hardly too difficult to replace (figures from "The Bite on Business," *The Sunday Times,* November 14, 1965). But when Mr. Levy, the oil expert, goes on to say that by the middle of 1966 the Rhodesian economy would be significantly affected and "that, on such a basis, there would be pressure on the regime, and the oil embargo could be of even greater political and psychological import than the immediate economic impact," then one wonders on what kind of data such conclusions are based (quotations from *UN Weekly News Summary,* Press Release WS/231, March 4, 1966, 3–4). According to the *Rand Daily Mail* (Johannesburg), February 16, 1966, about 150,000 liters of gasoline go into Rhodesia by car from South Africa and Mozambique every day, which is close to the normal consumption of about 300,000 liters. According to the *New York Times* (international edition, April 16–17, 1966, 1), the amount had risen to 50,000 *gallons* from South Africa alone by mid-April, but then the minimum daily consumption was estimated at 150,000 gallons a day.

28. Such theories, understandably, have also been very popular in Rhodesia. Thus, in a letter to the editor of the *Rhodesia Herald,* November 25, 1965, one writer asserts (rightly or not) that the food situation was better in Germany in 1918 than in 1917, that the Versailles Treaty led to the German experiments with rockets with their well-known consequences, that the reparations Germany had to pay to Serbia (such as trams for Belgrade) gave Germany a bridgehead on the economic market in that country because of the necessity for repairs, and so on—in short, stories of how sanctions may backfire and lead to unanticipated consequences. Stories of the same kind also cropped up in our interviews.

29. "Pluralistic ignorance" is what obtains when there is confusion about where the majority stands. In Rhodesia, even under the mildly authoritarian conditions reigning there now, it would be difficult for an opposition that happened to be in the majority to know that this was the case, since there is no adequate way of expressing such attitudes, and hence no incentive for action due to the feeling of being supported and strongly so.

30. For the first presentation of this theory, see L. Festinger, *A Theory of Cognitive Dissonance* (Evanston 1957), particularly chap. 1.

31. This was in January 1966.

32. See letter to the editor, *The New York Times,* January 28, 1966.

33. This Association was originally formed with the three goals of promoting tourism to Rhodesia, of encouraging the purchase of Rhodesian goods, and of acting as a pressure group by writing letters to the press, and so on.

34. The Proclamation of Independence, signed on "this eleventh day of November in the Year of Our Lord one thousand nine hundred and sixty-five" may sound quaint: "Now Therefore, We the Government of Rhodesia, in humble submission to Almighty God who controls the destinies of nations, conscious that the people of Rhodesia have always shown unswerving loyalty and devotion to Her Majesty the Queen and earnestly praying that we and the people of Rhodesia will not be hindered in our determination to continue exercising our undoubted right to

demonstrate the same loyalty and devotion, and seeking to promote the common good so that the dignity and freedom of all men may be assured, DO, BY THIS PROCLAMATION, adopt, enact and give to the people of Rhodesia the Constitution annexed hereto. GOD SAVE THE QUEEN."

There is style to that proclamation, and its expressive adequacy was fully appreciated by our informants. The same applies to the little document entitled *Rhodesia's Finest Hour*, showing the Smith government impeccably lined up for the signature ceremony, with the Queen's image watching them. We quote from Smith's speech: "Let there be no doubt that we in this country stand second to none in our loyalty to the Queen and whatever else other countries may have done or may yet do, it is our intention that the Union Jack will continue to fly in Rhodesia and the National Anthem continue to be sung. . . . We Rhodesians have rejected the doctrine of appeasement and surrender. The decision which we have taken today is a refusal by Rhodesians to sell their birth–right, and even if we were to surrender, does anyone believe that Rhodesia would be the last target of the Communists and the Afro–Asian bloc?"

35. Expression of such theories was very frequently found in Salisbury as well as London. Possibly the theories are quite valid—but then they are also valid in all other countries. Ghost-writers and -thinkers are found everywhere.

36. This is particularly true if one can even afford to use these resources to help others when one is in distress oneself. A typical example of the Smith government's strategy in this respect was demonstrated in connection with the cyclone in Mozambique at the beginning of January 1966: Smith sent a widely publicized cable to the Governor–General of Mozambique offering all kinds of assistance—at a period when Rhodesia itself was in a difficult situation (Rhodesia Ministry of Information, Press Statement 29/66, January 10, 1966).

37. Quoted in the *Rhodesia Herald*, February 11, 1966.

38. Let us pursue this parallel a little further. A basic point in sanction theory is *immediacy*; whether the sanctions take the form of reward or of punishment, they should ideally follow the actions to be rewarded or punished so closely that a clear connection is established. If there is a considerable delay, the learning effect may be considerably reduced. However, a characteristic of the international system is its long reaction-time, because of the generally weak level of integration and because of delays caused at the intranational level.

The case of Norwegian trade with Rhodesia may be suggestive in this respect. In this case, "all imports to and exports from Southern Rhodesia, except consignments contracted before November 27, 1965, have been banned." What then happened to Norwegian trade with Rhodesia can be seen from Table II.

39. This is a major perspective in the well–known content analyses of German actions and reactions before the outbreak of World War I made by R. C. North and his colleagues.

40. See footnote 5.

41. Thus, Norwegians would be most surprised and indignant if they heard that the Lapps had been influential enough to marshal nations into a boycott of Norway because of discriminatory practices. They would be less surprised, perhaps, but equally indignant if certain attitudes expressed at the UNCTAD confer-

ences about Norwegian shipping policies crystallized into boycott actions.

42. Shipping is of course also a "crop," putting a nation like Norway in the same position as many developing, raw-material-exporting countries where vulnerability is concerned.

TABLE 2.2

Monthly Value of Norwegian-Rhodesian Trade, 1966 Compared with
1965, in Thousands of Norwegian Kroner

| | Monthly Change in Trade,1966 Minus 1965 Values | Cumulative Change in Trade, 1966 Minus 1965 | |
		Values	*Percent*
January	1975	1975	258.1
February	216	2191	159.3
March	− 2347	− 156	− 3.7
April	644	488	11.0
May	224	712	14.5
June	1471	2183	36.7
July	− 3093	− 910	− 10.1
August	− 1911	− 2821	− 25.7
Total	− 2821	− 2821	− 25.7

The figures are for exports and imports combined. Thus, there was a quick *increase* in trade after UDI (mainly in imports from Rhodesia). Then there are some fluctuations in the cumulative pattern until the decrease became stabilized during the summer of 1966. In total trade statistics for 1966, a considerable decrease relative to 1965 will appear. But the pattern is similar to rewarding a child for its mischievous behavior at breakfast, punishing it in the afternoon and evening, and then announcing that the total day was worse for the child than the preceding day. (Trade statistics are from *Månedsstatisikk over untenrikshandelen*, Statistisk Sentralbyrå, Oslo.)

3

STRATEGIES FOR EVADING
ECONOMIC SANCTIONS*

Jerrold D. Green

INTRODUCTION

Economic coercion has been employed as an instrument of foreign policy by and against a variety of international entities. Such
coercive endeavors usually take the form of economic sanctions imposing embargoes or boycotts against a target state to induce it to
comply to a particular standard of political behavior. Although such
tactics have traditionally been considered as important instruments
of foreign policy, their effectiveness has, for some time, been subject
to question. A review of the literature in this area reveals that stu-
dents of economic sanctions almost uniformly conclude that sanctions are rarely effective and that they constitute symbolic acts
rather than dynamic instrumentalities. Margaret Doxey, for example, states that "one must concede that the deterrent and coercive
force of sanctions is weak on every count," while Peter Wallensteen
writes that "economic sanctions have been unsuccessful as a means
of influence in the international system."[1] Because such studies emphasize this effectiveness–ineffectiveness dichotomy, however,
they frequently overlook the more substantive question of why economic sanctions frequently do not achieve their objective. Thus, the
two central questions on which this chapter focuses are: 1) Why do

*For helpful comments on earlier drafts of this paper I would like to thank
David Deese, Ira Katznelson, Charles Lipson, Miroslav Nincic, and Peter Wallensteen.

economic sanctions fail?; and 2) What insights into the workings of the international system can be gained from the study of such failure?

Investigations of why economic sanctions are often less than fully successful tend to rely on two sets of separate, yet interrelated, explanations: First, the nature of the international economic system inherently allows for evasion since alternate trading partners can always be found; and second, such sanctions promote domestic cohesion and adaptation thus allowing a target state to weather the economic costs. These two explanations are by no means mutually exclusive. Indeed, it can be argued that evasion of economic sanctions usually relies on both domestic and external factors. Yet how do the two relate to one another? Is one likely to be more decisive than the other?

Johan Galtung is prominent among those paying special attention to the second explanation.[2] Like most scholars, he recognizes the general ineffectiveness of economic sanctions. But at the same time, and more importantly, he attempts to identify those factors that contribute to their failure. In his analysis, he presents a useful typology of economic sanctions and attempts to construct a general theoretical framework for their analysis. Furthermore, he discusses the functional characteristics of economic sanctions and relates these features to domestic psychological and social factors, using Rhodesia as an illustrative case.

Galtung identifies what he terms the "naive theory of sanctions" in which value–deprivation is thought to lead, almost automatically, to political disintegration. He counters this by his "revised theory," in which he posits that value–deprivation may, in some instances, lead to political *integration*. Restructuring the economy or smuggling may be employed to thwart the goals of the sender or even in the face of a universal sanction. Such strategies parallel the perspective of the sender yet, according to Galtung, are of little tangible value. Additionally, he indicates that these strategies ignore the ability of a population to adapt, not economically, but, more importantly, sociopsychologically. Thus, political integration rather than disintegration will occur when there are feelings that the collectivity is being threatened, when there is no identification with the attacker, and when there is a firm belief in one's own values.

Galtung suggests that the first set of strategies is obvious. Because of what he views as their limited promise, their import lies more within the parameters of the second set of psychological, domestic–based strategies than as significant economic solutions to a sanction. More specifically, Galtung states that such strategies as smuggling, joking about or otherwise adapting to deprivation can be valuable, because they will be what he terms "self–reinforcing." Economically they will mean little, but those engaged in such activities will derive satisfaction from their involvement in a collective national effort. Here the argument shifts subtly as Galtung argues that endogenous, social–psychologically based counterstrategies have more likelihood of success than do either economic adaptations, likely to be insignificant in scope, or attempts to find exogenous solutions to resolve endogenous suffering or deprivation. The value of self–reinforcing counterstrategies, according to Galtung, lies in the satisfaction derived from falling back on one's own resources without the necessity of believing in immediate victory or manifesting impotent feelings of dependence on a government whose behavior initially stimulated the imposition of the sanctions. In view of a target state's inability to respond in a concrete economic way to economic sanctions, the ensuing deprivation need not lead to political disintegration since there are strategies that are instead geared toward stimulating domestic unity and political integration. Going "through the moves" of responding to or resisting the sanction will serve such a self–reinforcing purpose. Simply speaking, economic sanctions may hurt yet they need not cause political turmoil as there are a variety of social "anesthetics" which can, for a time, dull or disguise the pain.

SANCTIONS AND THE INTERNATIONAL SYSTEM

Galtung's theory pays little attention to the target state's range of options as a member of the larger international economic system and tends to downgrade the political factors that play a dominant role in virtually all economic sanctions. Economic sanctions are dependent upon the economic system that usually contributes to their ultimate failure. This seeming paradox results from the complex nature of international economic relations, the frequent intertwining and separation of economic and political issues, and the practice, described by Stanley Hoffman, by which states play simultaneously on a number of "different chessboards" in their foreign relations. Such factors make theorizing about the operation of the international system extraordinarily difficult. Nonetheless, such complexity need not impede the formulation of some general theoretical propositions on the relative ineffectiveness of economic sanctions. And, we must ask how a theory of economic sanctions can pay short shrift to exogenous political and economic factors. These sanctions originate within the international economic system, and while not denying that "organisms have a certain self–maintaining potential," we must also recognize that no degree of self–reinforcement will produce needed commodities which might be denied a target state. In the throes of economic sanctions, it is unlikely that *joking*, *mysticism*, or *conspicuous sacrifice* can produce desperately needed fuel or food without which a society cannot exist.

Impediments to the ability of economic sanctions to induce compliance may best be understood through consideration of the following factors.

1) When the price of the compliance demanded by a sender entity outweighs the price of suffering economic sanctions, such compliance by the target state will not be induced. As we mentioned above and will demonstrate in more detail, this is supported by the cases of Rhodesia, Israel, and Cuba.

2) Comprehensive universal sanctions could achieve their goals because virtually no state can successfully enter into a period of sustained autarky. Yet:

3) The possibility of universal sanctions occurring is very remote. The degree of global coordination needed for such an undertaking could probably never be achieved. Thus, sanctions should be viewed against actual historical experience, in which all sanctions have been partial in scope and functional in character. We have yet to see universal sanctions anywhere or at any time. The concept of universal sanctions is a theoretical concept rather than an empirically achievable notion.

4) Particularistic economic sanctions can be successfully circumvented by the acquisition of exogenous, third party, trading partners. The character of the international system makes such a strategy both feasible and effective.

5) Whereas exogenous counterstrategies might lead to desirable endogenous outcomes (such as national unity), the obverse is not likely to hold true. In the face of sustained economic sanctions, political integration could not revitalize a rapidly failing economy although a revitalized economy might help to rejuvenate or stimulate the growth of national unity. The amount of time in which adaptation and self-reinforcement could successfully stave off economic disintegration and the political disintegration that would ultimately follow, at some point, is apt to be relatively short.

I attempt, below, to demonstrate the validity of the propositions through an examination of the Rhodesian, Israeli, and Cuban cases. It will be shown that in each case alternate trading arrangements were made and that without such arrangements no degree of national unity, sought through adaptation or self–reinforcement mechanisms, could successfully be mobilized as an effective counterstrategy.

THREE CASE STUDIES

The cases of Cuba, Israel, and Rhodesia were chosen for two reasons. First, these sanctions were imposed within roughly the same time period. Thus, they can be compared with due consideration for an international economic and political milieu whose basic functional characteristics remained essentially unchanged. This would not have been the case had we chosen to compare any of the above with other, earlier cases of sanctions such as those introduced by the League of Nations against Italy in 1935. Clearly, the international system has changed in the past 30 years, and, although a cross–time analysis might prove useful in some areas, it would accomplish little given the particular goals of our study. Second, the scope of our three cases is sufficiently different, ranging from unilateral American sanctions against Cuba to the multilateral Arab League boycott against Israel and finally to the more comprehensive United Nations sanctions against Rhodesia, which most closely approached the magnitude of universal sanctions. The variety of our cases allows us to deduce certain propositions about the nature of economic sanctions while avoiding the more tenuous and less persuasive approach of basing such deductions on a single case.

The concerns of our analysis necessitate a rather narrow perspective for the review of our three cases. We are concerned with the specific factors that minimized the effectiveness of the sanctions under examination rather than with a narrative of either day–to–day events or international legal machinations. Detailed, descriptive accounts of such processes have been provided elsewhere. Yet, it is our feeling that the inclusion of such material, extraneous to our central arguments, would serve to obfuscate rather than substantively inform our analysis.

United States Sanctions against Cuba

With the rise of Castro to power, United States–Cuban relations deteriorated rapidly. Castro's radical politics, his rabid anti–Americanism, and his desire for closer relations with the Soviet Union became sources of concern and frustration for U.S. policy–makers. In February 1960, within a year of his takeover, Castro moved Cuba even more closely to the Soviet Union by initiating a trade agreement that bartered Cuban sugar for Soviet petroleum. In response, in June of the same year, President Eisenhower altered the American sugar quota to Cuba's distinct disadvantage. This was followed, almost immediately, by the refusal of American petroleum companies (Standard Oil, Texaco) to refine Soviet crude oil in their Cuban–based refineries. Cuba responded by expropriating these facilities. This led, in July, to an American cancellation of its substantial yearly order for Cuban sugar. Castro's final response was the expropriation of additional American property whose value has been estimated, by Knorr (p. 148), to be one–half billion dollars. This action provoked the imposition, in October, of American economic sanctions that banned all United States exports to Cuba. Diplomatic ties between the two countries were severed in January of 1961. In addition, this period witnessed the unsuccessful Bay of Pigs invasion as well as attempts by the United States to garner support for its measures from the Organization of American States (OAS). Finally, the United States denied Cuba banking facilities and froze her assets while barring air or sea traffic, which had stopped in Cuba, from access to American ports. The embargo imposed was so strict that it prevented virtually all American exports from reaching Cuba, as well as Cuban goods making their way into the United

States. Travelers from this period may remember that items as insignificant as Cuban postage stamps, acquired abroad, were subject to confiscation by customs personnel at points of entry into the United States. In short, as of 1961, America's radical economic measures were aimed at humbling and inducing compliance from Cuba at almost any cost.

The extent to which economic and political relations had deteriorated becomes clear upon examination of Cuban–American trade patterns before Castro's ascent to power. In 1958, for example, American business interests had investments of over $1 billion in Cuba while 67 percent of Cuban exports and 70 percent of her imports directly involved the United States. Virtually all her technical and industrial equipment was produced in or acquired from the United States, as were almost all her energy requirements (Knorr, p. 138; Doxey, p. 42). Yet, by early 1961, the United States and Cuba, traditional trading partners, separated by only 90 miles of water, had become bitter adversaries.

What the United States hoped to accomplish through stringent economic sanctions is best summarized in statements made on different occasions by both George Ball and Dean Rusk in remarkably similar words. The first three goals of the sanctions were: "to reduce the will and ability of the present Cuban regime to export subversion . . . to other American states; to demonstrate . . . that Communism has no future in the Western Hemisphere; and to increase the cost to the Soviet Union of maintaining a Communist outpost in the Western Hemisphere" (Doxey, 1971, p. 41; Knorr, 1975, p. 149). The fourth and most instructive point, made by George Ball, was that through the sanctions the United States hoped to: "make plain to the people of Cuba and to elements of the regime that the present regime cannot serve their interests," or, as Rusk stated even more pointedly: "to make plain to the people of Cuba that *Castro's regime* (italics mine) cannot serve their interests" (Doxey, p. 41; Knorr, p. 149). The fourth point illustrates the ways in which sender states hope to incite political disintegration through the imposition of economic sanctions. Such sanctions will presumably cause economic disintegration while the sender entity, in this case represented by Ball and Rusk, informs the citizenry that they are suffering personal deprivation as a result of poor leadership. Once the population realizes this, it is hoped that they will compel political elites to make concessions to the sender state. As mentioned earlier, this process is what Galtung calls the "naive theory of economic sanctions" and, as we shall see, his rejection of this process is quite correct.

Another observation transpires from the above statement. For Castro, the costs of meeting U.S. demands was greater than the cost of enduring U.S. economic sanctions. Castro could not possibly comply while maintaining any degree of credibility with his people. After consistently and vehemently attacking the United States, it is unlikely that Castro could, even if he might have so desired, totally reverse his own position by allowing the United States to dictate how the Cuban polity should be ruled. Thus, in some sense, his choice was simple: "abdicate" or resist. Naturally, he chose the latter.

How did Castro choose to resist? In order to compare our notion of exogenous counterstrategies with Galtung's theory of endogenous measures, it should be determined which strategy played a dominant role in the Cuban case. As Schreiber (1973) writes:

> Cuban leaders actively sought new trade links within months of coming to power. The Castro regime believed from an early stage that the diversification of its trade patterns was essential if Cuba was to be fully independent and achieve social and economic development. As part of this effort, the Cuban leadership sought Soviet economic support. One analysis suggests that the Cubans deliberately radicalized their revolution in 1959 in order to win Soviet economic support. (p.390)

Doxey supports this by writing that "the reduction of the United States sugar quota to zero in 1960 forced a drastic re-orientation of Cuba's external trade" (p. 42). Cuba had few options other than to seek other trading partners, for without them her economy would be strangled. As a small island suffering a boycott imposed by her once closest trading partner, Cuba was, in Galtung's terms, extremely "vulnerable." With an economy that was "concentrated" on one major commodity, sugar, and having traditionally exported the vast bulk of that sugar to the United States, Cuba represents a classical case of an easily sanctioned economy. Yet, as history has demonstrated, these sanctions did not achieve their purpose. For, as Knorr writes:

It may well be that Cuba's economy would have utterly collapsed under the embargo if she had been isolated. But the Soviet Union and other Communist as well as non–Communist countries came to her help or traded with her. If this was a burden to the Soviet Union, as it surely must have been, its government is likely to have derived commensurate satisfaction from besting the United States "in her own backyard." (p. 149)

Knorr suggests, correctly, given Cuba's prior dependence on the United States, that without Soviet or other external aid the Cuban economy would have collapsed. Yet, he assesses incorrectly Soviet motivations in this regard. If not exactly a burden, Soviet support of Cuba was not a strategy based on an economic calculus. As Schreiber writes:

When the Soviet Union offered to buy much of the Cuban sugar that had been denied access to the United States market, the move was not based on need: the Soviet Union grew very large amounts of sugar at home. (p. 394)

It is unlikely that the Soviet Union would buy Cuban sugar which it really did not need merely "to best the United States" in the whimsical sense suggested by Knorr. Rather, the Soviet Union found a golden opportunity to increase her influence in the Western Hemisphere. Such an opportunity countered, in a sense, the American presence on the Soviet's own southern border in Turkey, a long-standing member of NATO. Indeed, the Soviet Union provided more military aid to Cuba than did the United States to all of Latin America in the time period 1955–67 ($750 million as opposed to $523 million) (Knorr, p. 180). Thus, Cuba successfully found an alternative trading partner. The partner became available, not out of economic necessity but rather from a complicated amalgam of political, strategic, and to some degree ideological ambitions and considerations.

Cuba was able to find a variety of other trading partners in addition to the Soviet Union. Members of the Eastern Bloc became involved in Cuban trade, and other states as well came to Cuba's aid primarily for economic reasons: among them Japan, Egypt, Morocco, Canada, France, Australia, New Zealand and, uncomfortably for both the United States and the Soviet Union, China. The United States attempted to arrest trade between Cuba and some of these states but with limited success. Indeed, trade with states such as those in Western Europe and North Africa increased after the imposition of the American sanctions. Most importantly, according to Doxey:

> In the three years from 1959 to 1962, the dominant position of the United States in Cuba's external trade was completely eliminated. Whereas in 1959 the United States supplied 68 percent of Cuban imports and took 69 percent of Cuban exports, by 1962 Cuban trade with the United States was negligible; 82 percent of Cuba's export trade and 85 percent of her import trade was conducted with Communist countries, particularly the Soviet Union, Czechoslovakia, and Mainland China. (p. 43)

None of this meant to indicate that American sanctions exacted no costs for Cuba, for this was not the case. In fact, most analysts agree that the sanctions, when coupled with Cuban errors in policy–making, contributed to a difficult economic situation. Nonetheless, Cuba withstood the rigors of the American sanctions far more effectively than she could have in the absence of alternate trading partners. In particular, it seems clear that without massive Soviet aid her economy would have collapsed.

On yet another level we find that smuggling and other unorthodox strategies significantly served to benefit Cuba, contrary to what Galtung suggests about the minimal economic value of such tactics. For example, when Cuba encountered a serious difficulty in acquiring spare parts for American machinery, international racketeers bought such parts in Canada and shipped them to Cuba via Morocco. Dummy corporations were started in Mexico from which spare parts were also sent. Gradually, Cuba began to use Soviet and Eastern European machinery as well as to obtain parts for U.S. machinery that were duplicated in Eastern Europe and later in Cuba (Schreiber, p. 396). The economic implications of such actions may seem minimal in strict dollar and cents terms, for a machine might merely lack a five-dollar part which prevents its operation. Yet, such a calculation ignores the economic bottlenecks that can appear for lack of even a minor and inexpensive part.

From the point of view of the new trading partners, motives for cooperating differed widely. The Soviets sought political gains, the Chinese found an opportunity to make both the Soviets and the Americans uncomfortable, and the Western European and North African countries found it economically expedient. The Mexicans and the Canadians may have considered the opportunity to trade with Cuba, in the face of vehement American opposition, an appropriate way to manifest their sovereignty in the face of a domineering and insensitive neighbor. The nature of the international system made the availability of the new trading partners virtually inevitable.

A comprehensive review of the descriptive literature concerning the Cuban case provides only one reference that seems to support, in part, Galtung's formulations on the value of endogenous counterstrategies. As Schreiber points out:

> The policy of economic coercion has given Castro a scapegoat to divert attention from internal problems and the errors of his regime. Cuban leaders admit their errors, but they also blame "the imperialist blockade" for some of their problems. The regime has made United States economic coercion a rallying point for the people as it attempts to bolster spirits and increase productivity. Standing up to the "North American giant" helps make Castro look like a hero. (p. 404)

Thus, notions of reinforcement have played a role, according to Schreiber, in Cuba's successful endurance of American economic sanctions. But it seems that without the availability of alternate trading partners such tactics would have accomplished little. For example, without massive infusions of Soviet aid, food could not have been available in adequate quantities and consumer goods would have rapidly disappeared from the shops. Indeed, until recently, even with Soviet aid, food and gasoline were strictly rationed as were consumer commodities such as soap and clothing. Even now, as Doxey writes, "it is clear that Cuba cannot yet finance her own development" (p. 44). Thus, endogenous counterstrategies, in the Cuban case, were less important than were alternate sources of supply and export. As we shall see, similar conditions obtained in our other two cases.

Arab League Sanctions against Israel

The details of the Arab–Israeli political and military crisis are by now so well known that we need not review them here. What concerns us is the less well-known *economic offensive* initiated by the Arab states to supplement largely ineffective political and military strategies against Israel. Surprisingly little has been written concerning these Arab sanctions, and much of the existing literature is of a polemical nature sponsored by such groups as B'nai Brith, the American Jewish Committee, or the Arab Boycott Office itself in Damascus. The reason for this dearth is clear because Arab sanctions against Israel have had limited success and have thus generated little academic interest. Jewish groups that deal with the issue are periodically concerned about particular instances in which international business organizations, in violation of U.S. law, discriminate against non–Israeli Jews in order to satisfy customers in the Arab world. The sanctions are of interest in this chapter, however, for they demonstrate the ability of a target state to circumvent attempts to strangle its economy.

In December, 1945, the Arab League Council committed all of its members to a collective boycott of goods produced in Palestine by Jewish (Zionist) firms. This was followed, in 1946, by the establishment of the permanent Arab League Boycott Committee which was headquartered first in Cairo and later in Damascus. After the inception of the state of Israel in 1948, the borders of all surrounding states were closed to Israel and a permanent state of war was declared. In the years immediately following Israeli independence the Suez Canal was closed to Israeli shippings as well as to ships of other nationalities bound to or from Israel; the Straits of Tiran and Aqaba were blockaded by Egypt to prevent Iranian oil from reaching the Israeli port of Eilat; overflight rights were denied air traffic destined to or from Israel; travelers with Israeli visas in their passports were not permitted entry to Arab states; and, finally, companies doing business with Israel were blacklisted and formally barred from Arab markets unless they ceased any and all involvement with the Zionist state. It is this last point, the blacklist, which is of greatest interest, for although the other actions listed above may have had certain economic implications, the blacklist represents the most significant attempt by the Arab states to involve other, non–Arab actors in their struggle with Israel. Indeed, the boycott in the form of blacklisting has been termed by Doxey as "economic cold war." She describes this "cold war" as follows:

> The Arab countries adapted the technique of blacklisting to widen the scope of their campaign of economic war against Israel. In addition to imposing a total embargo on all Arab dealings with Israel on a commercial or personal basis, the boycott extends to cover Arab trade with foreign firms who have close Israeli connections in the form of subsidiary companies, factories, or assembly plants in Israel, or who give technical assistance to Israeli industries. Such firms are given three months to sever their links with Israel or submit to the boycott themselves. (p. 28)

The blacklist extends to all levels of commerce and trade ranging from ships that have called at Israeli ports to a ban on the showing of Elizabeth Taylor's films in Arab countries because the actress had visited Israel and provided financial support to the Zionist cause. Robert McDonald, in his study of the Arab League, mentions incidents of blacklisting of a far greater magnitude. Attempts by the Boycott Office to exert pressure, with varying success, are mentioned. The targets of such pressure are financial giants which include Air France, Renault, Coca Cola, Ford, Hilton, Sheraton, RCA, and the British Union Insurance Company, a member of whose board of directors was compelled to resign because of Zionist sympathies (pp. 121–22). Individual states have also been pressured by the fear of Arab economic or political retribution: among them, Czechoslovakia, Hungary, Turkey, Cyprus, West Germany, Sierra Leone, and Ghana. A more recent example of the employment of such tactics was the refusal by Arab oil–producers to export petroleum to those states that might have supported Israel in the 1973 War. The strategy was so successful that only the Netherlands refused to comply. As a result, the United States was unable to arrange European fueling stops for military supply planes en route to Israel. Portugal alone allowed planes to refuel in exchange for American abstentions in United Nations votes condemning its colonialist policies in Angola. Thus, what was once the almost exclusive function of the Boycott Office had become a standard feature in the practice of Arab foreign policy and was focused both on private business concerns and individual states. The strategy employed was quite simply one of finding Israel's real or potential trading partners or political supporters, seeking out a weakness in the cooperator, and presenting an ultimatum—stop trading with or supporting Israel or a price will be incurred. This price may have been the withholding of oil or a raising of its price (Western Europe and Japan in 1973), a loss of Arab markets (various business concerns), Islamic religious interests (Pakistan, Uganda, Indonesia), or even vague statements hinting that the Arab world has more to offer to "its friends" than does Israel (African states that had close relations with Israel yet quickly dissolved ties with her after the 1973 War: Uganda, Zaire, etc.).

Admittedly, Israel has suffered slightly as a result of the Boycott Office's attempts to strangle her economy. Nelson and Prittie (1977, p. 14) suggest that the "combined Suez and Aqaba blockades may have cost Israel as much as $25 million between 1949 and 1956," a substantial sum for a developing country. Foreign trade was impeded; because of Israel's total geographic isolation, her nearest trading partners were 2,500 miles away in Europe or more than twice that distance in the United States. Through a combination of reasons this nation has become almost a pariah state, rejected and isolated, both economically and politically, by many international actors. Yet, paradoxically, Israel has not only survived Arab economic warfare but has prospered. We should attempt to reconcile this prosperity with the seemingly impressive array of economic weapons available to the Arab states.

The single most important factor that has contributed to Israel's successful endurance of Arab boycotts has been her close and profitable ties with the United States. This "special relationship" has insured a constant flow of funds, military supplies, consumer goods, technology, and even tourists to Israel. The influential American Jewish community and the American people at large, through the House and Senate, have firmly committed the United States to a strong and continuing support for Israel. This relationship, in spite of heavy Israeli dependence on the United States, has minimized her vulnerability to Arab boycotts. The Arab measures have had only marginal success in pressuring U.S. business interests and no effects at all within the U.S. governmental sector. Yet, Israel has attempted to establish or improve trade relations with other international actors more susceptible to Arab pressure. The reasons for this are two–fold: 1) Israel understands the dangers of becoming overdependent on the United States and would rather diversify than "put all her eggs" in the American basket; and 2) trade with the United States is at times economically awkward as it is difficult, expensive, and impractical to deal with a market that is over 6,000 miles away. Transportation and insurance costs involved in shipping goods to the United States often raise prices at a point at which these goods are no longer competitive in U.S. markets. In addition, some Israeli products are more suitable for non–U.S. markets. (Among these are military goods that are eagerly sought by Latin American and Asian states.) Unhappily for Israel, it is precisely in these other markets that Arab boycotts are likely to be most effective.

With regard to imports, Israel and the Arab states have divided up potential sources of supply. Thus, we find Coca Cola operating in Israel while Pepsi Cola does business in the Arab world. The Japanese automobile industry is similarly divided, with Subaru exporting to Israel and Toyota to the Arab states. The fact that Arabs import *any* automobiles from Japan, whose government allows export to Israel, exposes a serious flaw in the boycott: there are many instances in which Arab states ignore their *own* economic sanctions and the blacklist that they have so assiduously compiled. Japanese automobiles are quite simply often less expensive than comparably sized European vehicles. Thus, the Arab states prefer to turn a blind eye to one segment of the Japanese automobile industry rather than to deny themselves economically attractive products. There are more blatant examples such as Arab states which, in the face of a pressing need, involve themselves with companies that do direct business with Israel. Indeed, firms such as Avis, Hilton, Bank of America, Hertz, Raytheon, AT&T, Xerox, Eastman–Kodak, McDonnell-Douglas, General Motors, British Leyland, Volkswagen, and a variety of others do business both in Israel *and* the Arab world without impediment. Nelson and Prittie (1977) inform us that many of these companies have been asked to honor the boycott, but in almost all such cases the response was negative. Needing their products and services, and finding no adequate substitutes, the Arabs quietly let the matter rest. Lufthansa, Air France, and Swissair, by example, service both Israel and the Arab world although never on the same flights. Rejection of such airlines would virtually isolate the Arab states, whose own national airlines are small by comparison and service limited routes. The boycotts have also been circumvented, not by Arabs but by outsiders interested in dealing with Israel, by bribing influential boycott supervisory officials, by using falsified bills of lading and by various other forms of duplicity.

Two of the most blatant and well–known circumventions by the Arabs of their own boycott, are the "open–bridges" policy between Israel and Jordan and the post–1973 War injunction allowing the passage of Israeli goods on non–Israeli ships through the Suez Canal. The open Allenby Bridge is of mutual benefit to Israel and Jordan and, although the Boycott Office has considered closing it, it has been wary of the wrath of both West Bank and Jordanian Arabs who use the bridge for trade and family visits. In addition, it provides a profitable trade route for both Israeli and Jordanian economies, neither of which would be happy to forgo it. The Suez Canal issue was an important bargaining chip for the Israelis in negotiations with Egypt after the 1973 War. The Egyptians, in fact, were easily convinced to accept the new state of affairs which cost them little and increased canal revenues by expanding usage.

Israel also circumvented the boycotts by trading with other states considered as repugnant to the Arab world (e.g., South Africa) or with states that had demonstrated a willingness to mount political challenges to the Arab world (Pahlavi Iran). Little is known about the specifics or volume of such trade between pariahs, or near pariahs. Yet we do know that substantial quantities of Israeli weaponry have found their way to a South Africa able to make payment in the hard currency so badly needed by Israel. Until the fall of the Shah, Iran provided Israel with all of her domestic oil, thus flaunting Iranian independence and its growing economic, political, and military strength in the face of would–be Arab competitors such as Saudi Arabia. Israel, as Zonis (1972, p. 39) informs us, helped to train Iran's SAVAK (secret police), and it is common knowledge that Israeli firms, among them Solel Boneh, were actively involved in various Iranian construction projects including luxury hotels and roadways. Such relations were impervious to blacklisting or boycotts by the Arab world because, from the outset, Iranian and South African–Arab relations were either tenuous or hostile. These links between "outcasts" benefit both parties and may well expand in the future.

As we have shown, Israel has, for the most part, withstood Arab economic pressures. By seeking and being sought by a variety of exogenous trading partners who are able and willing to circumvent or ignore the boycotts, Israel has prospered. Admittedly, Galtung's notions of self–reinforcement and adaptation play an important role in a country whose population, with severe threats to its security, is unusually integrated and unified. Still, without the external availability of such crucial commodities as jet engines, ammunition, and other sophisticated U.S. armaments as well as substantial external economic relations, Israel could not survive.

United Nations Sanctions against Rhodesia

In order to analyze United Nations sanctions against Rhodesia, we shall first present a brief historical review of the events that brought them on. In 1961, the white Rhodesian government implemented a "new" voting system that limited the rights of black Africans to vote by basing suffrage on economic and educational qualifications that few of them could meet. Although the majority's enfranchisement was purportedly the aim of this system, it was actually evident that Rhodesia's white elites were attempting to deny it any influence on or entry into the political system. Most blacks were dissatisfied with this development, and their leadership refused to cooperate in the implementation of the new constitution that had been drafted collectively with the whites, under British supervision, earlier in the year. In response to the new electoral provisions, Britain refused to consider granting Rhodesia its independence until the white government had demonstrated its intention to move toward majority rule. On November 11, 1965, after two years of fruitless negotiations with Britain, Prime Minister Ian Smith promulgated the Unilateral Declaration of Independence (UDI), which Britain considered illegal and unconstitutional. After further unsuccessful negotiations with the Smith government, London referred the problem to the United Nations which, on December 16, 1966, imposed mandatory economic sanctions. This represented the first time in the history of the United Nations that such an action was taken. In 1968, the sanctions were broadened to include an almost total embargo on all trade and economic relations with Rhodesia.

As in our other cases, economic sanctions against Rhodesia were not fully successful. On the surface this may seem surprising given the virtual unanimity in the United Nations on the need for economic sanctions and given their mandatory nature. The scope of the measures seemed comprehensive as described by Doxey:

> ... the export of petroleum, arms, ammunition and military equipment, vehicles and aircraft was embargoed; members were also required to ban imports from Rhodesia of tobacco, sugar, meat and meat products, asbestos, copper, chrome ore, iron ore, hides and skins—key commodities which made up the bulk of her export trade. (p. 72)

Pressure was further intensified in 1968 and 1970 by additional provisions. Yet, as we shall see, "empty" condemnation of Rhodesia was more easily accomplished than was effective economic action against her.

Knorr notes that: "In this instance, too, the wall of trade sanctions has proved leaky. There are always traders who find evasion profitable" (p. 160). As in the Cuban and Israeli cases, some circumventions were motivated purely by financial criteria while others stemmed primarily from political considerations. In any case, the scope of such evasions was considerable. The House of Representatives' Subcommittee on International Organizations and Movements provides us with a partial list of offenders including *inter alia* Switzerland, Belgium, the Netherlands, West Germany, France, Japan, Australia, New Zealand, the United States, and Luxembourg (p. 155). Significantly, these states all enthusiastically supported the initial imposition of sanctions (with the exception of non–United Nations member Switzerland). Indeed, the Rhodesian case provided a rare opportunity for international cooperation and a unanimous show of concern for human rights. Only after the initial euphoria of self–righteousness did many states realize that Rhodesia was a valuable market as well as a source of rare and necessary minerals. The Security Council Sanctions Committee detected over 100 violations of the sanctions, while the House Subcommittee admitted, in concurrence with other informed observers, that only a small percentage of such violations were detected and documented.

As an example of such evasions, we might cite the United States which, shortly after the imposition of sanctions, experienced a substantial clash between political idealism and the desire for financial gain. This conflict originated in Detroit where automobile manufacturers became concerned about dwindling supplies of chrome ore as well as with the absence of alternate sources of supply. Applying pressure on the Congresss through its lobbies, the automobile industry successfully orchestrated the passage of the Byrd Amendment, which exempted Rhodesian chrome ore from the U.N. sanctions. Other states too circumvented the sanctions, either overtly or covertly. Evasions of this sort are illustrative, among other things, of the frequent conflict between economic sanctions and the senders' domestic economic needs. For example, had the United States needed Cuban sugar, it is likely that the history of Cuban–American relations would have taken a different course. The Byrd Amendment also illustrates the potential for competition and lack of communication that characterizes the parallel formulation of economic and political policies. Having discussed the evasions of sanctions by their initiators, let us now look at the more predictable and easily understood reactions of those who shunned the sanctions from the outset.

At the time of their imposition, the sanctions were opposed by South Africa and Portugal, each of which resented attempts to eradicate white colonialism from the African continent. As Doxey writes, regarding Rhodesia's links to these two states:

> The support of South Africa and Portugal has been crucial. The South African government has given backing to the Rhodesian regime; it has maintained friendly relations; it has supplied essential oil; it has permitted South African territory to be used as a supply route for Rhodesian exports and as a source of imports. (p. 87)

This support provided landlocked Rhodesia with an outlet to the sea for its foreign trade. Second, since Rhodesia and South Africa exported similar goods, the former's exports routed through South

Africa could be disguised as the latter's (Doxey cites the asbestos trade in which United Nations members admit importing 202,000 metric tons from South Africa, as South African, for Rhodesia [p. 80]). Similar tactics were employed for the illicit sale of gold, iron ore, copper, and chrome ore. As Curtin and Murray (1967) persuasively argue, Rhodesia's export capacity for export was $50 million a year, of which $35 million, in 1965, went to South Africa—it is unlikely that South Africa could consume vast quantities of Rhodesian exports which she herself produces.

Third, there was a constant flow of South African industrial capital into Rhodesia. Finally, South Africa and Rhodesia cooperated militarily in a defense against irredentist guerrilla activity from surrounding black nations. The South African Army is substantially larger and better equipped than was her Rhodesian counterpart and her aid importantly benefited the Rhodesians.

Another significant type of evasion came from an unexpected source—black states that border Rhodesia. Malawi and Zambia, in particular, have had traditionally close ties with Rhodesia since all three states once comprised a larger, "Greater Rhodesia." Both Malawi and Zambia found it desirable, yet nearly impossible, to unlink their economies from Rhodesia's. Thus, Zambia allowed the sanctioned nation access to her ports while Malawi imported her meat. Cooperation in a variety of other areas also persisted.

Here, as in the other two cases, economic sanctions took only a slight toll. In addition to the necessity of seeking alternate trading partners (or, more precisely, making new trading arrangements for dealing with old partners), Rhodesia had to diversify her economy somewhat. This diversification led to some structural unemployment, although ironically, mainly among the black population whose interests the sanctions had been designed to protect. Such diversification had its greatest impact in the agricultural sector where there was little success in finding alternate markets for a once flourishing export trade.

On the whole, however, Rhodesia managed to avoid the worst effects of the sanctions. This success can be attributed to South Africa and, to a lesser degree, to the other trading partners with whom Rhodesia dealt.

It is difficult to measure what contributions Galtung's notions of self–reinforcement made. Unfortunately, his study dealt only with the first year of the sanctions and no follow-up studies of a similar type were undertaken. Still, given the material deprivation to which the sanctions *could* have subjected Rhodesia, in the absence of exogenous aid, it is reasonable to assume that self–reinforcement mechanisms were less important than trade with South Africa.

CONCLUSIONS

In light of these three cases, let us briefly review our findings in an attempt to gauge the utility of various modes of evasion. It is generally recognized that economic coercion is often ineffective as a means of inducing compliance. Yet, authors such as Galtung attribute this lack of success to social–psychological, endogenous responses, while I have argued the primary importance of political and economic strategies of an international nature. Galtung bases his argument on a belief that "organisms subjected to stress change" and, although I accept this proposition, it seems that the nature of such change is different and less important than he asserts. I do not reject Galtung's conceptualization, merely his emphasis. A pattern emerges in our three cases which, while not refuting Galtung's claims, helps put them in a more accurate and realistic perspective.

In each of the three cases, the net costs of complying with the wishes of a sender entity were clearly outweighed by the risk of attempting to endure economic sanctions. Compliance in each case would have necessitated a virtual dismantlement of the target's political, social, and ideological systems. Thus, elites in each case had only one realistic option, *resistance*.

In order to successfully resist, each target was compelled to seek alternate markets. While Galtung pays little attention to such counterstrategies, it has been clear that Cuba, Israel, and Rhodesia were totally dependent on exogenous sources for energy and, to varying degrees, on a variety of other crucial commodities. By ignoring such economic factors, Galtung underestimates the material basis upon which all modern states depend. Certainly, domestic unity is important, yet it does not put food into our mouths or fuel into automobiles. *Economic* sanctions can effectively be negated *only* by *economic* measures. The importance of self–reinforcement mechanisms has, in each case, been subordinate to the far more crucial necessity of protecting the economy. There is a definite pattern to the evasion. In each case we find one major evader, the Soviet Union for Cuba, the United States for Israel, and South Africa for Rhodesia. In each of these instances, the "significant evader" intervened for essentially political or strategic reasons. The aid was offered not out of altruism but from a pragmatic and logical calculation that it would advance the evader's own interests: the Soviets helped Cuba in order to gain a foothold in the Western Hemisphere, the United States aided Israel to improve its footing in the Middle East, and South Africa came to Rhodesia's support in order to protect a kindred yet rapidly endangered form of white colonialism that reflected its own political system. Certain moral or ideological factors also motivated the assistance; these are self–evident and need not be enumerated here.

In addition to the politically motivated "significant evaders," each case received aid from a variety of smaller, economically stimulated evaders. These may be either private business concerns or individual states seeking profitable trade relations. In each case there were many actors who felt that "someone else's" political considerations should not interfere with their own search for profit. Even in the Rhodesian case, apparent supporters of the United Nations' sanctions eventually abandoned the sanctions in order to pursue their financial interests.

Another factor that emerges from the three cases is the irrelevance of a sanction's scope. Irrespective of their magnitude, from unilateral to multilateral to almost universal, each sanction was evaded with equal success which, incidentally, tells us that wherever there is a seller there is also a buyer (and vice versa).

By downplaying the possibilities for evasion provided by the international economic system Galtung neglects viable, effective, and relatively easily achieved counterstrategies. National integration is indeed a desirable goal and, *after attending to material needs*, a ruling elite must concentrate on maintaining national unity and political integration. But, self–reinforcement cannot grow food, although, when there *is* food, people can be, even in the face of an implacable foe, unified and integrated.

NOTES

1. These quotations are cited on page 3 of Olson's paper, "Expropriation and Economic Coercion: Theoretical Linkages and Case Illustrations." Please see the bibliography for full reference to this paper as well as for the studies by Doxey and Wallensteen.

2. Johan Galtung, "On the Effects of International Economic Sanctions: With Examples from the Case of Rhodesia." *World Politics* XIX (April 1967), 378–416.

SELECTED BIBLIOGRAPHY

Coser, Lewis. *The Functions of Social Conflict*. New York: The Free Press, 1956.

Curtin, Timothy, and Murray, David. *Economic Sanctions and Rhodesia*. London: The Institute of Economic Affairs, 1967.

Doxey, Margaret P. *Economic Sanctions and International Enforcement*. London: Oxford University Press, 1971.

Galtung, Johan. "On the Effects of International Economic Sanctions: With Examples from the Case of Rhodesia." *World Politics* XIX (April 1967), 378–416.

Harkavy, Robert. "The Pariah State Syndrome." *Orbis* XXI (Fall 1977), 623–49.

Inbar, Efraim. "The Pariah State." (Ph.D. dissertation, University of Chicago, 1976 unpublished).

Insight Team of the *London Sunday Times*. *The Yom Kippur War*. New York: Doubleday & Co., 1974.

Knorr, Klaus. *The Power of Nations: The Political Economy of International Relations.* New York: Basic Books, 1975.

Lipson, Charles, "Corporate Preferences and Public Policies: Foreign Aid Sanctions and Investment Protection." *World Politics* XXVIII (April 1976), 396–421.

McDonald, Robert. *The League of Arab States: A Study in the Dynamics of Regional Organization.* Princeton: Princeton University Press, 1965.

Nelson, Walter, and Prittie, Terence. *The Economic War against the Jews.* New York: Random House, 1977.

Olson, Richard Stuart. "Economic Coercion in International Disputes: The United States and Peru in the IPC Expropriation Dispute of 1968–1971." *The Journal of Developing Areas* IX (April 1975), 395–413.

_____. "Expropriation and Economic Coercion: Theoretical Linkages and Case Illustrations." (Paper delivered at 1978 meetings of the International Studies Association, Washington, D.C.).

Schirman, Shalom. "The Impact of the Arab Boycott on the Economy of the Middle East." (Unpublished monograph, Shiloh Institute of Tel Aviv University, n.d.).

Schreiber, Anna P. "Economic Coercion as an Instrument of Policy: U.S. Economic Measures against Cuba and the Dominican Republic." *World Politics* XXV (April 1973), 387–413.

Ullman, Richard H. "Human Rights and Economic Power: The United States Versus Idi Amin." *Foreign Affairs* LVI (April 1978), 529–43.

United States Government. *Sanctions as an Instrumentality of the United Nations: Rhodesia as a Case Study.* Washington, D.C.: United States Government Printing Office, 1972. (A report of hearings before the Subcommittee on International Organizations and Movements of the Committee on Foreign Affairs—House of Representatives).

Wallensteen, Peter. "Characteristics of Economic Sanctions." *Journal of Peace Research*, April 1968, 248–67.

Waltz, Kenneth. "The Myth of National Interdependence." *In* Charles P. Kindleberger, ed., *The International Corporation.* Cambridge: MIT Press, 1970.

Zonis, Marvin. *The Political Elite of Iran.* Princeton: Princeton University Press, 1972.

4

ECONOMIC SANCTIONS: TEN MODERN CASES AND THREE IMPORTANT LESSONS

Peter Wallensteen

WHAT DO WE WANT TO KNOW ABOUT ECONOMIC SANCTIONS?

The use of economic pressure between parties in conflict is well known throughout history: sieges, blockades and embargoes have often been part of military strategy. There has also been economic pressure without a concomitant resort to arms but it is only with the multifarious interdependencies between states and between consumers, middlemen and producers that it has become a credible tool of influence. Sanctions would, from this perspective, be preferable to other forms of influence because they do not involve the use of force. It could also be argued that they might help advance hitherto neglected interests. Thus, economic pressure could be at the same time less bloody and more "democratic" than military force. These are, therefore, two important reasons for being interested in sanctions: do they, first of all, provide an alternative to force leading, in the long–run, to a reduction in the use of military weapons in international relations (replacement rather than complement)? Second, are they a tool for states or interests that do not possess military force often deemed necessary to promote desired objectives? (Are they used by new interests, rather than being one more means in the hands of the old power holders?) Certainly these two questions present some general and broad issues for investigation. However, both might be premature unless a third and more basic question is answered: are economic sanctions at all successful? Obviously a rapid proliferation of sanctions would have to rest on their perceived utility for achieving a victorious outcome or a satisfactory conflict settlement.[1]

TEN CASES OF ECONOMIC SANCTIONS

Both the League of Nations and the United Nations have had the opportunity to use economic sanctions against member states. It was thought that, with the help of sanctions, aggressor states would be either deterred or forced to cease their aggression. The use of economic pressure to force Germany to submit to the Western powers during the First World War provided a major historical precedent for introducing sanctions into the Covenant of the League of Nations. The application of the logic in a very different situation, against Italy in 1935–36, shattered the simple faith in the efficacy of collective security arrangements in general and of economic sanctions in particular.

These experiences explain the more restrictive view of the utility of sanctions by the United Nations. Only once have sanctions been applied within the framework of collective security thinking: against China and North Korea in 1950 to punish their aggression against South Korea, but this time in conjunction with military force. Thus, neither of the world organizations have demonstrated the value of economic sanctions for the prevention of war or "aggression." Consequently, the use of economic sanctions by the world organization has been infrequent.

However, after 1945, economic sanctions have gained a different function: as a way of expressing discontent with the internal or external policies of states, whether or not they involve aggression. Indeed, since 1945 a number of such sanctions have been proposed and have been central to the international debate: South Africa, Rhodesia, Portugal, Greece, and Spain have all at one time or another had regimes that have been questionable by many international standards. All five have had, or still have regimes of either a fascist or racist complexion. Sanctions have also been implemented against other regimes, for being "Communist" (e.g., Cuba) or "revisionist" (e.g., Yugoslavia).

The concept of sanctions has frequently been applied in political science, jurisprudence, and sociology. Normally a sanction is an action that is carried out in order to maintain or achieve compliance with certain *laws or norms*.[2] Since the international system consists of a number of sovereign, although not entirely independent states, there is a great pluralism of norms and laws. Sanctions, could therefore be used by *any* state against other states that do not comply with the norms one of them believes to be significant. Since this could lead to a rapid breakdown of all kinds of economic and other types of transactions, sanctions tend to be channeled through international organizations because they express a wider international (although not necessarily global) consensus on the significance of particular norms. Of course, it is self–serving for the initiator to have its actions internationally endorsed since it increases the legitimacy of the initiator's norms, and increases the pressure on the alleged violator.

Sanctions can be either *positive* or *negative*, i.e., punishing or rewarding. In the sanctions debate the emphasis is often on negative actions: interruption of relations, isolation, applying pressure, and so forth. However, the scope of positive sanctions is as broad and would include economic rewards (foreign aid), reduction of pressure, integration, etc. As a matter of fact, studies of small groups show that such actions can be highly effective in splitting otherwise very closely knit target groups.[3] However, debates on norm compliance tend to concentrate on punishments rather than on rewards. This appears true for criminal policies within nations as well.

Sanctions can be applied by many different means, of which economics is only one. There are also diplomatic or military sanctions as well as less conventional forms such as popular demonstrations or mail campaigns. The more narrow category of economic sanctions is also highly unprecise. Since economic interaction between states tends to be multifaceted, it allows for varying types and combinations of sanctions. Thus, for some a demand to apply economic sanctions can appear a highly dramatic, punitive move whereas for others it may appear symbolic and moderate.[4] Most fre-

quently, economic sanctions refer to fairly general actions incorpo-
rating most of the economic exchange between states (although in
most cases there are exceptions such as medicine, news media, or
personal correspondence). The assumption is often that the more
comprehensive the action, the more intense the pressure, and, the
more likely the compliance. In this chapter only *negative, comprehensive economic sanctions* imposed by governments are investigated,
whether termed trade bans, boycotts or embargoes.

A further, fundamental idea to the sanctions debate is that the
economic sanctions should be the *main instrument* used by one party
against another. Thus, an attempt to evaluate the recent performance of economic sanctions would have to locate cases corresponding as closely as possible to this notion and exclude situations
in which the outcome is too intertwined with other simultaneously
occurring events.

Departing from these assumptions, it has been concluded that a
complete list of economic sanctions since at least the advent of
"Keynesianism" would reveal why and how economic sanctions fail
or succeed. Thus, leading international archives have been
searched for cases of economic sanctions, trade bans, trade embargoes, blockades, and boycotts from 1932 onward. Economic sanctions were defined as a severe reduction in trade accompanied by
publicly declared political demands of at least one party (the initiator, here called the sender) on the other party (the target, here called
the receiver). With this definition the ten modern cases of economic
sanctions listed in Table 4.1 were compiled.

Some well-known situations have not been included. Thus, the
Arab oil embargo on the United States and other Western states in
1973–74 was omitted because the noticeable change in American
attitudes to Israel and the Palestinians could be explained by the
military and psychological impact of the October War as well as the
embargo.

Some other important events have not been included because of
the accompanying onset of war or the early escalation of the conflict
to war. Such cases were the United States embargoes on Japan, resulting in the attack on Pearl Harbor in 1941, and the UN sanctions
against China and North Korea where the military actions obviously
were more important. The embargo on strategic exports from the
West to the Soviet bloc and the interruption of Soviet assistance and

TABLE 4.1

Cases of Economic Sanctions since 1932

Time	Sender	Receiver	Issue
1933	United Kingdom	Soviet Union	Release of British citizens
1935–36	League of Nations	Italy	Stop war on Ethiopia
1945	Arab League	Israel	Stop Jewish settlements/ Prevent consolidation of Israel
1948–55	Soviet Union	Yugoslavia	Install pro–Soviet regime
1960	African states	South Africa	Abolish apartheid
1960	United States	Cuba	Undermine Castro regime
1960–62	United States	Dominican Republic	Create democratic regime
1961	Soviet Union	Albania	Prevent pro–China policy
1963–75	Org. of African Unity	Portugal	Achieve decolonization
1965–80	United Kingdom (UN)	Rhodesia	Return to legal rule

trade to China around 1960 were two additional cases for which other means (diplomacy, military confrontation, subversion) were judged to be more important than the economic measures. Thus, these cases were not included.

Still, the ten cases are not entirely "pure" since some military action has been present in some them (notably the Arab–Israel wars and Southern Africa). However, in these cases the sanctions effort had consistently constituted the major activity undertaken by a large number of states against the target; hence, they were included in the investigation.

The list of ten cases is a complete set of sanctions given our criteria and the period selected. They should help address the issues raised in the debate on international sanctions and tell us what history teaches about uses, effects, and consequences of economic sanction.

Since no country has been exposed to economic sanctions twice but several countries have initiated sanctions on several occasions, it is convenient in the following to name the cases after the receivers.

SUCCESS AND FAILURE OF ECONOMIC SANCTIONS

Success and Failure

The major issue for international economic sanctions concerns their effectiveness. However, this may refer to many different aspects of a conflict, for instance, the degree of international support for the effort, the economic impact of the actions, or their success in bringing about the desired political change. The third criterion will be the one used here: their success in bringing about the political changes in or by the receiver desired by the sender.

Still, this leaves a great problem of implementation. First of all, we have to assume that the receiver is the only target of the sanctions. This is not always entirely the case. Thus, when the League of Nations imposed sanctions on Italy, the aim was not only to stop Italy's aggression against Ethiopia, but other potential aggressors were also targets (to send a signal to Germany, for instance). In other situations, a target might have been a big power supporting the receiver. This appears true for the U.S. sanctions on Cuba (an additional target being the Soviet Union) or the Soviet actions on Albania (a target being China). However, in such situations we still have to content ourselves with observing the direct relationship between sender and receiver. If sanctions do not change receiver policy, the effects on other targets may also be reduced, as the credibility of the sender using sanction again is lowered. Thus, although the scope might be broader, success should be measured in the sender–receiver relationship.

Second, even when concentrating on the sender–receiver relationship it may be difficult to determine the sender's real motives. What the latter claims publicly might be its bargaining position and, thus, if the final outcome appears less than successful from the sender's perspective, it might actually have achieved what it intended.

Again, we end up with the difficulty inherent in defining success in terms of the sender's objective. We simply cannot, with a sufficient degree of certainty, know what these motives are. Let us then approach the question of success from a different angle: that of the sender's *actions*.

The sender, if satisfied with the political changes forced upon the receiver, would naturally cease to apply sanctions. Thus, one could infer that when sanctions continue to be applied the sender still feels a need to inflict punishment. Whatever changes result, there is little question about the sender's dissatisfaction. This means that cases in which sanctions have not been terminated are, by the sender's actions, considered unsuccessful. Our list of ten cases, in this way, results in at least four unsuccessful cases: the sanctions against Israel, South Africa, Cuba, and Albania. In each case, the sender has continously reaffirmed a commitment to the sanctions, normally with much rhetoric and citing new events to justify the measures. In the case of Israel, the peace treaty with Egypt also led to sanctions against Egypt. In the case of South Africa, events in Soweto and incursions into Angola, have confirmed the need for sanctions. In the case of Cuba, the revolution in Nicaragua and the internal war in El Salvador have provided similar supporting evidence. Only in the case of Albania has the verbal tension been significantly reduced.

Let us, then, scrutinize the six cases in which sanctions have ended. The fact that action is terminated does not, in and of itself, mean that success has been achieved. For example, the sender could admit that the sanctions have failed and, rather than continuing with them, reestablish normal relations with the receiver. At least two cases fall into this category: the sanctions against Italy and Yugoslavia. The first one is the most clearcut. Italy occupied Ethiopia in spite of the sanctions, and within two months the League of Nations decided to terminate its actions.

The case of Yugoslavia is somewhat different. Sanctions were imposed by the Soviet Union in order to force Yugoslavia to "conform with Marxism–Leninism." In actual fact, this meant the replacement of Marshal Tito with a more pro–Soviet regime. After the death of Stalin, however, the new Soviet leadership ceased verbal criticism of the Yugoslav leader and in 1955 Nikita Krushchev visited Yugoslavia, declaring that the accusations against Yugoslavia were based on material "produced by enemies of the people, the . . . agents of imperialism."[5] In essence, Krushchev stated that the sanctions were unjustified and, thus, should never have been imposed. He, thus, not only demonstrated that the sanctions were a failure, but also attributed this failure to his predecessors who imposed them in the first place.

In both cases, senders expressed dissatisfaction with the sanctions' effect. The League readily admitted failure, while Krushchev chose to explain away the failure by blaming Stalin. However, had Tito been overthrown, there is little reason to believe that Krushchev would have expressed regret.

In two other cases, the sender expressed satisfaction with the outcome while terminating the sanctions. Nevertheless, the contribution of the sanctions to the desired outcome can be doubted since, in both instances, the escalation of military violence appeared more significant. The two cases are the sanctions against Portugal and against Rhodesia.

In the case of Portugal, the OAU imposed sanctions were terminated in 1975 following the successful coup that overthrew the Caetano regime. The OAU (Organization of African Unity) did not itself vigorously claim that its sanctions had, to a significant degree, contributed to this. Instead, most observers would agree that the liberation struggles in the Portuguese possessions of Angola, Guinea, and Mozambique were more instrumental in ousting the regime. These seemingly endless wars without victory eventually made segments of the Portuguese armed forces turn against the central authorities.

The Rhodesian case is more complex since the sanctions were terminated in a process whereby the illegally declared independent state was, for a brief period, returned to colonial status. This then met Britain's original demands. Furthermore, the elections with broad participation supervised by the British and other international observers, resulted in a clear majority for one of the African liberation leaders, Robert Mugabe, producing majority rule within a parliamentary system.

Thus, the outcome in 1980 appeared to be what the British government wanted when imposing sanctions in 1965. However, here the problem of causality is fully evident. Obviously, a number of other events took place between 1965 and 1980. Although the sanctions might have played a role, more important was the armed liberation struggle itself. Initiated in 1975, following the inability of the sanctions to bring about change, the violence, after some years threatened the economic viability of the society itself. Indeed, the final agreement, reached in London in December 1979, dealt more with questions of troop disengagements than with the restoration of legality and economic relations. Second, a new political environment was created with the fall of the Portuguese colonial empire. It now became possible for the liberation movements to operate from bases in an adjacent country. What this suggests is that, although the sanctions remained the principal tool used by the British government in dealing with Rhodesia, other parties to the conflict ceased to rely on them. Weapons and armed support became more important. We still have to regard this as a sanction case, but it could be argued that, by the mid 1970s, the sanctions were no longer the main element of influence. This means, furthermore, that Britain itself was no longer the leading actor in the situation. By maintaining sanctions, and upholding its legal claim on Rhodesia, Britain could usefully serve as a mediator and negotiator between the white minority and the black groups in the country. Thus, here we again find a case of unsuccessful sanctions, in spite of the fact that the sanctions were terminated and the sender expressed satisfaction with the final outcome. This case, however, does highlight the problem of causality, present, of course, in all social science research. There always are intervening factors in a historical process. The more time lapses, the more such intervening factors there will be. And incidentally, when sanctions are initiated, the sender probably expects fairly rapid results. It was hardly envisioned by the British leadership that the sanctions would last for almost 15 years and end in the restoration of colonial control for only two months.

This leaves us with two cases in which termination was achieved, the sender expressed satisfaction, the receiver carried out or experienced policy changes, and the time span was short enough to argue that the sanctions were crucial to bringing about this state of affairs: the Soviet Union and the Dominican Republic. However, a close analysis still suggests some ambiguous conclusions. In 1933, Britain demanded that the Soviet Union immediately release some British merchants who had been arrested on espionage charges.

The Soviet Union, however, went ahead with the trials, convicted the merchants, and held them for several months before agreeing to the British demands and, by that time, trade between the two countries had been brought to a halt. It appears that the Soviet Union simply could not accept a solution to the conflict that too obviously meant a surrender to British demands. The sentences were, however, shortened quite considerably. Thus, although not a complete success for Britain, the Soviet Union agreed to release the merchants after some face–saving maneuvers. The sanctions lasted less than four months.

In the Dominican case the sanctions, which were imposed because of the suppression of human rights and the lack of representative democracy in the island republic, were terminated 16 months later when completely new political conditions had emerged. The dictatorship, led by Trujillo, had been severely shaken, Trujillo himself was killed in 1961, and a regime, although composed of some political figures from the Trujillo era, had promised free elections by late 1962. Again the success was not complete, but a process was initiated that justified ending the sanctions.

Although internal development could play a role in explaining the outcome in these two cases, it seems plausible to suggest that the external pressure was highly important in bringing about change. Furthermore, the time span from the initiation to the termination of the sanctions is relatively short meaning that fewer intervening factors were present. Thus, the cases of sanctions against the Soviet Union in 1933 and the Dominican Republic in 1960–62 are the only successful ones.

Drawing this together, success occurred in two cases out of ten. This is obviously not a very striking record. The relative ineffectiveness of sanctions will have to be understood more fully before we can draw a more general conclusion. By systematically comparing the two successful cases to the eight that were unsuccessful, light can be shed on the correlates of success and failure.[6]

Theories of Success and Failure

A case of sanctions embodies a conflict between the sender (who initiates the actions) and the receiver (the target of the actions). The outcome of the sanctions, thus, may depend on the (lack of) actions taken by the former and the counteractions (or lack thereof) of the latter. This means that the success and failure of the sanctions can be explained from both sides of the conflict and that a clear understanding of the outcome would have to incorporate the two perspectives. It is, however, typical of sanction debates that they tend to focus on only one side and, then, mainly on the sender side.

There are at least two additional plausible explanations: the relationship between the sender and the receiver and the reactions of other actors in the international system (i.e., the environment). This means that, altogether, there are four possible ways of explaining the outcome of sanctions. In the international sanctions debate, a great number of ideas are suggested, all falling into one of the four categories. We will treat here such ideas as hypotheses. In all, we have been able to locate approximately 50 different theories, or fragments of theories, that can be used to explain the outcome. In order to organize these properly, the following categories will be used:

> *Sender–oriented explanations*: such theories emphasize the (in)action of the sender, for instance, intentions, commitment, other involvements.
> *Receiver-oriented explanations* suggest that the (in)action of the target is decisive, including factors like capacity for adaption, strength of regime, and economic countermeasures.
> *Relation–oriented explanations* pointing to dependencies, interactions, comparative advantages and perceptions, among other variables, as significant.
> *Environment–oriented explanations,* finally, focus on the activities of other actors, existence of alliances, sanction breakers, etc.

Thus, equipped with ten cases of economic sanctions, a clear definition of successful and unsuccessful cases and four major groups of explanations, we can embark on a complete evaluation of the modern record of economic sanctions.

Explanations Emphasizing the Sender

In most analysis of the outcome of the sanctions the motives of the sender rank high as an explanation. However, the power of the sender, as well as dependence on the receiver, can be equally important.

Motives

The concept of motive is not necessarily very precise. Thus, when an unsuccessful outcome is explained by the sender's disinterest, this may refer to many different aspects of what is commonly termed "motive" or "interest." First, it may mean the instrumentality of the actions. The sender might be interested in bringing about a solution (an instrumental approach) or in making a symbolic manifestation (an expressive approach). Second, "interest" can refer to the salience of the issue at stake. The more salient the issue, the more motivated the sender would be to achieve a successful conclusion of the conflict. Third, the sender might have other "motives" in mind, apart from the successful outcome of the sanctions conflict. Thus, the sender government might find itself involved in internal or international conflicts that "overshadow" the dispute with the receiver. The sender would then be correspondingly less interested in the outcome of the sanctions. Let us discuss these three different sets of motives as possible explanations for the success and failure of the sanctions.

Sociological research often makes a distinction between instrumental and expressive actions. Instrumental actions are those that attempt to achieve a solution to a given problem or a given conflict. Such actions would, for instance, be accompanied by statements pointing to the issue of contention and indicating ways out of the present impasse. Expressive actions, however, aim at releasing accumulated tension and finding solutions is not primarily important. Working from this distinction, the initial sender declarations have been analyzed and the ten cases grouped along the instrumental–expressive dimension.[7] A case of instrumental sanctions is the League's actions against Italy, when it was continuously underlined that the sanctions should be carried out in a friendly spirit without interrupting normal relations and without disrupting the possibilities for a compromise settlement.[8] A typical case of expressive sanctions were those imposed on the Dominican Republic by the United States and OAS. It was explicitly stated that the sanctions would end only when the government of the Dominican Republic ceased to constitute a danger to peace and security in the Western Hemisphere.[9] Eight of the ten cases are of an expressive rather than instrumental nature. This means that the declaration accompanying the sanctions seldom made clear to the receiver how compliance was to be achieved.

Thus, we find that, on the whole, the sender is particularly interested in a moral condemnation of the receiver for its violation of norms important to the sender. To what extent does this help to understand the outcome of the sanctions? There is little evidence that this has any explanatory value at all. Of the eight expressive cases one was successful (actually the most expressive of them all, the case of the Dominican Republic). Of the two instrumental cases one scored a success (the case of the Soviet Union, not being the most instrumental, however). Thus, no correlation between the sender's motive, as measured here, and the outcome of the sanctions was found.

However, we have suggested that the question of motives can be approached by trying to estimate the salience of the issues at stake. We can again scrutinize the initial declarations. Thus, if the sender points to the wider implications of the actions taken by either the sender or the receiver, this presumably increases the sanctions' salience to the sender. In the case of Cuba, for example, the United States did not primarily emphasize Cuban nationalizations of American property but pointed to the dangers of "Communism." In the case of Yugoslavia, the Soviet Union found the deviations from Marxism–Leninism to be the issue. In the South Africa and Portugal cases, the fight against colonialism was pointed to by the African states, etc. In all these cases, broader concerns have been invoked, making the matter relevant to all those sharing the sender's values. In this way the issue is made more salient and fundamental. However, in the cases of Italy and the Soviet Union, such generalizations are virtually absent. In neither case did the British government suggest that the sanctions were part of a fight against "Communism" or in defense of democracy. Rather, the significance of the issue was minimized. It is not difficult to see why, since as overall relations with the Soviet Union were less important to Britain at the time, and the question of the Horn of Africa was probably less significant than the issue of German rearmament.

Thus, we find that the salience of the issue was stressed in eight cases and not emphasized in the other two. Again, there is no correlation with the outcome. Instead, salience correlates with instrumentality: matters of high significance are also matters for expressive sanctions, whereas in less fundamental matters instrumental sanctions were applied. It does not mean, however, that the sanctions become more successful.

However, if the issues are perceived by the sender to be of such high importance, why would economic sanctions be preferred to military action? After all, fundamental issues require, it could be argued, fundamental action. In a thought–provoking investigation, Frederick Hoffmann suggests that internal tensions within the sender would explain why economic sanctions are preferred to other forms of actions (ranging from inaction to military intervention). The sanctions resolve that tension by satisfying those who want only moderate action and those who demand radical measures, while making the sender government appear firm and allowing it to maintain power.[10]

Internal stress can be of two different types: one concerning the goals of the actions (whether the issue warrants firm reaction or not), the other concerning the capability for action (whether one has the resources for a firm reaction or not). In situations where the goals are controversial but where the capabilities are available, expressive sanctions would be preferred in order to blur the internal goal conflict. This argument would in particular apply to major powers that have substantial military capabilities. The capability conflict would be more acute for resource–poor countries that have a strong need for action but are unable to take effective military measures.

In our ten cases of sanctions, there is relatively little intrasender disagreement in five situations (the Soviet Union, Italy, Israel, South Africa and Portugal cases), whereas in the remaining five cases, the patterns are less clear–cut.

In the Yugoslavian case, some material suggests that the sanctions were actually linked to power competition within the Kremlin between a more orthodox and a more "revisionist" grouping (including Malenkov and Khrushchev?). The link between this power struggle and the sanctions, of course, remains obscure, but it is of interest that in 1955 Krushchev blamed one faction for the sanctions (rather than the whole leadership).

The Cuban and Dominican cases are clearer. Both sanctions were announced during the presidential campaign when Kennedy accused his rival, Nixon, of softness toward Cuba. The American embargo against Cuba was announced in October, 1960, shortly before the elections. Previous actions were timed with an eye to the Democratic and Republican National Conventions. The sanctions against the Dominican Republic were imposed as part of an effort to make the policy of opposing *all* types of dictatorial regimes in the Caribbean more credible.

Finally, the case of Albania obviously was related to the Sino–Soviet conflict which, at the time, was mostly phrased in terms of Communist ideology. Again, information is scarce, but several writers point out that this conflict created sharp disagreement within the Soviet leadership, notably between a more orthodox line (Suslov) and a more revisionist one (Khrushchev).[11]

Hoffmann (1967) has documented the disagreements within the British Parliament and within the governing Labour Party at the time of the Rhodesian crisis. Furthermore, he clarified that the sanctions, being perceived very differently in terms of "firmness" actually managed to diffuse some of the internal tension within the Party and secure the Cabinet's position in the Parliament. In February, 1966, the Labour Party, benefiting in part from perceived success in dealing with the Rhodesian crisis, achieved a major victory in the general elections.

Thus, there is some pattern of internal tension in five of the ten cases and, thus, we could theoretically explain the outcome in the following way: when there are contradictory interests within the sender, the sanctions might be less vigorously pursued whereas in case of unanimous support, they might be more forcefully brought to a successful conclusion. Again, however, we have to be disappointed: in the five cases of internal consensus, success was achieved only in one instance; in the five less consensual cases, sanctions again were successful but once.

This brings us to a second type of internal conflict, that between a need to react and a lack of capability to do so with military force. This, we suggested, is more frequently true of small powers. Indeed, in the cases of Israel, South Africa and Portugal, the senders have all been comparatively poor and with little military capacity. Thus, sanctions may well have been one way to resolve this tension; indeed, the high expressive content of the initial declarations may be a way of compensating for the lack of force.

However, we should also search for motivating factors in the *international* system and ask whether the sender was involved in another international conflict at the same time because this would affect the sender's interest in pursuing the sanctions. Here, too, this was the case in five instances. At the time sanctions were imposed on the Soviet Union, Japanese aggression in China, and the international economic crisis seemed to have captured most of British attention. With regard to the sanctions against Yugoslavia, the Soviet Union was simultaneously involved in the Berlin blockade and the German question probably had highest priority.

Similarly, at the time of the sanctions against Cuba and the Dominican Republic, the United States was heavily involved in conflicts with the Soviet Union over the U2, over Berlin, over the collapsed summit meeting in Paris, and over the unfolding Congo crisis. Finally, in 1961 Albania was only one of all Soviet conflict involvements, others being Berlin, nuclear tests, and increasing controversies with China. Thus, in these five conflicts, the sanction issue probably was not the most important involvement.

The remaining five conflicts are different, however, since they were important issues to the senders at the time: Italy claimed most of Britain's attention; similarly, the Rhodesian situation was Britain's major international conflict engagement in 1965. Finally, the conflicts with Israel, South Africa, and Portugal were the primary international activities of the small states imposing the sanctions.

However, the determinants of success have not become clearer from any of this. In each of the five cases in which the sanctions were the dominant external conflict involvement the sanctions were unsuccessful. In the cases in which the sanctions were equally important to or less important than other involvements, two were successful while three clearly were not. Thus, having analysed the motives of the sender in three different ways, we have to conclude that the motives do not strongly determine the outcome of the sanctions.

Power

It is often suggested that the power of the sender will be decisive to the sanction's outcome. Big powers, in other words, would more likely be successful than small ones and, indeed, big powers are frequent initiators (seven cases have big powers as main senders). Three big powers are particularly partial to this weapon: the United Kingdom, the United States, and the Soviet Union. However, the record of success is not striking since five of these big power sanctions ended in failure. The three sanctions initiated by smaller states met with no success at all. Still, this suggests that there is no automatic power effect: big powers may be mighty but not almighty.

If we combine the different variables treated in this section we find that the sanctions fall empirically into three categories. These help us understand why sanctions were initiated but do not explain the outcome of sanctions.

First, there is a set of expressive, big power initiated sanctions. These are the situations when the sender has experienced internal cleavages about how to react to the receiver's infractions of important norms. We suggest that the highly expressive content of the initial declarations makes the actions look firm, although they do not involve the use of force. The internal tension, in fact, would restrain the sender from actually using open military violence against the receiver.

Second, there is a group of expressive, small power initiated sanctions, where the sanctions are non-controversial within the sender, and the action chosen stems from a lack of other alternatives.

Third, there are the instrumental, big power initiated sanctions, when the issue is less salient, the need for a settlement is clearly emphasized by the sender, and there is less controversy within the sender about the sanctions.

A more general trait of all the sanctions is that they have been imposed on countries that have not been economically very significant to the sender. On average, the senders conducted only 1.8 percent of their total trade with the receiver. The highest dependence seems to have been the Soviet reliance on Yugoslavia (about 5 percent of the Soviet external trade involved that country in 1948). This

means that the sender could expect little internal economic dislocation from the sanctions and problems (if any) could be solved by
turning to other trading partners.

To sum up: Explanations emphasizing the sender shed light on
the origins of the sanctions, they do not, however, account for the
outcome of the sanctions. That might perhaps be better answered
by focusing on the receiver, the target of the sender's action.

Explanations Emphasizing the Receiver

With economic sanctions the sender hopes to exploit the receiver's dependence on international trade. However, we also need
to consider countermeasures by the receiver and the political impact
on the target nation, as well as the receiver government's interpretation of the conflict.

Trade Dependence

The receivers were, in some cases, very dependent on the
sender before the imposition of sanctions. In the ten cases, the average share of the receiver's total trade with the sender was 29.0 percent. This means that some countries, notably Cuba and the
Dominican Republic, were extremely dependent on the United
States (68.9 percent and 57.9 percent, respectively). Other highly
sender–dependent states were Albania (50 percent of its total trade
going to the Soviet Union) and Rhodesia (29.0 percent going to the
United Kingdom). In the remaining cases the dependence was less
marked (for instance, South Africa's and Portugal's trade with the
African senders amounted to 5.0 percent and 3.5 percent respectively). However, high dependence has no immediate correlation
with success. On average, in the successful cases the receiver's dependence on the sender was 32 percent, whereas the unsuccessful
ones averaged 27 percent. In fact, several highly dependent states
such as Cuba and Albania successfully withstood the pressure
whereas a less dependent state like the Soviet Union yielded to the
sender.

Thus, we need to pursue the analysis a step further by examining the *actual reduction* of trade occasioned by the sanctions. Calcu-
lating this reduction during the first year of sanctions (which in

some cases is the only year of sanctions, and in some cases may underestimate the more dramatic reduction during the first few months of sanctions), we find an average reduction of approximately 13 percent.[12]

The picture emerging from Table 4.2 is quite clear: the sanctions have not achieved a complete reduction of trade in any single case. Obviously, such an expectation is unrealistic since few states are that dependent on a few suppliers. However, sharp reductions have nevertheless taken place. The most publicized cases, the Italian and Rhodesian ones, are, as can be seen from Table 4.2, among the most effective: about one–third of their total trade was reduced during the first (in the case of Italy also the only) year of sanctions. Only in two other cases did the sanctions result in a two–digit reduction of trade: the Dominican Republic and Yugoslavia. How do we explain the discrepancy between the generally high dependence on the sender (approximately 29 percent) and the much lower actual reduction of total trade (approximately 13 percent)?

The first explanation is that the sender has not always cut off all trade, either because of deliberate policy (as was the case in the US

TABLE 4.2

Actual Reduction of Receiver's Total Trade

Reduction of total trade at end of first year of sanction calculated as percentage of total trade year before sanctions.

Receiver	Total Reduction in Percent
Soviet Union	7
Italy	32
Israel	n.a.
Yugoslavia	13
Cuba	5
Dominican Republic	21
South Africa	0
Albania	7
Portugal	+2
Rhodesia	31

Mean (out of nine cases) 13, mode 7

sanctions on the Dominican Republic) or because all transactions simply cannot be immediately halted. The second, and more important, explanation is that the receiver has been able to find new trading partners. Most sanctions will be initially slow to implement; there will always be other states which, for economic or other reasons are not willing (immediately) to comply or join the sanction effort, and trade with the receiver might become economically lucrative (smuggling).

Let us illustrate the abilities of the receivers to circumvent sanctions. The case of Italy is the only one in which the sanctions actually achieved a more drastic reduction of trade than might have been expected from the dependence on the sender. Italy's trade with Britain was about 10 percent of its total trade before the sanctions. With the support of other members of the League of Nations, the reduction was more than three times this amount. Most accounts suggest that Italy did not strongly compensate for this with non–sending nations (such as Germany, Switzerland or the United States) but kept trade at a "normal level." In this case, the Italian authorities used the sanctions rather as an opportunity to enhance their program of increasing autarky for the Italian economy.[13]

Yugoslavia intensified its trade with the Western world, increasing the share of West European and North American states from about 40 percent of total Yugoslav trade in 1948 to about 68 percent in 1949, at the same time reducing the share of the Soviet Union and Eastern Europe from about 50 percent to 14 percent in 1949.[14]

In a similar fashion, Cuban exports to the United States were almost entirely replaced by sales to the Soviet Union. As a matter of fact, one of the reasons for American sanctions was the already increasing trade with the Soviet Union which, U.S. authorities claimed, might result in reduction of sales to the United States. What happened was a dramatic intensification of an already initiated process. The Soviet actions against Albania followed a parallel pattern: the Soviet Union protesting increased Albanian ties with China, reducing trade, and seeing Soviet trade entirely replaced by China. Finally, in the case of Rhodesia, South Africa, Portugal, and other states took the role previously played by the United Kingdom, either purchasing Rhodesian goods or making it possible for such goods to enter the world market through their territories.

Let us now relate this to the question of success. A reduction of one–third or one–fifth of total international trade is a substantial loss. It might not be what the sender hoped for, but it certainly places any government in a difficult position. The significant conclusion is that even a reduction of this magnitude is not necessarily associated with success: neither the Italian nor the Rhodesian cases were successful. On the contrary, these failures have made world organizations reluctant to attempt economic sanctions in other circumstances. Success, however, occurred in a case with considerable impact: the Dominican Republic. This does not suggest, however, that there is a generally valid relationship between the actual reduction of trade and the outcome of the sanctions. In fact, the economic impact was probably greater in the unsuccessful cases of Yugoslavia and Albania than in the successful case of the Soviet Union.

Moreover, a government facing the ambitious task of drastically rearranging trade from one set of trading partners to another would also be politically vulnerable. The four cases with the sharpest reallocation of trade (Yugoslavia, Cuba, Albania and Rhodesia) were all highly unsuccessful.

Of course, it could be argued that the impact would not be felt during the first year of sanctions, and that, if only the sanctions continued over time, the impact would be greater. The relevant data suggest the opposite. The longer the sanctions are applied, the more modest is their economic impact.[15]

In the cases of Yugoslavia and Albania, the second year of sanctions created the most severe situation: the total trade was then reduced by 26 and 19 percent respectively, compared to the presanction level. This means that some of the actions taken by the Soviet Union and its allies (in the case of Yugoslavia) did not take immediate effect and that the Western trade was not able to make up for the losses. Similarly, Albania's trade with China could not compensate for the reductions. During the third year, however, both countries reported a total trade higher than the presanction level. Thus, at most, the trade reduction had a severe impact during the first two years.

The patterns for Cuba and Rhodesia are less uniform. In the former case the second year of sanctions showed a total trade at almost the level of the presanction year, whereas some reduction was experienced during the third year. The figures for Rhodesia emerge from Table 4.3, relying on a time series produced by the U.N. Security Council Committee on Sanctions.

The first year of sanctions obviously was the most difficult economically for Rhodesia. In the second year imports began to increase, and in the fifth year of sanctions total trade was again on the level with presanction figures. Of all the cases we have reviewed, the Rhodesian one shows the longest sustained effect on the receiver's international trade. By the early 1970s, however, it appears that Rhodesia had increasingly found ways to trade with the world and, as a matter of fact, the first half of the 1970s appears to have been almost an economic boom.

Rhodesia's difficulties were greater than any of the other receivers': there were no neutral countries to rely upon and very few countries explicitly admitted trading with Rhodesia. No major power or major bloc was willing to openly side with the receiver (as was the case for Yugoslavia, Cuba, and Albania). In practice, clandestine trade through South Africa served to supply Rhodesia with the necessary economic exchanges. Also, from a world perspective, Rhodesian trade was very small and thus more easily disguised.

TABLE 4.3

Rhodesia's International Trade, 1965–1975
(in millions of dollars)

Year	Total Export (excl. gold)	Total Import
1965	399	334
1966	238	236
1967	238	262
1968	234	290
1969	297	278
1970	346	329
1971	379	395
1972	474	404
1973	625	480
1974	600	515
1975	640	588

Source: SCOR S/12265, Vol. III, Tables 2 and 4.

However, this illustrates that the long–term impact of sanctions does not necessarily go in the direction of making economic conditions worse. To the contrary: this investigation suggests that the impact is reduced over time, the techniques for circumventing sanctions improve, political and economic conditions change which can be exploited by the receiver, and as a consequence the sanctions become weaker. In other words, the first year(s) of sanctions are the most important, providing the receiver government with the most problems and giving rise to the most serious political challenges. However, even so, there is no correlation between the serious immediate impact on trade and outcome: even countries experiencing sharp reductions in the first year have not complied with the wishes of the sender.

Political Effects

An interesting sociological theory suggests that where internal cohesion is fairly high, external pressure will further reinforce it. This suggests that there is an important threshold: pressure on states with low cohesion would result in disintegration, pressure on states with high cohesion results in the opposite.[16] It is difficult to measure cohesion in a society, but some important factors can be suggested, such as: strength of popular opposition against government, cohesion within leading circles, and governmental control over means of violence (police, military forces). A government that does not face serious opposition would probably have less to fear from external sanctions. Let us approach this question with a case–by–case discussion.

It appears that the governments were in firm control in nine of the ten cases. By 1933, Stalin had eliminated most opponents and his control over the police was probably unquestioned. Similarly, in 1935 Mussolini was riding a wave of renewed popularity, partly because of the conflict over Ethiopia. The unity among Jews in Palestine favoring the creation of Israel was obvious at the end of the Second World War. Tito in 1948 was the unquestioned leader of Yugoslavia, during the early part of 1948 actually eliminating from power more pro–Soviet politicians. Castro had a similar position in Cuba; he was a popular liberation hero, who had stood up against American pressure and replaced the disliked Batista regime. In Portugal, the government resting on the military establishment was probably secure and unchallenged, as indeed was the Nationalist Party in South Africa. The opposition parties repeatedly lost in the elections during the 1950s, while the white population increasingly favored the apartheid policy pursued by the Nationalists. In Rhodesia, the first part of the 1960s saw a drastic shift in the white electorate away from Liberal policies to white nationalism culminating in the elections with a total victory for the Rhodesian Front led by Ian Smith in 1965. In Portugal, South Africa, and Rhodesia, furthermore, the white governments maintained tight control over the armed forces and played on the cleavages between different African opponents. In the case of Albania, the internal situation is the most difficult to evaluate, but the Albanian Communist Party very explicitly used the fear of Yugoslavia to explain its policy toward the Soviet Union. This might well have made any opposition difficult.

We, thus, have nine politically secure regimes faced with external pressure which they, in accordance with the theory mentioned initially, should have been able to resist. The tenth case contrasts sharply with the others: the Dominican Republic. Obviously, the dictator, Trujillo, relied on the police to maintain himself in power, and terror was frequent. However, the opposition seems also to have been active. Attempts on Trujillo's life were reported in 1947, 1949, 1956, 1959, and 1960. In January, 1960, the influential Catholic Church changed its earlier positive attitude and instead criticized the dictator. Thus, there appears to have been great and popular disenchantment with the dictatorship before the sanctions were imposed. Indications of opposition were present in other situations as well. Thus, Stalin had pushed the collectivization of Soviet agriculture to an extreme by 1933, resulting in starvation for peasants and food shortages for the cities. Although the regime maintained control over its armed forces, it was certainly under severe strain. Organized opposition existed in the cases of South Africa, Portugal and Rhodesia. However, the dominant group, the white population, showed an increasing determination to maintain its own privileges in the face of this opposition. Sanctions, specifically aimed at curtailing these privileges could hardly have served to reduce that determination.

Thus, the impact of the sanctions is partially determined by the situation immediately prior to their imposition. A government whose popularity is built on a war in Africa will be reluctant to change that policy in the face of international opposition; rather, it will be tempted to exploit the situation to maintain or increase support for itself. Interestingly enough, the two successful cases of sanctions (the Soviet and Dominican ones) were also those in which the cohesion and strength of the regime was doubtful. In all other cases there was important support behind the regime just prior to the sanctions. This means, in effect, that the conflict preceding the sanctions tends to generate support for the receiver government, improving its position. Thus, by the time the sanctions are imposed they are least likely to have the desired effect.

Furthermore, it is not surprising that after the sanctions have been imposed, the political support for the government is maintained or even increased. Galtung has pointed to this adaptive potential, particularly to its sociopsychological aspect.[17] From most cases of economic sanctions such effects can be exemplified. In Italy, about 10 million Italians donated their wedding rings to the state in order to improve the gold reserve, lunch hours were eliminated in order to save gasoline (preventing civil servants from going home for lunch in their own cars), and Christmas trees were declared to be "un–Italian" in order to reduce imports.[18] In Yugoslavia, it was often pointed out that the condemnation of Yugoslavia by the other Communist states was published on St. Vitus Day, commemorating a heroic Serbian battle in 1389.

All these developments are part of a more or less conscious policy of the government to make the hardships following the imposition of economic sanctions appear as sufferings for a good cause. If, at the same time, the economic impact can be reduced, the government is in a good position during the first period of sanctions which, in accordance with our analysis above, is also the most important one. Furthermore, the government can acquire increased legitimacy which allows it to take measures that would normally not have been allowed. It can assume control over the economy (withholding publication of crucial statistics, controls over trade, balance of payment, involvement in investment programs, operate in clandestine economic transactions, etc.) and it can restrict the freedom of the mass media (if previously existing). Most importantly, political opposition can legitimately be defined as "unpatriotic" and suppressed by all kinds of measures. Yugoslavia officially admitted to having arrested approximately 8,000 opponents, but the real numbers were probably higher. Similarly, mass arrests were carried out in Cuba and the Dominican Republic. Obviously, such measures were regarded as normal in South Africa and Portugal whereas in Israel and Rhodesia major sections of the population were defined as unreliable and kept under special surveillance.

This means that, in general, the opposition will have a much more difficult time operating immediately after the imposition of sanctions. National loyalties will restrict its scope of action as will the police measures taken by the government. Ultimately, it could mean expelling existing opposition from the country. That was a deliberate policy in Cuba following Castro's taking of power. In 1965 a special air connection was created between Cuba and the United States, primarily to allow opponents of the regime to leave. Parallel developments occurred in the Rhodesian, South African, and Portuguese cases (where not only white opponents but also blacks were forced to emigrate). As a matter of fact, often the most vocal opposition is to be found outside the country: in the Yugoslav case, exiled politicians were active throughout Eastern Europe against Tito; the invasion of Cuba in 1961, organized by the United States, was carried out by exiled Cubans; the leading anti–Trujillo opponent, Juan Bosch, consistently lived outside the Dominican Republic; and the democratic opposition against Mussolini was based in democratic countries. The same is true for many of the more well–organized opponents of the white minority regimes in Southern Africa. Thus, we have to conclude that the immediate effect of the sanction is to improve the position of the government and to worsen conditions for the opposition, contrary to the sender's expectations.

The improved position of the receiver government has paradoxical effects. On the one hand, it increases the options available to that government; on the other hand, it reduces those very options. Thus, a stronger government will also be able to strike a deal with the sender government. As it is in control and opposition is reduced, it can work out arrangements that cannot be seriously questioned. On the other hand, the government's position might rest on its strong desire to withstand all outside pressure, and entering into deals with the sender might erode its support basis. Either way, the receiver government will be in a very strong bargaining position vis–à–vis the sender since it can argue that its options are limited (but not nonexistent). The sender, in other words, will lose some of its leverage on the receiver through the sanctions; what it can do is to use the lifting of the sanctions as a *reward* for compliance, but the punishment already inflicted certainly does not make such rewards highly attractive.

All this, of course, assumes that the receiver government is at the same time capable of maintaining its own power position and of coping with the economic problems created by the sanctions. In general, this appears possible, and the only clearly deviant case is the Dominican Republic where the rapidly eroding support for the Trujillo regime also curbed its ability to handle the economic crises and ultimately led to political chaos. In this case, the expectation of the sanction theory was borne out but only because the regime was weak and illegitimate to begin with.

Significance of the Issue of Contention

The sender demands changes in the receiver's policies as a condition to lifting the sanctions. From the receiver's point of view the significance of the demanded concessions will be measured against the damage inflicted by the sanctions: as long as the latter appear to be smaller than the former, the receiver will resist.

How would we, then, estimate the significance of the issue for the receiver government. First, let us examine the importance of the sender's demands with respect to the entire political structure of the receiver. Second, an investigation of the receiver's interpretation of those very demands is needed.

Let us assume that the issues can be either very specific or very general. The sender might demand some clearly defined concessions or more general and vague ones. Furthermore, the issue can concern changes in foreign policy or in domestic policies. On the whole it could be argued that specific changes in foreign policy (for instance, trade concessions or tariff modifications) are least significant, whereas general changes in domestic policy (demanding changes in constitution or resignation of government) are most significant. This means that the more specific the issue, the more likely a settlement, whereas the more general the issue, the more likely a continued struggle. Among the ten cases, five certainly concern highly fundamental changes. The sender was, in effect, demanding not only the government's resignation but also substantial changes in the country's political, economic, and social structure (Israel, South Africa, Cuba, Portugal, and Rhodesia all belong to this category). In two cases, the sender demanded (de facto) the resignation of the incumbent government (Yugoslavia, Dominican Republic); in one case the sender wanted changes in central political orientation (Albania, meaning eventually also a change of government). Thus, in eight of the ten cases, the demands were very fundamental. Consequently, the receiver government, which is responsible for the existing political structure and derives its own power from it, has every reason to resist. Thus, the sanctions would not only have to inflict considerable damage but a destruction so comprehensive that the government would be unable to operate and would prefer to capitulate. As we have just noted, this did occur only in one case, the Dominican Republic. It suggests, furthermore, that the demands raised are often unattainable with the means chosen by the sender.

In two cases, however, the issues were more specific. In the Soviet case, Britain demanded concrete concessions with respect to the arrested British merchants, and in the Italian case, the issue centered on the war in Ethiopia. The demands were clear and the concessions would not, per se, threaten the survival of the regime. On the contrary, negotiations could be carried out between the conflicting parties. The receiver government had a choice and, in fact, concessions were soon offered in the first case, but rejected in the second case.

This analysis suggests that the more fundamental the issue the more unlikely it is that the sanctions will be successful. However, one fundamental sanction was successful (the Dominican Republic) and one fairly specific sanction failed (the Italian case), suggesting that different mechanisms are operative depending on the nature of the issue of contention.

However, the issue might be more important to the receiver than it would seem to an outside observer. Thus, in cases that appear to deal with rather minor issues (like the Soviet case) the official interpretation was less sanguine. The Soviet government considered the British demands unacceptable to an independent and sovereign state. Some interpretations also suggested that the real goal was to launch an anti–Soviet drive, rather than to deal with the alleged issue. Similarly, Mussolini spoke of a plan to suffocate the

Italian people economically, to humiliate them, and to undermine their right to self–defense.[19]

Thus, the receiver's strategy was to interpret the sanctions as directed against the independence of the state or against the people as a whole. This means that the issues become even more fundamental than they would objectively have appeared. As a matter of fact, a very general feature of the sanctions literature is the complaint by the sender that the intentions of the sender have not been understood correctly by the receiver. Certainly, the receiver will see the conflict only from its perspective. If is, of course, not unexpected that someone exposed to punishments from another party would fail to see the situation from the punisher's angle rather than its own.

In summary we have seen that sanctions are, generally, directed against countries that are highly dependent on the sender, but that their impact on trade is seldom as dramatic as might be expected. The receiver can often circumvent the sanctions by finding new trading partners or can absorb some of the economic effects by appropriate economic policies. If the receiver government is well in control at the outset of the conflict, it is often able to strengthen its position and to make the necessary economic adjustments. Only when the regime has been weakened *before* the imposition of sanctions does it either collapse or make concessions. Finally, we have seen that the issues involved are frequently very fundamental and, if more specific, their salience is magnified by interpreting the issue as one concerning the sovereignty and/or the existence of the state or the nation as a whole.

Explanations Emphasizing the Relations between the Sender and the Receiver

Relation–oriented explanations attempt typically to address questions on the impact of unequal power, interdependence, and conflict escalation on the outcome of the sanctions. A short discussion on these aspects is consequently warranted.

Relative Power and Interdependence

We have noted that economic sanctions are principally used by powerful states whereas, for the most part, the targets are smaller states. This means that sanctions either occur in highly asymmetric situations (major powers vs. smaller ones) or in more symmetric ones (major powers vs. other major powers or smaller states vs. other smaller states). Success is not more frequent in any of these relations. It is perhaps most surprising to note the ability of smaller states to resist the pressures from major powers, something which is possible to explain from the strength of the regime, as we have just done, or from the reaction of other members of the international system, something we will shortly return to.

However, it is interesting to study the interrelationship between the two protagonists. We have already noted that the receivers in general are highly dependent on the sender whereas the reverse seldom is true. If we also include noneconomic ties between the two (military and/or diplomatic relations) we find that the sanctions group themselves into three major, highly distinct categories. In three of the cases there was very little previous contact between the parties, and the sanctions were basically taking place between smaller states (South Africa, Israel, and Portugal). In two other cases, some contacts existed but it was largely of a formal sort (diplomatic relations, some trade, no military collaboration): Italy and the Soviet Union. The remaining five cases are similar in one important respect: the contact between the sender and the receiver was very intense prior to the imposition of the sanctions. Since the senders were major powers, the relationship was in essence "colonial" and the conflicts had a distinct element of smaller states objecting to major power policies (Yugoslavia, Cuba, Dominican Republic, Albania, and Rhodesia all being receivers of the dislike of a major power upon which the country had previously relied very heavily). Furthermore, we find that in these cases the senders have been internally divided over how to deal with the opposition from the smaller country. Indeed, it does not seem farfetched to suggest that there is a particular dynamics of interdependence: there will, most likely, be groups inside the sender who know something about the receiver and, in one way or another, regard its policies with sympathy or understanding. At the same time, however, the activities of the receiver might antagonize other groups also with links to the receiver, and consequently dialogue is created within the sender about how to perceive the receiver's present policies. However, in

the cases of little interaction, a consensus can probably be more easily established within the sender about the optimal course of action.

This would also suggest that the repercussions within the receiver would vary. In cases in which the receivers are highly dependent on the senders, the internal conflicts would be sharper,
particularly in cases of a "colonial" character. Indeed, it might be
the aim of the sender to play on such cleavages within the receiver.
However, as we have seen in the previous sections, this rarely is
successful. One possible additional explanation might now be
added: within the receiver the sanctions shift power away from the
sender–dependent groups to sender–independent ones. Thus,
groups particularly favorable to the sender are those with a vested
interest in continued trade, contact, and cooperation. Examples of
such groups are pro–Soviet loyalists in the cases of Yugoslavia and
Albania, drawing their power and influence from a continued Soviet
presence in the country, or businessmen involved in international
transactions such as trade or tourism, in the cases of Cuba, the
Dominican Republic, and Rhodesia. These groups are, however, the
first victims once the sanctions have been imposed, making it difficult for them to continue economic or political cooperation with the
sender. They are forced either to leave the country, to engage in
clandestine activities, or to participate in the country's effort to
adapt to the sanctions. Interestingly enough, leaders of the most recalcitrant receiver governments have often built their power on
groups independent of interaction with the sender. Thus, Tito could
draw support from peasants or workers, rather than party bureau-
crats, and Castro similarly did not rely on the American hotel interests or plantation owners. Ian Smith's support basis was primarily
white farmers not intellectuals, merchants, or Africans. Only in the
case of the Trujillo regime did the sanction actually aim at the resource base of the regime, making the withdrawal of American support more effective.

Conflict Escalation

The conflicts that ultimately lead to the implementation of economic sanctions are also characterized by other types of conflict behavior. Some argue for instance that a threat of sanctions would be

more successful than the actually implemented sanctions. The ten cases are all situations in which threats were not enough, though they may at times have been expected to suffice. Thus, the League of Nations collective security system suggested that the threat of collective action against a potential aggressor would deter the aggressor from action. This, however, did not deter the Italian leaders forcing an unprepared League to implement the threat.

In the case of Rhodesia, the threat of sanctions was first issued in October 1964 when Rhodesia seemed on the verge of making a unilateral declaration of independence. This initially appeared effective: the Rhodesians retreated, but also undertook a serious investigation of the effects of sanctions on the economy. Thus, a year later they were more confident and better prepared and, consequently, were no longer deterred by the renewed threat of sanctions. As a matter of fact, the British government did not appear to be prepared to launch a major sanctions effort (which affected their initial effectiveness).

At most, we would suggest, a threat of sanctions will have a modifying effect on the receiver. Often, in trying to read the intentions of the sender, the receiver may predict that sanctions may be the toughest action likely to be taken. Thus, if convinced that adaptation or evasion is possible, the receiver will not be deterred.

This bears out our previous observation that most senders select sanctions because military means are unavailable or impractical. To what extent does military action nonetheless follow sanctions? The selection of cases makes such an investigation impossible because we have excluded those cases in which a rapid military escalation took place (for instance, the U.S.–Japan relations in the years leading up to Pearl Harbor in 1941). Still, observations can be offered. First of all, sanctions are often part of a polarization process, whereby not only economic interactions but also other types of contacts are reduced. When the sender's motive was expressive, diplomatic relations have been curtailed and military cooperation ended. Thus, after a short period of time virtually all political interaction has been eliminated. This can create difficulties in communication between the conflicting parties. Even during a crisis, a need for some contacts will exist. Consequently, *ad hoc* channels have had to be invented.

This process, leading to an almost complete breakdown of inter-action, could be seen as a first phase of "stripping for action": the parties prepare themselves for more militant behavior. But it could also mean a reduction in irritation resulting in a stalemate, a "freez-ing" of action: the tension arising from too close contact ceases and the conflict can be "forgotten," and eventually seem no longer sig-nificant. The case of Israel is closer to the escalating situation, whereas Yugoslavia approximates the freezing process. In the other cases, characterized by drastically reduced relations, room has been left for other parties to act—in particular, guerilla actions. Also, the sender might still contemplate some military action.

Thus, there are cases of some limited military actions: the Brit-ish flying in air force units to Zambia to exert pressure on Rhodesia and the Soviet Union making threatening military maneuvers to-ward Yugoslavia. There are also examples of covert actions (the United States organizing, through the CIA, an invasion of Cuba in 1961). These cases, which incidentally also belong to those of high asymmetric dependence (the "colonial" situations), contrast with those of actual guerilla warfare in which the senders take action to express solidarity with indigenous forces (Portugal, South Africa). Sanctions arising in asymmetric situations appear to limit the need for a rapid military escalation of the conflict, the sender being un-willing to involve itself in open military fighting. In the symmetric situation of smaller countries boycotting other smaller countries the escalating potential is probably higher. In such cases, as already noted, the sanctions grow out of a lack of military capability, and when such a capability emerges, there will be fewer restrictions on its use.

This leaves the two cases of instrumental sanctions directed against Italy and the Soviet Union. In no case was military action contemplated. Obviously, the Italian war in Ethiopia could have been made difficult if, for instance, Italian access through the Suez Canal had been restricted. However, such actions would have had an immediate escalatory effect and consequently were not seriously considered. In both of these cases sanctions were the highest level of action that the senders could conceive.

Explanations emphasizing the relations between the sender and the receiver do not further clarify the outcome of sanctions. However, they do make it possible to understand more clearly why the senders opt for sanctions in the first place and to relate sanctions to the international hierarchy of states. Most often these measures have been used by strong states to retain control over "their" areas of influence, in situations where military means have, mostly for internal reasons, been unavailable. In these situations military action has not been applied at later stages of the conflict either. Rather, apart from threats and concealed actions, the sanctions have resulted in a freezing of the situation, ultimately preparing the public for a reestablishment of contacts.

Sanctions used in symmetric relations have, in the case of big powers imposing them, been the highest level of pressure and, in cases of small states imposing them, an initial level of action. In the former situation sanctions could be expected to lead to negotiations and settlement, in the latter to escalation of military violence.

Explanations Emphasizing the Environment of the Conflicting Parties

What is the role of surrounding states? How many would support the sender? What support could the receiver expect? How strong is the cohesion among the senders, and what degree of international economical and political isolation can be achieved?

Number of Co-Senders

In eight of ten cases, the main senders sought and received international support for economic sanctions. Only two cases remained bilateral (the sanctions against the Soviet Union and Albania) in terms of implemented economic actions. This is in accordance with our expectations: when issues are deemed to be of universal and fundamental significance, it is logical to aim for the broadest possible international support. Also, when the issue is more specific (as in the case of sanctions against the Soviet Union), international support is less necessary and is probably not readily forthcoming. However, it is remarkable to find that most East European countries continued to trade with Albania after 1961 in spite of the sanctions imposed by the Soviet Union.

International governmental organizations continually play an important role in implementing or broadening international support for sanctions. Thus, world organizations were involved in the sanctions against Italy, Rhodesia, and South Africa (arms embargo); major regional organizations in sanctions against Cuba and the Dominican Republic (OAS); Portugal and South Africa (OAU); Israel (Arab League); and international political organizations against Yugoslavia (Cominform). Sanctions also provide an opportunity for IGOs (International Governmental Organizations) to demonstrate their utility. In most of the organizations mentioned, special boycott offices have been created that more or less actively contribute to the international effort. International support, however, is not decisive for the outcome of the sanctions. One case of sanctions lacking such support was successful (the Soviet Union) as was one with regional support (the Dominican Republic). All actions by world organizations were unsuccessful (Italy and Rhodesia; the arms embargo on South Africa could also be questioned).

Cohesion Among the Senders

In our section emphasizing the relations between the sender and the receiver, we noted that five cases of sanctions arose from "colonial" types of relations: big–power senders imposed sanctions on "disobedient" and dependent smaller states. In each case the receiver was only one among a number of states in a similar position. This suggests an interesting additional impetus for the use of sanctions: they are not only aimed at bringing the deviant state back into line but also at *increasing the cohesion within the big power's zone of influence*. Obviously, Yugoslavia or Albania were not the only Soviet–bloc states manifesting resistance to Soviet control. On the contrary, following the expulsion of Yugoslavia in 1948, purges of "Titoist" elements occurred throughout Eastern Europe. The sanctions against Albania were also aimed at reducing the impact of China on Eastern Europe or among international communist parties.

Similarly, the American sanctions against Cuba and the Dominican Republic were partly designed to set the limits of permissible political orientations and to counter the influence of "Castroism" in

Central and South America. The British actions against Rhodesia served, in part, to maintain cohesion within the Commonwealth, thus preserving British influence. In these five cases, the big powers, by "temporarily" sacrificing one dependent country, hoped to consolidate or enhance their influence over those remaining.

Similarly, the sanctions imposed by smaller states were meant to enhance unity among otherwise quarreling states. Pan–Africanism or Pan–Arabism, both diluted by the daily pursuit of particularistic interests, could at least require joint action against a state clearly antagonistic to these group principles, such South Africa and Portugal (racial discrimination) or Israel (occupation of Arab land).

Thus, the five sanctions imposed by big states against small ones, as well as the three cases of small states directing sanctions against other small states, are all highly expressive. This approach, of course, is meant to emphasize the significance of the threatened principles not only to the receiver but to the senders themselves. Participation in sanctions, in other words, becomes a way of demonstrating allegiance to the group.

Effects on Trade Patterns

The international environment can both contribute to the sanctions effort or help sabotage it. On balance, the second effect appears the more powerful of the two. In eight of the ten cases the receivers have had relatively little difficulty in developing alternative suppliers or markets.

In the case of Italy, two important trading partners, Germany and the United States, together accounting for about one–fourth of total Italian trade, did not participate in the sanctions because they were not members of the League. Additionally, important trading partners like Switzerland and Argentina or neighboring countries like Austria and Hungary did not comply. Apart from France, the only neighbor making a deliberate effort, at considerable cost, to implement sanctions was Yugoslavia.

Similar conclusions can be drawn from almost all the other cases. Sometimes major powers have little interest in participating in sanctions or actually expect to benefit from actively sabotaging them. Thus, the West supported Israel, Yugoslavia, Portugal, and

South Africa in the face of Arab, Soviet, and African sanctions, respectively. The Soviet Union replaced the United States as Cuba's main trading partner, and China replaced the Soviet Union as Albania's. Sometimes neighboring countries find it economically and politically very difficult to participate in the sanction. As we have seen, this was the case with the sanctions against Italy, but it was equally true for Rhodesia or South Africa.

Often such shifts in trading patterns can be discerned before the sanctions are imposed, and later developments are a fairly predictable reinforcement of existing trends. A major change was difficult to predict for Yugoslavia: after all, Tito was regarded by the West as more Stalinist than Stalin himself, and it was some time before American leaders could appreciate the significance of the rupture with the Soviet Union. However, it was not surprising that Germany exploited the conflict between the League and Italy; it actually made many British and French leaders hesitant about sanctions in the first place. That Cuba would receive support from the Soviet Union was also obvious by the time of the American sanctions. That South Africa would have multiple interests in trying to sabotage the sanctions against Rhodesia was also evident at the outset. Sometimes, however, a scale of support has been difficult to predict; China, for instance, carried a considerable burden in sustaining Albania.

Thus, major powers normally had an interest in supporting receivers, even across considerable distances. All current major powers have done so (United States, Soviet Union, and China). Also, neighboring countries have sometimes found economic or political reasons not to participate.

Indeed, sanctions have not only provided an opportunity for rival powers to exploit, but have actually driven the receiver to the opposite camp. The West rapidly became a most important source for military equipment, assistance, and collaboration in the case of Israel as well as Yugoslavia (even joining the NATO–linked Balkan Pact). Cuba became militarily dependent on the Soviet Union following the abortive invasion in 1961 (even to the point where it became a tempting launching pad for Soviet medium–range missiles in 1962). Political cooperation with Germany followed Italy's exposure to sanctions (leading, ultimately, to Germany's invasion with Italian acquiescence of Austria in 1938). Also, by 1967, close military cooperation had been established between the Rhodesian and South African armed forces.

Thus, in eight of the ten cases, sanctions set in motion forces that have reshaped international relations. Two situations are nevertheless dramatically different, the cases of the Soviet Union and the Dominican Republic. In neither case could these countries rearrange their trading patterns: they had nowhere to turn. In 1933, the Soviet Union was the only Communist state. In January, 1933, Hitler had taken control in Germany with a strongly anti-Communist program. Italy was governed by Fascists, Japan, Britain and France were hardly friendly toward the Soviet Union and still had no diplomatic relations with the United States. Thus, the Soviet Union chose to yield to the British demands, avoiding a worsening of its own situation.

Similarly, the Dominican Republic, run by a ruthless and unpopular political family since the 1930s, had few friends in the Western world. Few countries were willing to risk for support this regime once the United States had withdrawn its own blessing; neither West European countries (not unwilling to trade with Cuba), nor the Soviet Union could see much point in backing Trujillo.

This leads us to two important general conclusions: first, the relative political isolation of a country is very significant to the outcome of sanctions. Countries that are, at the outset, politically isolated will be more willing to make specific concessions, as seen in the case of the Soviet Union. Also, such isolation will serve to undermine a government, in particular one already weakened by internal resistance.

Second, given sufficient political isolation, it does not seem necessary to reduce *all* trade. Neither Britain nor the United States did so. In all other cases, however, the main sender consciously eliminated almost all elements of trade with the receiver without apparent success. This suggests that graduated sanctions are more efficient because they leave additional leverage: the sender can inflict added damage after the first wave of the sanction's effect has been absorbed. Also, by not eliminating all trade, the sender might be able to play a more intelligent game, using the divergent interests existing on the receiver side. Big, broad–sided sanctions would certainly create more immediate damage but would also convince all groups within the receiver nation that the sender does not really care about *any* of them. Furthermore, these two points act in conjunction with each other. If isolation is not forthcoming, the sanctions can be undermined fairly quickly by the receiver.

THREE IMPORTANT LESSONS

Three major questions have been addressed: first, the likelihood that sanctions will be successful (i.e., will achieve the changes in the receiver's policy sought by the sender); second, whether sanctions represent alternatives to violence; and third, whether they provide a means for "new" interests to exert influence. The emphasis, of course, has been on the success/failure of sanctions, whereas the other two questions have been approached indirectly by reconstructing the senders' motives for sanctions (rather than being passive or taking military action) and by delimiting different categories of sanctions. From this, three important lessons emerge:

1. *Economic sanction can be successful, but only under very restrictive conditions that can be met before the sanctions are imposed.* We have to conclude that, historically, economic sanctions tend to be unsuccessful. However, it can be argued that this was because they were not correctly applied and that economic sanctions could become more successful if the correct inferences were drawn from historical evidence. Specifically, it should be understood that their success depends on the following three conditions. First, the receiver government must be fairly weak at the outset. A strong government only will benefit from sanctions because it can use them to rally support, eliminate opposition, and take appropriate countermeasures. A government with significant domestic opposition or in charge of an economy in serious trouble will have considerable difficulty in embarking on such a necessary counterprogram. It might still be able to do so, but it is more likely that it will prefer to make some early concessions in order to avoid such risks. The historical record shows that sanctions have often been used against regimes of rising popularity (partially a result of conflict with the sender) who have taken determined actions to secure control over vital elements of the political arsenal prior to the imposition of sanctions.

Second, the country must be politically isolated. A regime without friends will lack the resources to deal with the economic problems created by the sanctions. Thus, weak and politically isolated regimes will, in general, be most vulnerable to economic pressure.

Add to this a third point: it is not necessary to immediately eliminate *all* trade with the receiver. On the contrary, given the previous two conditions a gradual reduction is probably the most effective way of proceeding.

This suggests that the internal political situation of the receiver is what matters most. It is only when a strong internal opposition exists that the sender can really hope to change the receiver's policy. In its absence or if it is weak, the government will have little incentive to yield and the chances of its being replaced will be slight.

2. *Economic sanctions supplement rather than replace military action.* The economic sanctions imposed during the last 40 years have not arisen from a nonviolent philosophy; rather, they have stemmed from political expediency. Military courses of action have been blocked, the pressure to "do something" has been great, and sanctions have, consequently, been seen as a suitable course of action. Countries using economic sanctions have not been reluctant to use military action in other situations.

Thus, in several cases in which major powers have used economic sanctions, their incentive for military action might have been great. The internal debate over appropriate courses of action, thus, could reduce the political support behind military measures. However, in the long term, sanctions would only constitute a plausible alternative if they have an acceptable record of success. Without that, their credibility would be low in a parallel future situation.

For smaller states, the sanctions have often grown out of the lack of military means. Thus, we find it quite consistent that sanctions are gradually replaced by military action when such capabilities emerge. The fact that the sanctions have not achieved a broader, in particular Western, support not only has colored the relationship between these states and the West, but also has made guerilla or conventional warfare appear a more effective means.

In a world of increasing armaments and an abundance of armed conflicts, economic sanctions of course are preferable. However, military means probably continue to occupy the first place in strategic planning, and economic means only attract the same attention when their utility has been demonstrated or when military action is ruled out by other considerations.

3. *Successful economic sanctions would not change the global distribution of power.* In this study we have seen that economic sanctions have been used primarily by major powers. This is, of course, what would be expected, since they have global interests and are at the center of economic networks. If economic sanctions were more effective, would this not result in the enhancement of their control in the world? Alternatively, it could be argued that more effective economic sanctions would give more power to previously powerless groups. The case of the Dominican Republic exemplifies the former and the oil weapon the latter.

Probably, the overall power enhancing effect would be slight, but there would be other benefits: less human sacrifice, less danger of escalation, and less incentive for military armament. Major powers always have a military option and, if highly motivated, will prefer military means. Thus, effective economic sanctions would, in some situations, reduce the incentive for military action. This is so because, some arguments favoring military action, such as weak internal support for the recalcitrant regime, also suggest the possibility for economic sanctions to be effective. By and large, the powers vested in the present major powers would not be reduced, nor would they be enhanced, but the scale of preferred action might be modified.

The same also applies to smaller states. The record shows that small power sanctions have been unsuccessful. However, there might be particular situations in which the combined action of many smaller states might affect other smaller states. Whether such collective action also could influence major powers seems more doubtful. Obviously, the oil weapon had some impact on the attitude of the West toward the Palestinian question, but in many other situations, the attention given to smaller states has been slight.

This then is to suggest that the distribution of power between states is hardly affected by the intensified use of economic sanctions. Still, economic sanctions, if effectively and prudently used, could play a role in making international relations less brutal. Seldom, however, do they seem preferable to genuine dialogue across conflicting lines.

NOTES

1. This article is an updated summary of a study published in Swedish only, Peter Wallensteen, *Ekonomiska Sanktioner* (Stockholm: Prisma, 1971). Details on methodology, operationalization, and sources are found in this volume.

2. See G. D. Mitschell, *A Dictionary of Sociology* (London: Routledge & Kegan Paul, 1968), p. 156.

3. L. Coser, *The Functions of Social Conflict* (Glencoe: Free Press, 1956), p. 87f; and B. Berelson and G. A. Steiner, *Human Behavior: An Inventory of Scientific Findings* (New York: Harcourt, Brace & World, 1964), p. 613f.

4. See F. Hoffmann, The Functions of Economic Sanctions, *Journal of Peace Research*, 4 (1967): 140–60.

5. *Documents on International Affairs*, 1955, p. 265f.

6. To assure that the generalizations made are not based on complete randomness, Fisher's exact test has been used and only distributions with a probability below 0.05 have been accepted when establishing correlations with the outcome variable. The small number of cases has also made it necessary to work, mostly, only with dichotomies. On Fisher's exact test, see Siegel, N., *Non–Parametric Statistics* (New York: McGraw–Hill, 1956) and for probability values see Wallensteen, 1971. Basically, for a variable to correlate with the outcome the two successful cases have to be found in one category and the eight other in the other category of the dichotomized variable.

7. The initial declarations were searched for the following items here formulated according to their extreme, expressive form: moral condemnation of the receiver, reference to the uselessness of continued relations, indications of possible disruption of diplomatic relations, indications of other negative sanctions, no indication of possible sanctions, no reference to possible settlement, no indication of possible future coexistence. Each item was graded on a four–point scale going from the most instrumental to the most expressive. The initial declaration used was the first publicly available statement by the sender to explain why trade with the receiver was reduced. Mean and mode were strongly within the expressive part of the continuum. For details on methods and sources, see Wallensteen, 1971, pp. 64–65, 194–95.

8. Walters, F. P., *A History of the League of Nations*, London, 1958, p. 657.

9. *Documents on American Foreign Relations, 1960*, p. 490ff.

10. Hoffmann, 1967.

11. See Pano, N.C., *The People's Republic of Albania*, Baltimore, 1968, p. 152ff and n. 47.

12. Several of these figures are uncertain because many receivers have not published reliable statistics. Thus, Rhodesia reported a reduction in total trade of 17 percent during the first year of sanctions, whereas British estimates suggested 45 percent. Here 31 percent has been used as the Solomonic mean between the two. This actually comes close to the figures given by the United Nations Sanctions Committee, which is 35.7 percent.

13. Taubenfeld, H. J., *Economic Sanctions: An Appraisal and Case Study* (New York: Columbia University, dissertation, 1958), p. 91f.

14. Pertot, V., Yugoslavia's Economic Relations with Eastern Countries, *Co–Existence*, 4 (1967): 7ff.

15. The long–term impact can only be studied in four cases since three were of a very short duration (Soviet Union, Italy and the Dominican Republic) and three saw very little economic impact from the beginning (Israel, South Africa and Portugal).

16. Cf. Coser, 1956, p. 87f.

17. Galtung, J., On the Effects of International Economic Sanctions, *World Politics*, 19 (1967): 378–416, reproduced in this volume. See also the discussion by Green, G., Evading sanctions, in this volume.

18. Taubenfeld, 1958, p. 203f, p. 240 n. 72 gives a number of examples of this form in the case of Italy.

19. *Soviet Documents on Foreign Policy*, ed. by J. Degras, Vol. III, 1933–1941, London, 1953, p. 9f (Litvinov), *Documents on British Foreign Policy*, 1919–1939, Second Series, Vol. VII, 1929–1934, London, 1958. Message 496 (Soviet spokesperson), *Documents on International Affairs*, 1935, Vol. II, p. 169ff (Mussolini).

5

USING FOOD POWER: OPPORTUNITIES, APPEARANCES, AND DAMAGE CONTROL

Robert L. Paarlberg

Back when the U.S. enjoyed unchallenged military supremacy, self–sufficiency in energy supplies, most of the world's gold reserves, a consistently strong currency, and a dominant position in the export of manufactured goods, the makers of U.S. foreign policy did not think or talk much about "food power." Only as their supply of traditional diplomatic assets dwindled did U.S. policy makers begin to take an active interest in the so–called food weapon. As the U.S. trade position in raw materials, energy, and manufactured goods weakened, and as productivity growth in most sectors of the U.S. economy fell sharply, U.S. agricultural productivity—and export earnings—continued a sustained increase. In the all important world grain market, the United States emerged as an unchallenged superpower, capturing an ever larger share of total exports. Meantime a significant variety of U.S. adversaries, including the Soviet Union and most of the OPEC countries, were becoming more dependent upon grain imports. This curious combination of adverse and apparently advantageous developments inspired a hope that food resources, if properly managed and manipulated, could serve the U.S. as a corrective to diplomatic weakness.

U.S. foreign policy makers will be tempted by their own hopes and expectations, and also obliged, in response to popular hopes and

Reprinted with permission from the *Proceedings of the Academy of Political Science* 34, no. 3 (1982): 25–39.

expectations, to make what use they can of their purported food power in the years ahead. We anticipate here the lessons they will learn, as well as some of the guidlines they might adopt to control the likely damage.

U.S. FOOD POWER STRATEGIES:
THE APPARENT RANGE OF OPTIONS

Those seeking external advantages from U.S. food abundance appear to enjoy a wide range of strategic and tactical options. First considering only economic advantages, the foreign exchange earned from commercial food exports can help to compensate the United States for its weakened position in the trade of many manufactured goods and for its need to import large quantities of expensive foreign oil. Apart from internal gains to U.S. producers, food exports contribute to a stronger U.S. trade and payments balance and to a stronger U.S. currency. In pursuit of such gains, a purely economic U.S. food power strategy would require continued U.S. food exports to all paying customers, friend and foe alike, even in times of tight domestic supply. To sustain export growth in times of abundant supply abroad, a variety of market interventions would prove necessary. Bilateral purchase and sale agreements, export credits, and export subsidies might be needed to maintain and to expand U.S. market shares. Only an indirect diplomatic payoff would accompany this first food power strategy, by way of an implied U.S. option to adopt a different strategy, and to cut back on commercial exports for diplomatic reasons, at some later date.

As an alternative to seeking economic gains through unrestrained export promotion, direct diplomatic gains might be sought through a strategy of conditional exports. In its extreme form, this alternative strategy would tie all U.S. food exports to the short run political behavior of U.S. food customers. Friendly behavior would be rewarded with concessional food aid, credits, or preferential commercial trade; unfriendly actions would result in food aid cutoffs or commercial export embargoes. The intended payoff from this conditional export strategy would be increased U.S. control over the behavior of foreign governments, or at least over the well–being of those governments, through a direct augmentation of U.S. capabilities to punish and reward.

Against the backdrop of this broad strategic choice between foreign economic and diplomatic food power objectives, only a weak combination of ethical constraints appears to arise. Some U.S. foreign policy officials, sensitive to global nutritional needs, might hesitate to conduct a foreign food policy in exclusive pursuit of their own economic or diplomaic interests. Tactics of food denial, at least in peacetime, might be shunned as a policy taboo. Presuming such ethical inhibitions against use of the "food weapon" can be overcome, the range of possible food power strategies open to U.S. policy makers appears to be quite broad.

CONSTRAINTS ON THE EXERCISE OF U.S. FOOD POWER

In fact, the range of food power strategies open to U.S. foreign policy makers is quite narrow. Ethical inhibitions are probably the least significant of the many constraints that combine to diminish the usability and the impact of the U.S. food weapon. Because of the character of world food markets, the character of the U.S. economic system, due to the character of the U.S. political system, and due to a fundamental incompatibility between the two principal objectives of U.S. food power, efforts to use the food weapon will usually produce disappointing, and even damaging results.

The Character of World Food Markets

U.S. exports appear to dominate today's world food markets. The U.S. supplies more than 40 percent of all wheat and two–thirds of all coarse grains entering international trade. U.S. grain exports have grown to be almost six times as large as those of its closest export competitors.

This dominant U.S. export position, in a rapidly expanding world grain market, obviously contributes to a strengthened U.S. trade and payments balance (except insofar as the growth of U.S. food exports was itself stimulated by falling currency values, such as in the aftermath of dollar devaluations in 1971 and 1973). Paced by its strong performance in world grain markets, the U.S. is now enjoying a thirteenth straight year of record farm sales abroad. Total U.S. agricultural export earnings for fiscal year 1982 are projected at $45.5 billion; the U.S. agricultural trade surplus is projected at $28 billion.[1]

Commercial benefits notwithstanding, this U.S. dominance of world food markets is less than meets the eye. Because of the character of world food markets, a dominant share of exports does not by itself translate into diplomatic leverage.

First of all, for most importers food from international markets seldom supplies a critical share of total consumption. Reliance on world food markets has grown, but the vast proportion of the world's food supplies are still produced, marketed, and consumed entirely within national boundaries. By one estimate, more than 80 percent of the world's citizens live in nations that are still more than 95 percent self–sufficient in food supplies.[2] Even among grains, the most widely traded of all foods, international trade satisfies only about 17 percent of total world consumption.

Even the Soviet Union, which has recently emerged as the world's largest grain importer, experiences only a modest dependence on imports and therefore suffers only a modest vulnerability to politically motivated trade interruptions. Soviet grain imports have grown dramatically over the past decade to a record level of 34 million tons in 1980/81. Following their third poor harvest in a row, the Soviets are now projected to import an astonishing 42 million tons of wheat and coarse grain in the current 1981/82 marketing year. Even so, imported grain will be satisfying a relatively small share—roughly 20 percent—of total Soviet grain consumption.[3] Annual fluctuations in Soviet domestic grain production, caused by weather, can still be several times the size of annual Soviet imports, and it is the danger of a harvest failure at home, rather than the possibility of a trade embargo from abroad, that most concerns Soviet planners.

The Soviet Union is the world's largest wheat producing nation and does not depend upon imports to provide its accustomed and more than ample rations of bread. Imported grain is now used exclusively by the Soviets to feed livestock. Even so, only about one–third of annual Soviet feed use is supplied by grain imports, and isolated grain embargoes do not add much to the difficulties of increasing meat production in the Soviet Union. Soviet meat and milk production did decline, at a rate of about 3 percent during the 16 months of the 1980–81 U.S. grain embargo, but meat and milk production had begun this decline in 1979, the year before the embargo, despite high imports from abroad. Domestic shortfalls and not the embargo were to blame for the decline. Even before the U.S. embargo, Brezhnev's meat program was going nowhere; per capita meat consumption in the Soviet Union had stopped growing in 1975. For this we can blame the harsh Russian climate, slower growth rates throughout the troubled Soviet economy, the needless inefficiencies of state farming, and unbalanced feed rations, but we cannot blame Soviet vulnerability to a U.S. food weapon.

By switching to other suppliers during the 16 months of the U.S. embargo, the Soviet Union found it possible to escape the punitive intent of U.S. grain trade sanctions. As grain imports from the United States were reduced, Soviet purchasing agents paid whatever price premiums were necessary to attract larger grain imports from a variety of smaller suppliers—including Argentina, Canada, Australia, the European Community, Thailand, Spain, and Sweden. As a consequence, Soviet grain imports actually doubled during the first marketing year affected by the U.S. embargo (1979/80) to a record level above 30 million tons. Feed use was expanded as well, thanks in part to the availability of grain from domestic reserves, and livestock herds were maintained. In December 1980, after one year of the U.S. grain embargo, Soviet livestock inventories were larger than they had been in December 1979, the month before the embargo was imposed.

Beyond the Soviet Union, the fastest growing customers for U.S. food exports have been the OPEC countries. For these countries, food imports do tend to satisfy a much larger share of total internal consumption. But once again the flexible character of world food markets protects them from any unilateral exercise of U.S. food power. Much like the Soviet Union (which is itself flush with hard currency earned through the export of petroleum), the OPEC countries have ample purchasing power to compete for needed imports even in a tight world market. Moreover, they import food in quantities that are small enough to be had from a wide variety of individual suppliers. Iran, for example, the largest OPEC food importer, had no trouble getting the 3.4 million tons of cereals that it required in 1980 despite trade interruptions occasioned by the ongoing hostage crisis with the United States. This was a record quantity of food imports for Iran, 35 percent above the previous year's import total. But it was a small amount by any other standard, being equivalent to less than 1 percent of the world trade total, and hence easily available from other suppliers.

Before the hostage crisis, the United States had appeared to enjoy an awesome measure of "food power" over Iran, having supplied as much as 80 percent of Iran's imported wheat and rice. But when trade with the United States was cut (the U.S. share of Iran's total agricultural imports dropped to less than 1 percent during the crisis), a number of smaller suppliers were more than willing to step in to fill the food gap. Australian farm exports to Iran tripled, European Community farm sales to Iran increased by 45 percent, and additional food supplies reached Iran from Turkey, Argentina, Canada, and even India. Some U.S. food also reached Iran during the hostage crisis, indirectly by transshipment through Dubai, and directly as well, through export firm deceptions.[4]

Food market dominance not only fails to confer diplomatic leverage. Export dominance itself can be reduced through any attempt to maximize short run foreign exchange earnings or through any attempt to use food to gain diplomatic advantage.

World food production is responsive to higher prices, and at slightly higher prices the United States could easily lose a part of its competitive edge in world markets. Those who propose to take maximum external economic advantage of U.S. market dominance in the short run, by funneling U.S. exports through a single and high-priced government marketing board, overestimate the durability of U.S. food market dominance. Today's expanded U.S. share of world markets could shrink, and U.S. export earnings could fall, if U.S. grain were once again priced out of world markets, as was the case several decades ago.

Today's expanded U.S. share of world markets could also shrink if too many political conditions are attached to the purchase of U.S. food. If the United States comes to be viewed as an unreliable supplier, or one whose grain can only be secured at the risk of diplomatic blackmail, importing nations can seek to permanently reduce or diversify their trade away from the U.S. Both Iran and the

Soviet Union have already done so, to a significant degree, since their experience with U.S. economic sanctions in 1980.

The permanent diversification of Soviet grain imports, away from the U.S., following the 1980-81 grain embargo, is particularly instructive in this regard. Within months of the embargo announcement the Soviet Union had signed a five–year agreement with Argentina, providing a guarantee of access to a minimum annual purchase of 4.5 million tons of Argentine corn, grain sorghum, and soybeans. A year later the Soviets signed a similar agreement making available at least 60,000 metric tons, yearly, of Argentine beef.[5] Encouraged by its new access to the Soviet market, Argentina made plans to increase both grain and meat production, increasing acreage devoted to grain by 13 percent, and producing a grain crop in 1980/81 that was nearly 30 percent higher than its production average of the previous five years. Most of this increased production was exported to the Soviet Union in place of grain shipments that might otherwise have come from the U.S.

Even after the U.S. embargo was lifted in 1981, the Soviets persisted in this import diversification strategy. In May 1981, they signed a bilateral agreement with Canada guaranteeing them a minimum 25 million tons of Canadian wheat and barley over the five–year period 1981–85. The Canadian reaction was to develop an investment program designed to expand exportable wheat supplies by 50 percent by 1985.[6] In July 1981, still aggressively pressing for supply diversification so as never again to be so vulnerable to a U.S. grain embargo, the Soviets signed yet another five–year food supply agreement with Brazil, this one guaranteeing them access to a minimum 2.5 million tons of Brazilian soybeans, plus a minimum 2.5 million tons of Brazilian corn.[7] Agreements to receive grain from Hungary and rice from India were also concluded. By 1982, despite its projected import needs of 42 million tons of grain, the Soviet Union had significantly reduced the share of this grain coming from the United States and hence its exposure to a renewed U.S. grain embargo. More important to the United States in the long run, it was stimulating investments in the production of exportable supplies of non–U.S. grain, threatening to cut into the U.S. share of exports worldwide.

Grain importing nations do not have to be the target of a U.S. food power exercise to react in this manner. President Lopez Portillo of Mexico, upon witnessing President Carter's embargo against the Soviet Union, announced an ambitious and expensive new agricultural development plan (SAM) designed to make his country self–sufficient in corn and beans by 1982 and in other staples by 1985. "It is becoming clear," he said, "that the definitive strategic instrument of the superpowers is . . . food."[8] In order to reduce Mexican vulnerability to the possible exercise of U.S. food power in future years (most likely, in the form of demands for preferential access to Mexican oil—"food for crude"), Mexico was seeking, before the fact, to diminish its reliance on food imports. It also sought to diversify those imports away from the United States. For example, in 1981/82 U.S. wheat exports to Mexico were expected to decline by 35 percent, while Mexico's wheat imports from Canada were to increase by roughly 75 percent.[9]

The Character of the U.S. Economic System

The U.S. economic system, founded as it is upon private enterprise, is a second barrier to the official exercise of U.S. "food power." Unlike most other large food exporters, the United States does not channel its foreign grain sales through a single government marketing board. There is no institutional counterpart in the U.S. to the Canadian Wheat Board or to the Australian Wheat Board, which have been granted sole authority to export grains from these two smaller producers. U.S. food producers and export firms are long accustomed to the use of individual marketing strategies and are opposed, for reasons of habit and ideology as well as self–interest, to the rigid procedures (production–delivery quotas, collective marketing, and averaged pooled prices) that a government marketing board might entail. Proposals to create a U.S. grain marketing board or to give equivalent powers to the existing Commodity Credit Corporation (CCC) have been routinely defeated in the Congress. The spectacular growth of U.S. grain exports, in contrast to the sluggish export performance of Canada and Australia, has appeared to vindicate this U.S. preference for lightly regulated exports.

Lightly regulated food exports are well adapted for earning foreign exchange, but they are not well adapted for manipulation in the service of U.S. foreign policy. Foreign policy officials lack the means to fine tune either the volume or the direction of U.S. food exports. Prior to the embarrassment of the ill–timed 1972 grain sale to the Soviet Union (the "Great Grain Robbery"), U.S. officials did not even know, on a timely basis, how much U.S. grain was being sold by private firms, when, or to whom. Official monitoring of exports was subsequently tightened, and Presidential authority to deny validated grain export licenses for reasons of foreign policy was plainly conferred under the 1979 Export Administration Act. But when President Carter sought to use this authority in 1980, he discovered how difficult it can be to put a sudden halt to U.S. food exports moving through the various stages of the private export chain. In order to avert a panic sale of grain futures contracts, which would have been followed by catastrophic losses for U.S. grain export firms and an eventual collapse of farm prices, the CCC had to step in to assume the contractual obligations of those firms that had already purchased large quantities of grain earmarked for delivery to the Soviet Union at a short term cost to the government of about $2 billion. According to a Government Accounting Office study released in 1981, this hastily improvised procedure incurred needless costs and generally failed to mitigate those private market losses that were occasioned by the embargo.[10]

There are several links in the private grain export chain that the U.S. government cannot control. Loading U.S. grain at East coast ports onto ships destined for overseas customers is an activity controlled by the International Longshoremen's Association (ILA), a labor organization with a long history of injecting its own views into the conduct of U.S. export policy. Ever since President Kennedy first sought to promote U.S. grain sales to the Soviet Union, in 1963, the ILA has successfully used its considerable power to block the loading of grain as a lever to gain self–serving publicity for its leadership plus greater influence over U.S. maritime policy. In this regard, President Carter's decision to embargo U.S. grain sales to the Soviets in 1980 was not entirely his own; it was made in haste, amid growing threats from the ILA to cut off all grain trade with the Russians, with or without the President's command. Even after the President acted, the ILA was not satisfied with a partial embargo, and for a number of months the longshoremen refused to load some remaining quantities of the 8 million tons of grain that the United States was obliged to sell (and that the President wanted to sell, under the terms of a previously negotiated and still valued long–term agreement with the Soviets). Several months earlier, the ILA had imposed a similar wildcat embargo on food shipments to Iran, in reaction to the hostage taking, despite a White House preference that food and medicine should be permitted to go through.

In the Iranian case, however, while the dockworkers were defying the White House, some resourceful private grain export firms were defying everyone, including the dockworkers. These firms transshipped significant quantities of U.S. rice to Iran through Dubai. Several smaller export firms in Portland, Oregon (according to the Treasury Department's customs service office there) were able to ship at least four boatloads of U.S. wheat directly to Iran, in 1980, by deliberately filing false shipping documents. The shipments were posted for a Nigerian flour mill that was yet to begin operation.[11]

The very large U.S. food export firms do not have to resort to such petty deceptions to market U.S. food products when and where they choose. The five largest grain trading companies (Cargill, Continental, Bunge, Louis–Dreyfus, and Andre) are still privately owned by just seven European and American families, thereby preserving for themselves a much greater degree of secrecy and autonomy in their operations than would otherwise be tolerated.[12] These five private firms, which together handle about 85 percent of all grain exported from the United States, describe themselves as "citizens of the world." They are genuinely multinational in character, with much that they sell from the United States going through overseas subsidiaries.[13] It was only through the device of a "gentleman's agreement," rather than through the effective reach of U.S. government power or information, that the U.S. Department of Agriculture persuaded these companies to refrain from using overseas subsidiary sales to "leak" U.S. grain into the Soviet Union at the time of the 1980 embargo.

The Character of the U.S. Political System

When government officials do intervene in the private food export chain, they usually do so to solve political problems at home rather than diplomatic problems abroad. U.S. food export policy has traditionally been hostage to domestic political forces, and only with great difficulty can U.S. foreign policy leaders institute new appropriate food policies to serve their own external purposes, economic or diplomatic. Producer and consumer groups within the United States usually fight battles and strike bargains over food export policy while paying little attention to any sort of foreign policy objective.

Complaints from farm state legislators and threatened lawsuits from outraged producer associations were the reason that President Ford finally lifted his own brief embargo on grain sales to the Soviet Union, late in 1975. (This embargo had been made necessary, in turn, by an earlier round of complaints from domestic consumer groups, fearful of the higher food prices that further grain sales to the Russians might imply.) Jimmy Carter, then a presidential candidate, seized the opportunity to win farm votes away from Ford, in 1976, with a promise of "no more embargoes." When Carter went back on this promise in 1980, it was candidate Reagan's turn to benefit. Reagan's campaign pledge to terminate the grain embargo, although at variance with the rest of his foreign policy, was nonetheless honored just three months following his inauguration. Political operatives in the White House persuaded the President to yield to domestic producers, despite the vigorous objections and unconcealed displeasure of the Secretary of State.

Domestic consumer groups have tried to exercise an opposing sort of veto power over food export policies, blocking any food trade strategy that might seem to imply expanded U.S. food sales abroad in times of short supply and high prices at home. U.S. food exports were suspended on three separate occasions in the early 1970s (the 1973 soybean embargo, then grain export suspensions to the Soviet Union in 1974, and 1975), each time in direct response to consumer pressures voiced through the President's Cost of Living Council and through a variety of self-appointed inflation fighters and consumer advocates in the U.S. Congress and within the organized labor movement. Particularly in 1975, with U.S. food prices still high following the food crisis experience of the early 1970s, food exports to the Soviet Union momentarily fell hostage to consumers. Both the Department of State and the Department of Agriculture were pushed aside, in August 1975, as George Meany, then President of the AFL–CIO (using the threat of another ILA boycott) negotiated the terms of a temporary export suspension on grain sales to the

Soviet Union with the Labor Department and the President's Council of Economic Advisors.

As noted above, producers fought back, forcing the President to lift the 1975 embargo before he could negotiate any significant concessions from the Soviets. Then, two years later, to protect themselves in the future, producer groups added an extraordinary insurance clause—Section 1002—to the 1977 Food and Agriculture Act, which required that the Secretary of Agriculture set farm "loan rates" at a budget breaking 90 percent of parity in the event of any future embargo decision based upon a finding of tight domestic food supplies. When surprised by President Carter's 1980 embargo— undertaken for reasons of foreign policy rather than tight domestic supplies—producer groups wrote into law an even more extreme form of embargo protection. They added to the Agriculture and Food Act of 1981 a Section 1204, which requires that producers be compensated at 100 percent of parity in the event of any export suspension that singles out agricultural products for reasons of national security or foreign policy and that does not include all U.S. exports to the target country.[14] In early 1982, the additional cost to the U.S. Treasury implied by this provision, had the U.S. reimposed a selective food embargo on the Soviet Union, was estimated at more than $30 billion. The authors of the provision explained that their purpose was not so much to compensate producers in the event of a renewed embargo, as it was to prevent a renewed embargo in the first place by making it impossibly expensive.

In the end, consumers are more numerous than producers and are not without their own trump cards to play. It is arguable that President Carter might have been forced, by consumers, to suspend grain exports to the Soviet Union in 1980, even without an invasion of Afghanistan, and even without a threatened ILA boycott. The hopes of the Agriculture Department to sell an all time record quantity of grain to the Soviet Union in 1980, 25 million tons, would have become a serious political liability for the President by mid–1980, following the severe drought that withered U.S. corn and soybean harvests that summer. This latest Soviet grain deal (much larger than the still remembered 1972 sale) would have been described by the President's enemies as a contributing factor to double digit inflation, all this on the eve of the November presidential election. Electoral politics might have required a partial suspension of grain exports to the Soviet Union, especially exports of corn, even without a foreign policy motive or a Soviet foreign policy provocation. Even with Section 1204 now in place, domestic political pressures to cut off all grain exports to the Soviet Union, in the event of some future diplomatic or economic provocation, might be satisfied at an affordable price to the U.S. Treasury simply by expanding any future embargo to encompass nonagricultural sales to the Soviets.

The Incompatibility of Economic and Diplomatic Food Power Objectives

Transcending these specific constraints, perhaps the strongest and most persistent inhibition against the use of food power is the obvious incompatibility between economic and diplomatic food power objectives. The unrestrained promotion of U.S. food exports, to strengthen the nation's trade and payments balance, makes impossible a conditional export strategy, conditional on diplomatic or security objectives, and vice versa. The conflict is obvious between selling as much food as possible to a large importer such as the Soviet Union, to earn foreign exchange, and also conditioning those sales upon acceptable Soviet policies in Afghanistan, in the START talks, in El Salvador, or in Poland. The economic imperative to sell will too often collide with the diplomatic imperative to deny.

The diplomatic benefits to be had from exercising food power may also, at times, be accompanied by even larger diplomatic costs. If it pursues the most effective kind of food sanction—a multilateral food export embargo—the United States must be prepared to accept a heavier strain upon its own alliance network. Some U.S. food exporting allies may decline to go along, apart from the diplomatic merits of the case, because their food exports constitute a larger component of total foreign exchange earnings and are more costly to sacrifice. The result can be a level of diplomatic friction within the alliance that undercuts whatever diplomatic pressure is being brought to bear upon the adversary. In the case of the 1980–81 grain embargo, which was never joined by Argentina and therefore ineffective from the start, allied governments in Canada, Australia, and in Western Europe all gradually withdrew from their initial promise to maintain grain exports to the Soviet Union within normal bounds. By the time the embargo was finally lifted, Australian, Canadian, and EC grain sales to the Soviet Union were running at roughly four times the pre-embargo (1978/79) level.[15] As these allied exports to the Soviet Union increased the embargo was further weakened, the U.S. lost a still larger share of the Soviet market, and acrimonious charges of profiteering, answered by charges of coercion, were exchanged among allies. Japan, whose trading companies had held back from selling grain to the Soviet Union during the embargo, took offense at the manner in which the embargo was finally lifted.[16]

Pursuing a U.S. food power strategy of unrestrained export promotion can also cause diplomatic friction among allies. If the United States were to promote grain exports with all of the resources at its disposal, diplomatic protests would be heard from direct export competitors such as Canada and Australia. The EC, while guilty in its own right of dumping food onto world markets, would surely complain as well. Once again, a larger collateral price might outweigh the intended short run benefit. (As a parallel consideration, if foreign exchange earnings were to become the one overriding objective of U.S. food export policy, concessional food aid shipments might wither to nothing, and diplomatic relations with some friendly nations that are too poor to buy large quantities of U.S. food, such as Egypt, might suffer as well.)

The other side of this incompatibility between economic and diplomatic food power objectives has already been mentioned. If U.S. food export policy were tied exclusively to diplomatic objectives, and if it became known that all U.S. food sales were conditioned upon foreign policy behavior pleasing to the United States, the reliance of foreign governments upon U.S. exports would likely diminish. When Lyndon Johnson attempted, in the 1960s, to secure diplomatic concessions from nations such as Egypt and India by putting U.S. food aid on what he called a "short tether," the short run result, in each case, was an aversion to further food aid or food trade from the United States (as well as an added measure of diplomatic defiance).[17] To avoid being a target of U.S. food power, even poor and powerless nations can seek to diversify their imports or retreat into an artificial and premature state of "self–sufficiency." The case of Mexico has already been discussed. If the United States appears an undependable source of supply, reliance upon U.S. exports and U.S. export earnings could eventually decline.

FORGET FOOD POWER?

In view of these many barriers to the satisfactory exercise of U.S. food power, perhaps frustrated policy officials should wish the notion out of existence. Rather than seeking unlikely satisfactions from food power, U.S. foreign policy makers might do well to concentrate all of their energies upon a restoration of their more traditional military, industrial, and financial power assets. Why not forget food power?

The choice does not exist. Even if it were the preference of foreign policy makers, the notion of food power would not so easily disappear. Use of the "food weapon" is too much alive as a popular concept, having been widely discussed in print for nearly a decade, having been endorsed, in one form or another, by the last three Secretaries of Agriculture, and having been visibly embraced and stubbornly defended as presidential policy after the Soviet invasion of Afghanistan. Officials who now decline to seek a diplomatic advantage from U.S. food abundance would have too much explaining to do. As long as an attentive public believes in food power, national leaders—whatever their own enthusiasm for the concept—will feel some obligation to try to use it. If stung by another Soviet provocation, the American people would pay no heed to the recently demonstrated futility of denying food to the Soviet Union; they would expect their leaders to try again. Amid the intensification of the Polish crisis, late in 1981, the U.S. Senate passed by a vote of 67 to 27 a resolution calling for a total U.S. trade embargo against the Soviet Union should that country send its own troops, or other Warsaw Pact troops, into Poland to quell unrest there. In February 1982, the AFL–CIO endorsed across the board economic sanctions against the Soviet Union, to include a renewed grain embargo, on the basis of martial law alone.

This sort of public insistence that the food weapon be used may at times be useful to policy makers. In the realm of appearances, and as a convenient form of symbolic or surrogate action, the food weapon can have its attractions. Whether or not the food weapon has its intended effect upon the adversary may matter very little alongside the appearance of such an effect, or alongside the symbolic satisfaction gained from the announcing of its use. Recourse to a food embargo, even an ineffectual embargo, can sometimes present to policy makers a satisfactory middle ground between doing nothing at all and doing something even more costly or even more dangerous. With some luck, officials adept in the timing of their policies, and in the public presentation of those policies, might be able to minimize the damage of an obligatory food power initiative. In the realm of appearances, they might even be able to take credit for a food power success. The food power obligation presents those who make U.S. foreign policy with a difficult task of securing substantial interests in the realm of trade while seeking apparent gains and symbolic victories in the realm of domestic politics and external diplomacy.

MAKING THE MOST OF THE FOOD POWER OBLIGATION

To make the most of their sometimes unhappy obligation to use food power, U.S. officials should begin by protecting the economic substance of the issue, seeking always to preserve a steady rate of U.S. food export growth beneath the turbulent surface of political symbolism or diplomatic appearance. As a rule, food power payoffs in the more elusive world of symbol or appearance should only be sought after securing a continued payoff in the real world of economic substance.

Joining symbol and appearance with a continued commercial reward is not always an impossible chore. Thanks to the enormous flexibility of world food markets, isolated U.S. food embargoes designed for the sake of diplomatic appearance need not result in a commensurate loss of food export opportunities. The U.S. grain embargo of 1980–81 is a case in point. Just as that embargo failed to prevent the continued growth of Soviet grain imports in 1980, it also failed—at least in the short run—to prevent the continued growth of U.S. grain exports. U.S. grain prices did fall during the first six months of the embargo, but it is difficult to blame the embargo for this price slump since U.S. grain exports were still growing, even with the embargo in place. U.S. grain exports to all customers, in the first marketing year affected by the embargo (1979/80), increased by 22 percent, in terms of volume, over the level of the previous year. Total U.S. grain exports then continued to increase in the next marketing year (1980/81), even though the embargo continued, and even though a summer drought in 1980 had cut U.S. grain production by 11 percent. Embargo critics tried to argue that by suspending sales to the Soviet Union, the United States had only "shot itself in the foot." In fact, to the extent that export growth was maintained, we missed even our own foot.

U.S. grain had not "leaked" through the embargo. It did not have to. With only one channel of trade shut down, exporters as well as importers were able to work around the embargo. As a greater quantity of non–U.S. grain was attracted to the Soviet market, larger quantities of U.S. grain moved, in reciprocal fashion, toward non–Soviet customers. As a result of these compensating trade shifts, the U.S. share of grain sales worldwide was not immediately reduced by the embargo, the complaints of U.S. grain farmers and exporters notwithstanding. In fact, the U.S. share of total world wheat and coarse grain exports increased from 55 percent in the year before the embargo (1978/79) to 57 percent in the year the embargo was lifted (1980/81). Only in time, perhaps, with the expanded production in Argentina and in Canada inspired by the embargo, would U.S. market shares worldwide be adversely affected.

The shift in trade patterns occasioned by the unilateral Carter grain embargo, although doing little or no damage to U.S. market shares in the short run, even had its advantageous aspect from a U.S. perspective. While this trade shift may have diminished the impact of the embargo on the Soviet Union, it also reduced the danger, to the United States, of economic disruptions caused by highly variable and unpredictable Soviet grain purchases. Before the embargo, the United States had been carrying most of the burden of having to absorb or outguess such disruptions. With the partial embargo in place, this burden was spread more evenly across a large number of smaller suppliers. Moreover, the trade shifts occasioned by the embargo made it far more difficult for the Soviets to surprise and disrupt world markets in the first place, through massive purchases made—or not made—in the United States alone. The Soviet Union must now tip its hand earlier, because it fills a larger part of its needs through a series of purchases, throughout the year, from a half–dozen smaller suppliers.

In its substantial economic impact, therefore, the U.S. grain embargo of 1980–81 was hardly the total calamity for U.S. trade and producer interests that its critics have argued. Had it not been for the inauguration, in January 1981, of a President solemnly pledged to lift the embargo, it might have been permitted to continue, at least for symbolic purposes (to avoid the appearance of U.S. indifference to the Soviet threat in Poland). Had the embargo continued through the summer of 1981, during which the Soviet Union experienced their third bad grain harvest in a row, a U.S. president might have finally been able to make a believable claim, at least to the semi-informed, that the embargo was having an impact on Soviet meat production. Additional meat production setbacks that would have occurred in any case could now be claimed as a payoff from the continuing U.S. grain embargo.

In any one individual instance, the juggling of real and apparent food power effects will require a unique set of policy calculations. Still, a few crude tactical guidelines could be offered.

First, select food power tactics that are properly adapted to short run market conditions. Do not attempt to curtail exports in years of abundant domestic or world supply. To do so is to ensure immediate food power failure abroad in combination with magnified producer discontent at home. Applying this rule strictly, it might be that only one year in four—a year of simultaneous short crops in the U.S. and in the target nation—will provide an acceptable market context for a sustainable tactic of food denial: see Figure 5.1.

Since both U.S. and target nation grain production can fluctuate considerably from one year to the next, the market conditions needed to sustain even the appearance of a successful food power exercise can quickly come and go. To prolong the period of dependable policy effects, the choice of a food power tactic should therefore be made as soon as possible after the result of each year's harvest is known.

A second bit of tactical guidance is related to the first. Because year by year changes in market conditions are so likely, avoid open ended commitments to promote or restrict trade. Also, when seeking the appearance of having imposed punitive trade sanctions for diplomatic purposes, remember that most of the diplomatic payoffs will be realized very soon after a symbolic action has been taken, so announce the kind of export stoppage that can be self–terminating. The contrast between President Carter's symbolic Olympic boycott (which died a quiet death with the completion of the summer

FIGURE 5.1

Harvest Conditions Appropriate to Food Trade Denial
(U.S.–Target Nation)

| | | Results of U.S. Harvest | |
		Above Average	Below Average
Result of Harvest in Target Country	Above Average	Worst Conditions for Food Trade Denial	Food Trade Denial More Acceptable Within U.S., but Little Impact on Target Nation
	Below Average	Food Trade Denial Might Have Some Impact on Target Nation, but Less Acceptable to Producer Groups in the U.S.	Best Market Conditions for Food Trade Denial

games), and his symbolic grain embargo (which was announced without a specified point of termination) is instructive in this regard. In 1981 an awkward decision was required, by Carter's successor, to lift the embargo. This diluted its early symbolic value, reminded the public of its failed impact, and highlighted the apparent inconsistency with President Reagan's uncompromising policies toward the Soviet Union in other areas.

Third, anticipate that food power embargoes, in particular, are likely to be short–lived but repetitive by nature. They are destined to be imposed, lifted, and then reimposed by policy makers trying to stay ahead of constantly changing configurations of domestic, diplomatic, and economic forces. Be aware, then, of a repetitive "cycle" of food trade relations with adversary states, and be alert to the variety of leverage seeking opportunities found at the different points in this cycle: see Figure 5.2.

Within the confines of this hypothesized cycle of food exports between the United States and target nation X, U.S. officials will enjoy a different mix of food power advantages and disadvantages

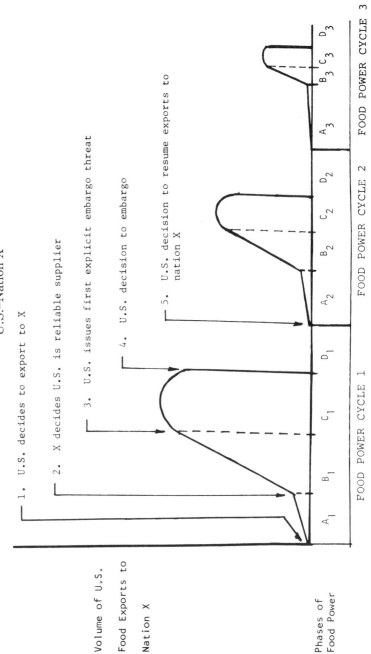

FIGURE 5.2

A Generalized Cycle of Food Power
U.S.–Nation X

1. U.S. decides to export to X

2. X decides U.S. is reliable supplier

3. U.S. issues first explicit embargo threat

4. U.S. decision to embargo

5. U.S. decision to resume exports to
   nation X

Volume of U.S.

Food Exports to

Nation X

Phases of
Food Power

FOOD POWER CYCLE 1

FOOD POWER CYCLE 2

FOOD POWER CYCLE 3

A_1 B_1 C_1 D_1 A_2 B_2 C_2 D_2 A_3 B_3 C_3 D_3

at different times. The substantial economic benefits of food power will grow most rapidly during Phase B, they will be sacrificed during Phase C, and they might be reduced to nothing during Phase D (unless exports can be immediately redirected to other overseas customers).

Substantial diplomatic benefits from food power, always difficult to realize, will be greatest just prior to the initial decision to export, when the promise of future sales can represent a significant inducement, and then also during Phase B, when dependence is growing rapidly and the danger of a trade interruption can be implied. During Phase C, however, following explicit threats of a trade interruption, the target nation may be forced, by the need to resist public blackmail, to adopt a posture of diplomatic defiance, and real diplomatic leverage may actually decline. A further reduction of real leverage will then take place as the target nation reduces or diversifies its trade. Once the decision to terminate sales has actually been made, in Phase D, diplomatic leverage is reduced to nothing.

Food power payoffs that are purely symbolic or only apparent in nature are usually found in Phases C and D of this food power cycle. Some symbolic or apparent payoffs might also be found, with luck, in Phase A or B, if the growth of exports can be artfully construed by clever officials as a "reward for good behavior" on the part of the target nation. Efforts to secure this sort of apparent food power payoff were made, with some success, by officials within the Nixon administration when they asserted that Soviet diplomatic restraint, in the Middle East and elsewhere, particularly in 1974 and 1975, was being effectively encouraged by the reward of ever larger U.S. grain exports. Official U.S. assertions made in 1981–82, that continued U.S. grain sales to the Soviet Union had provided the Soviets with a critical incentive to stay out of Poland, were of the same order.

Whenever the food power cycle repeats itself (whenever a renewed U.S. offer to sell brings to an end the final phase of denial), we can guess that the rate of growth of renewed food sales to the target nation (if they occur), and also the magnitude of renewed U.S. food power over that nation, will be somewhat reduced. After a recent experience with U.S. food power, most target nations will be slow to accept the United States, once again, as a reliable supplier, and the renewal or rapid growth of exports will probably be delayed.

If only to deny the United States an appearance of victory, embargoed nations may decide against an immediate return to the U.S. market. It is therefore likely that the total volume of exports achieved before the next explicit embargo threat will be diminished as well. Additional long run economic and diplomatic benefits may be permanently sacrificed following each subsequent phase of denial. The symbolic and apparent benefits from repeated denial can dwindle as well. Lower volumes of trade will be involved, and the limited impact of each previous trade cutoff will probably be brought to the public mind with every new decision to return to a cutoff policy. U.S. opportunities to gain apparent as well as real benefits from renewed food power sanctions against the Soviet Union, in 1982, were somewhat reduced from the opportunity level that prevailed in 1980 for just this reason. Other things equal, the food weapon loses value with every repetition of its use, depending somewhat upon the memory span of domestic and diplomatic audience groups.

CONCLUSION: THE EXERCISE OF FOOD POWER AS DAMAGE CONTROL

The odds are heavy against a successful food power exercise. Yet the obligation felt by officials to wield food power will probably continue to grow, as long as their inventory of traditional foreign policy assets continues to decline. Pending the restoration of those traditional assets, officials must exercise food power as best they can, mindful of the failure they will likely meet, and grateful for every apparent or symbolic success. The correct official attitude toward food power will be one of modesty and circumspection, not adding to the mythology of food power, never promising too much in advance. The correct official strategy will be vigilant damage control, maintaining substantial economic gains first of all, and seizing upon symbolic or apparent diplomatic victories whenever possible, claiming victory if necessary to allow termination of any particularly damaging food trade interruption. Perhaps when the substantial foreign policy capabilities of the United States have been revived, the unhappy official obligation to use "food power" will be diminished, thus bringing to an end the cyclical dissipation of real benefits available to all from U.S. food exports to which no presumption of power is attached.

NOTES

1. U.S. Department of Agriculture, *Foreign Agriculture,* Vol. XX, No. 1 (January, 1982), p. 4.

2. J. P. O'Hagan, "National Self–Sufficiency in Food," *Food Policy,* Vol. 1, No. 5 (November 1976), pp. 355–66.

3. U.S. Department of Agriculture, FG–41–81, November 16, 1981.

4. U.S. Department of Agriculture, "Iran's Farm Imports Could Hit Record High in 1981," *Foreign Agriculture,* Vol. XIX, No. 4 (April 1981), pp. 7–9.

5. Dan Morgan, *Merchants of Grain* (New York: Viking, 1979), p. 151.

6. *Journal of Commerce,* January 12, 1982, p. 5A.

7. *Boston Globe,* July 16, 1981, p. 3.

8. Quoted in John J. Bailey, "Agrarian Reform in Mexico: the Quest for Self-Sufficiency," *Current History,* November 1981, p. 359.

9. U.S. Department of Agriculture, *Foreign Agriculture* (February, 1982), p. 2.

10. *U.S. Wheat Associates Newsletter,* August 7, 1981, pp. 2–3.

11. *U.S. Wheat Associates Newsletter,* February 20, 1981, p. 1.

12. Morgan, *Merchants of Grain,* p. 7.

13. Gary L. Seevers, "Food Markets and Their Regulation," in Raymond F. Hopkins and Donald J. Puchala, eds., *The Global Political Economy of Food* (Madison: University of Wisconsin Press, 1978), p. 164.

14. U.S. Senate, 90th Congress, 1st Session, Report No. 97–290, Agriculture and Food Act of 1981, Conference Report, pp. 66–67.

15. U.S. Department of Agriculture, *Foreign Agriculture Circular,* August 13, 1981.

16. *Journal of Commerce,* December 10, 1981, p. 3A.

17. Mitchel B. Wallerstein, *Food for War—Food for Peace* (Cambridge: MIT Press, 1980).

6

THE VULNERABILITY
OF MODERN NATIONS:
ECONOMIC DIPLOMACY
IN EAST-WEST RELATIONS

David A. Deese

INTRODUCTION

At least since the dawn of the modern nation–state in the 1500s, wealth and power have been the most prominent and interactive of national objectives. Nations' diplomatic and military strategies have frequently exploited domestic economic resources, trade, aid, and international finance in the projection of power worldwide. During peace, crises, and war, nations have relied on everything from subtle implicit pressure to intensive strategic bombing. In the twentieth century economic sanctions have become a tool of diplomacy and warfare. Yet, carefully conceived and well executed economic diplomacy, or its avoidance when appropriate, remains the exception rather than the rule in international relations.

Understanding the use and abuse of economic diplomacy seems more urgent than ever under the relatively unique and threatening circumstances that have emerged over the past decade. Simultaneous with increasing awareness and debate over relative U.S. decline in worldwide political–economic power, economic growth rates have slowed worldwide and protectionism seems to be increasing, even among the OECD (Organization of Economic Cooperation and Development) nations (Vernon, 1982; Dahrendorf, 1983). This increasingly complex and uncertain economic environment joins a difficult set of political–military issues confronting the major powers in the 1980s. The competitive and at times still hostile

Eastern and Western blocs find themselves interlocked in a political–economic web presenting serious vulnerabilities and opportunities. Although the superpowers remain relatively immune to economic diplomacy, both are potentially vulnerable to some direct threats and particularly susceptible to indirect pressure through the weaknesses or divergence in positions of their allies. Government officials seem increasingly prone to resort to economic coercion or persuasion, even when alliance cohesion is threatened and further implications are uncertain.

A significant gap exists between the theory, data, and case analyses of economic diplomacy on the one hand and the continuing practice of states, corporations, and international institutions on the other. Although there are inconsistencies and other limitations in the scholarly literature on economic sanctions, coercive diplomacy, and economic warfare, important progress has been made over the past four decades. Scholars can now offer a serious body of analyses across economic diplomacy in trade, aid, finance, and the multinational corporation, although the emphasis has been on trade. In bringing practice into line with existing analyses, however, the relevant literature must be carefully screened for precision in defining and analyzing the objectives, contexts, and outcomes of economic diplomacy.

My working hypothesis runs against much of the conventional wisdom that economic coercion has almost always failed as a diplomatic measure. Much of the existing literature makes two heroic and dubious assumptions (or assertions) concerning the objectives of sanctions. First, it is assumed that the initiating nation aims its action primarily at the target nation. This misses or underemphasizes objectives involving international markets and domestic politics, both at home and in other nations. Second, most sanctions are said to be intended to change the target nation's policy, rather than to punish, discredit, or embarrass. Yet the primary objective can be even more subtle—simply to avoid what might be interpreted as a reward soon after a specific action or event. President Carter's denial of additional options for grain sales to the Soviets after the invasion of Afghanistan in 1979 appears to fit best into this latter category. Furthermore, this action may have been aimed more at domestic audiences worldwide, including Afghanistan, than at Soviet political elites. Until we have better specified what a nation intended to accomplish with economic coercion, it makes little sense to focus on what it failed to do.

I expect economic coercion to be a potentially effective element of foreign policy and grand strategy, if it is carefully planned, timed, and executed. Yet, if used too often or hastily—perhaps frequently the case—it may accelerate or even precipitate damaging instability in international political–economic and military relations. Instead of substituting for military coercion, economic diplomacy might endanger important arms control negotiations, escalate superpower conflict, and undercut the longer term power position of the initiating state. Manipulating the Soviet and Polish vulnerability in international finance may, for example, be more effective for the West than refusing or drastically curtailing all future access to Western liquidity, including other nations in Eastern Europe. It is therefore necessary to apply a carefully structured framework for defining and assessing both vulnerability to economic diplomacy and the implications of its use.

Central to this approach are careful delineation of likely multiple and shifting objectives in past cases, avoiding heavy reliance on publicly announced national objectives, and consistent distinction of the concept of dependence from that of vulnerability. Whereas dependence is the degree of actual physical reliance of a country on external sources of trade, aid, or finance, vulnerability represents the liability to political, economic, or military damage as a result of its dependence. These definitions are intended to emphasize that a nation can be highly dependent on another without necessarily incurring significant vulnerability, or only marginally dependent on another nation and yet seriously vulnerable. The similarity or difference between the two concepts in a given situation is a function of conditions at home, in international markets and systems, and in other nations.

Context is the central element in analysis of the comparative vulnerability of modern economies. It is first essential to define general conditions in the international arena. Are conclusions being drawn from experiences before the 1800s, before World War I, during or between the World Wars, during the Cold War or Détente, or the early 1980s? For useful direct comparison of East–West vulnerabilities, it may be imperative to highlight experience from the past decade when there were trade and financial flows among the blocs

that approached the levels existing today. Yet it is obviously important that we draw upon all possible earlier experience to assess both
the resilience of Eastern and Western economies under peacetime
and wartime conditions, and the possibility of drawing inferences
from similar or analogous situations.

The focus here is economic diplomacy during peacetime and, to
some extent, crisis and wartime conditions. Most relevant past
cases, including both quantitative and qualitative analyses, involve
economies that were not mobilized for war. In some instances these
studies of peacetime economic diplomacy may reveal findings relevant to economic warfare. In cases of international crises or limited
wars, such as the Korean War, the Suez crisis of 1956–57, the Vietnam War, and the oil crises of 1973–74 and 1979, results are more
easily extrapolated to wartime conditions. A more comprehensive
literature is beginning to be available on the importance of supply
restrictions, mobilization, and battlefield logistics during war
(Milward, 1977; van Creveld, 1977).

One major constraint on applying crisis, and especially wartime,
experience to peacetime conditions is the generally lower levels during peacetime of popular and regime commitment in both initiating
and target states and of regime control over the economy and political system.

The comparative assessment of vulnerability in the context of
East–West power remains elusive. Complexity and controversy
defy reasonably complete description, classification, and explanation of how overall economic leverage balances out. The literature
to date fails to define and analyze carefully the purposes, contexts,
and outcomes of economic diplomacy, and the explanatory power of
the associated East–West literature tends to be especially diluted by
advocacy. With few exceptions, the literature concentrates on a relatively small number of the most publicly visible and highly controversial cases, usually involving only trade and negative sanctions,
and frequently in a North–South rather than East–West context.

This results from the post–World War II evolution of two almost
entirely separate economic systems. Under the extreme Cold War
conditions of the 1950s there was very little interchange between
the blocs in trade or finance. The growth of two largely separate
post–Word War II economic systems was led by the U.S. effort, especially through the Coordinating Committee on East–West Trade

(COCOM), to enforce relatively tight restrictions on technology transfer to the East. Economic exchange was ruled out as a result of ideological, diplomatic, and military hostility.

Economic barriers were gradually lowered in the mid– to late 1960s as part of the easing of tensions following the Cuban Missile crisis in 1963. By 1969, in response to external and internal pressure, the Brandt government formally instituted Ostpolitik. A long–term trade agreement of July 1972 between Bonn and Moscow led to the lifting of restrictions on 84 percent of all goods traded. Over the period 1970 to 1976, when overall West German trade doubled, trade with the Soviets increased in value by 400 percent. For the first three quarters of 1979, West German exports to the Soviet Union exceeded those to the United States.

While the overall volumes of economic transactions continue to be predominantly within the separate blocs, the rate of change and qualitative significance of relatively limited inter–bloc flows have been dramatic. In annual debt service, for example, Table 6.3 shows an eight–fold increase for the Soviet bloc and a ten–fold increase for the Soviet Union between 1972 and 1979. Highly aggregated data also miss the large proportions of total official export credits to the CMEA (Council for Mutual Economic Assistance) for example, from West Germany, France, and the United Kingdom, including especially high levels from West Germany to East Germany and from France and West Germany to the Soviet Union.

Yet even this grand opening and rapid development of economic relations in the late 1960s and early 1970s, which is both recent and unprecedented in the overall history of East–West relations since 1945, did not usher in an entirely new era of behavior by either superpower. In 1967 and 1968, for example, the U.S. Congress explicitly linked the granting of access to U.S. markets to Soviet behavior toward the Vietnam War. Nixon and Kissinger decreased and increased trade concessions during 1971 and 1972 in attempts to punish, deter, or induce specific Soviet actions, from the emigration of Jews to steps in Vietnam and other third world areas (Kissinger, 1979). Even by 1974, concessions in the major U.S. trade act were again explicitly linked to the emigration of Jews from the Soviet Union.

The peak of détente from 1975 to 1978 reduced the use of such economic diplomacy, but the Soviet invasion of Afghanistan in 1979 triggered an even more intense reliance by the Carter Administration on sanctions as frontline elements of foreign policy. The Reagan Administration has gone even further in erecting economic sanctions as a fundamental premise of its East–West policies. These have become a central instrument during not only crisis conditions, such as those surrounding martial law in Poland, but also steady state relations. When progress on forcing the allies to back down on the East–West natural gas pipeline deals appeared impossible, the Administration shifted its campaign toward building a common policy to restrict official export credits in East–West trade. In place of selective manipulation of concessions that are important to the Soviets, the Administration seems to have adopted the assumption that everything from scientific exchanges to commercial loans provide unwise degrees of assistance to the East's economic and military development.

Yet the members of each bloc are searching for a new equilibrium somewhere between the old restrictions of the Cold War and the recent zenith of détente. There may be some leveling off in the rates of increase in East–West transactions, but given the depth of commitment to what started with Brandt's Ostpolitik in 1969 for West Germany and is paralleled in the rest of Western Europe, there certainly will be no returning to the days of isolated blocs. Trade statistics for 1981 and 1982 even show increases in U.S.–Soviet trade.

Energy markets and policies demonstrate the limits to drawing on most post–World War II experience. Only since the early 1970s has the Western bloc been heavily reliant on oil supplies from far beyond its own national borders, and only since the late 1970s have Eastern European nations been significantly reliant on oil from external sources at full world market prices. As shown in Table 6.4, about 11 percent of total oil use in Eastern Europe was imported in 1979, and the prices paid and foreign exchange consumed for this oil were escalating rapidly. Furthermore, the Soviet Union is now providing smaller increases in oil exports to Eastern Europe each year. It now appears, for example, that Czechoslovakia, as well as Poland, Romania and Hungary, face energy shortages and direct economic and financial repercussions.

During wartime or even crisis conditions, this now means that much imported oil, especially the 30 to 35 percent of Western oil from the Persian Gulf, may well not be available. This puts definite limits, for example, on the potential duration of a conventional war in Europe or even in the Persian Gulf, and leads to relatively early pressure on Western nations to use nuclear weapons. It also gives tremendous potential economic and strategic leverage to oil producing nations that maintain the capacity to export during crises or war.

Short of war, the Soviet Union, for example, could become a much more critical source of petroleum and natural gas to Western Europe. Concerted action by the Western Alliance under such conditions, especially in areas such as the Persian Gulf, which are beyond the formal NATO operating boundaries, could become extremely difficult. Only under a clear and present danger of war would the Alliance be likely to pull together and act decisively. Yet East–West economic flows are much deeper than energy alone. The Soviets and Eastern Europe stand to lose access to a wide variety of manufactured equipment and machinery, and tremendous financial resources if all ties are cut when conflict starts.

COMPARATIVE ECONOMIC LEVERAGE

A further essential element in defining context for economic diplomacy and warfare is the paradox inherent in the current web interlocking economies in the East and West. If we hold the crucial Western vulnerability in oil and gas supplies constant for a moment, we can establish a rough qualitative measure of comparative U.S.–Soviet economic leverage. The United States appears to hold some net advantage under both peace and wartime conditions because of some important degrees of control over international liquidity, high technology exports, world foodgrain exports, and world phosphate exports. Yet, any such attempted coercion will involve reciprocal costs for the United States.

The East–West context may make objectives particularly difficult to assess. Although it is quite true that the Soviet Union has carefully minimized its vulnerability, if not always its dependence in economic relations with the West (Finlayson and Marantz, 1982), it is clearly not immune (Portes, 1976/1977; and Goldman, 1975 and 1979). Certainly the decentralization and politicization of control over foreign economic policy in the major Western nations and the associated increase in need for domestic decision-makers to establish domestic political support (Destler, 1980; Katzenstein, 1977; Kohl, 1977) have not affected the Soviets as strongly. Yet there is clearly considerable bureaucratic maneuvering and domestic political sensitivity to Soviet macroeconomic decisions. This situation is likely to be aggravated in the 1980s, with slowed rates of economic growth and a continuing commitment to the military sector.

Beyond Soviet sensitivity to fluctuations in Western business cycles, weather, and the market prices for gold and oil, there are also some important direct vulnerabilities to the West. In energy the nation seems to be gradually losing the capability to continue exports at current levels, although domestic needs should be adequately satisfied for the foreseeable future. Table 6.4 focuses on the increasing need for Eastern European nations to import OPEC oil at prices much higher than those paid to the Soviets. Since exports to third world nations such as Cuba, Vietnam and India remain relatively small, the key problem is how to balance the critical needs for exports to the West for hard currency and technology and exports to Eastern Europe for economic and political stability.

The Soviets are also vulnerable to some extent in international finance, since Western loans are essential to their ability to import needed goods and carry out large scale projects such as the Yamal natural gas pipeline. Foreign exchange is their central limiting factor since their export markets are unstable. By far the most important and fastest growing export—oil—may drop off if no further near term disruptions occur in world oil markets. Declining world oil prices in 1982 and 1983 are already reducing foreign exchange earnings. The key question for Soviet energy exports is whether natural gas exports will increase at a rate that is rapid enough to replace decreasing crude oil exports.

The areas of continuing discussion, such as high technology for industrial and military uses, and foodgrain and phosphates, are also vulnerabilities, although of highly controversial significance. These are highlighted in Tables 6.5 and 6.6. Most of these potential vulnerabilities are, however, vis-à-vis the West in a collective sense much more than the United States alone. Coordinated action by at least the three or four most involved nations is necessary to carry out any real threat or use of economic coercion against the Soviets. Western policy coordination is likely to be both increasingly difficult and increasingly essential to economic coercion, especially in trade, against the Soviet Union.

Even more important, of course, to Soviet vulnerability are indirect threats through Eastern Europe. The degree of political–economic hardship that can be imposed on Poland, Romania, Hungary, Czechoslovakia, and even East Germany may be considerably greater than on the Soviet Union. Economic effects of Western sanctions or CMEA decisions may be translated into political problems much more rapidly.

The Soviet Union already faces serious and heavy economic costs through bloc economies, opposition from bloc leaders to economically costly steps, and political breakdown in the bloc that is aggravated by Western economic diplomacy.

The Soviets face a longer term paradox in maintaining control over Eastern European economic relations with the West. Compared to the West, the Soviets have much greater economic, political, and military leverage over Eastern Europe. Yet Western economic support is critical to the Soviet ability to keep the existing Eastern economies, and thus political systems, functioning. As recent events in Poland have well demonstrated, over the longer term even simple dependence, as opposed to vulnerability, on the West can stimulate liberalizing economic and political trends that may threaten Soviet control. Although Soviet and Eastern European diplomatic action or reaction to Western economic diplomacy may therefore not be significantly contingent on public support, the range and duration of measures to reduce domestic consumption may be seriously constrained. Major Western governments must generate support for embargoing grain, computers or high technology projects, while Eastern European governments must at least be careful not to exceed consumer tolerance.

East–West economic relations also present a special situation with respect to ideology and the flow of information. Responses in the East to Western economic threats must be tailored within the constraints of established dogma on the goals of multinational corporations and Western governments, thus leaving little room for admitting harmful effects from Western economic diplomacy. It is difficult to understand actual results of past cases both because information is frequently not published or unavailable, and because real economic effects can be at least partially masked. In particular, in the past positive sanctions seem to have been more effective than negative ones, perhaps because the Soviet regime can quietly provide a *quid pro quo* to the West, such as permitting more Jews to migrate, which is not visible to its population.

It is thus essential to emphasize that the overwhelming elements of leverage, available to each superpower beyond their own borders, apply primarily through influencing the behavior of nations in the opposing bloc. The United States and several Western nations can readily exert much more leverage over individual Eastern European nations such as Poland, Romania, and Hungary than over the Soviet Union. Similarly, individual Western European nations are much more vulnerable than the United States to Soviet leverage.

Table 6.1 shows the relatively minor overall U.S. position in East–West trade. Soviet imports from the United States were steady at only 2 percent of their total imports, and total bloc imports from the United States averaged only about 4 percent for 1978–1980. The United States averaged only 16 percent of all Western exports to the Soviets and about 13 percent to the bloc for 1978–1980. These are very small proportions given that total U.S. exports in this period were about one–third of total European NATO exports.

Table 6.2 shows that with the exception of Turkey, and perhaps also Greece and Iceland, trade by individual NATO countries with the Eastern bloc nations remains a small fraction of total trade. Although only exports are shown, Western imports from the bloc are generally even a smaller fraction. For the United States, only an average of 2.4 percent of total exports in 1979–1980 went to European CMEA countries.

Although the financial data in Table 6.3 are only estimated, they illustrate that the Soviets have been cautious. Their almost $5 billion annual debt service to the West is important but still relatively small when compared to the other major CMEA members. Soviet debt service in 1979 was about 28 percent of the total for CMEA, or less than 40 percent of the total for non–Soviet CMEA. This is relatively low considering the size of the Soviet economy compared to the rest of CMEA. It also reflects the generally greater caution of the Soviets in trade with the West.

The superpowers are considerably less reliant on international trade than their allies. By the late 1970s, for example, Soviet foreign trade contributed only about 5 to 10 percent of the GNP. This contrasts sharply with about 12 percent for Poland, 15 percent for East Germany, over 15 percent for Hungary, Czechoslovakia, and Yugoslavia, and over 20 percent for Bulgaria and Romania. While Bulgaria and Yugoslavia were deeply involved in international trade throughout the 1970s, all the others made a rapid transition during the decade. Over the period 1970 to 1978, the trade as a percentage of GNP indicator roughly doubled for Romania and the Soviet Union and increased by 50 percent for Poland.

The two superpowers thus remain relatively immune from direct economic attack, even though selected U.S. high technology and grain exports and international financial support may, at least temporarily, be important to the Soviets. A complex and vital question thus arises: how does each bloc gain or lose the most from the potential exploitation of this economic web?

The answer to this question for each specific case must reflect the fact that both superpowers lack major direct leverage over each other and therefore need the support of their own trading bloc. There are at least two important results of this situation. First, it is increasingly difficult for the United States to make use of its potential leverage, especially with negative sanctions. Western European nations are reluctant to take action against Eastern Europe because of the importance of existing trade and financial relations and their view that this is an inappropriate, if not ineffectual means of leverage over the Soviets. Furthermore, U.S. unilateral action against Eastern Europe in conditions short of war is considerably less effective than joint Western efforts.

Finally, even if Eastern Europe is affected by U.S. action, the results could be counterproductive. It is usually not Eastern Europe as much as the Soviet Union that Western nations want to influence, and this of course provides Soviet and Eastern European regimes with a clear excuse and scapegoat for harsh domestic countermeasures such as strict rationing. Yet there are some situations, such as in the transfer of high technology with military applications, in which it may be not only appropriate but essential to act against Eastern Europe in order to affect the Soviet Union. At least for militarily significant technologies and equipment, it seems clear that the Soviets have access throughout Eastern Europe.

The second result of the superpowers' need for support among their bloc members includes the relatively greater leverage available to the Soviet Union through unilateral negative action against Western Europe. The West may in some cases be unable, short of war, to effectively impose negative sanctions on Eastern Europe in order to get at the Soviets. Yet, although the Soviet Union may be able to constrain or punish the United States through action, or at least implied threats against Western Europe, we must carefully assess the limits on such potential Soviet leverage.

ENERGY SUPPLY AS LEVERAGE

In oil and gas supplies the difference between war and all other situations may be important. Although we must assume the loss of Soviet supplies to Western Europe during war, under most other circumstances the Soviets would be reluctant to stop, or even explicitly threaten energy flows. This is because of short–term losses in foreign exchange which, in the case of gas, do not start until the 1990s (if Western exporters are careful to make payment arrangements only on a quarterly or semiannual basis), in important imports from the West, especially from Western Europe, and longer term loss of high technology, private investment capital, and credibility as a reliable business partner.

If, as the U.S. government now argues strongly, these exports and imports are crucial to the Soviets, then it must also follow that they will be extremely reluctant to forego them. There remains, however, at least one important possibility—that the Soviets gain an immediate bargaining advantage by threatening to cut off energy supplies to Western Europe, whereas the West only gains offsetting leverage in an intermediate to longer term context.

An absolutely crucial response for this case may be available in the West: emergency preparedness. Offsetting domestic and international measures can be taken in advance to further minimize vulnerability despite dependence on Soviet natural gas. For example, natural gas pipeline networks can be designed to allow regional and international diversion of supplies. Dual use burners can be installed in major plants, where consumption may also be concentrated for ease in fuel switching. Stockpiling of supplies beyond normal operational levels is also feasible in some regions (Deese and Nye, 1981).

The most interesting case may therefore be potential modification of behavior by Western European nations as a result of implicit or very subtle threats, or positive sanctions, from the Soviet Union or through bloc nations such as East Germany. West Germany is especially sensitive to any change in the status of its relations with East Germany, especially if West Berlin is involved. Since Soviet deliveries of energy supplies to West European nations slow at times in the winter, for example in the winter of 1980–1981 when volumes were down as much as 30 percent over a short period of time (Stern, 1982; Blau & Kircheimer, 1981), it could be difficult to assess Soviet motives during future supply restrictions. This question could be further complicated at any time by a Soviet claim that supplies were diverted to offset shortages in Eastern Europe—a continuing and serious possibility. This makes it easier for the Soviets to manipulate energy flows for political purposes and perhaps split Western Europe from the United States over the interpretation of Soviet motives.

Yet, it remains unclear whether the Soviets would ever find it in their best interest to send such signals to Western Europe. It has already been suggested within the Reagan administration that the restrictions in 1980–1981 were related to U.S. attempts to gain Western European support for sanctions against the Soviets after the invasion of Afghanistan. Some officials and analysts point to Soviet use of economic sanctions against China in 1962, Albania in the 1960s, Czechoslovakia in 1968, and threat of use against Poland in 1981–82 (which has not been documented) as evidence that they are ready to use them against Western Europe in the future. These cases are, however, all confined to defections, or attempted defections, from the Soviet bloc when there were no real countermeasures available. Given Soviet, and especially Eastern European economic needs from the West, economic diplomacy against Western Europe may make little or no sense.

Is some form of Soviet influence over Western European nations at all probable? Or is it likely that Western nations will gain offsetting leverage against the Soviets under nonwartime conditions? If structured carefully, it is clearly possible that flows of foreign exchange, high technology, and private investment from Western Europe will be as important to the Soviets as the exchanged gas supplies will be to the Allies. There may also be offsetting energy options available to the West since Austria may export increasing supplies of electricity to the Eastern bloc and the Soviets may face decreasing foreign exchange earnings from energy exports. Under wartime conditions, furthermore, most energy flows to Western Europe must be assumed to be disrupted so the specific source of imports may not be overly important.

Resisting implicit or very subtle Soviet threats may demand common action by Western nations. Offsetting Western power in East–West relations is monitored carefully in the Soviet Union. The Soviets seem to be increasingly skillful at playing off companies bidding for business ventures in the East, keeping negotiations secret, and insuring that trade and foreign exchange balances are maintained within safe limits. Western Europe in particular may therefore have to carefully seek terms for maintaining control over flows of foreign exchange, energy, and technology. The position of Western European nations, both individually and collectively, is greatly strengthened if they can interrupt these flows, including any increased electricity exports, assistance in nuclear power, and all other important high technology exports to Eastern Europe as well as the Soviet Union. The challenge, of course, lies in establishing at least a minimal degree of coordination, if not cooperation, in Western deals with the Soviet bloc. Without serious and continuing consultation and coordination, the temptation could be overwhelming for individual nations to quietly accept Soviet conditions in order to gain special treatment, especially under ambiguous circumstances. It turns out, for example, that France did indeed reap positive benefits, in the form of sharply increased oil imports, during the critical months of the oil embargo of 1973–1974 and the Iranian crisis in 1979 (Colglazier, *et al.*, 1983).

The analysis becomes more complex if we relax the assumption that the West must obtain large quantities of oil and gas supplies from imports and consider the possibly greater resilience of market economies in the West to wartime conditions. Under extreme crisis, conflict, or wartime conditions, the Soviet Union can certainly make at least temporary interruptions in oil tanker routes, thus making Western governments highly uncertain about their oil and natural gas supplies from overseas. In a crisis, a simple overflight of the Straits of Hormuz by Soviet aircraft capable of laying mines could cause panic in the West and freeze tanker traffic if the major shipping insurance companies revoke coverage of vessels in these waters.

In any such scenario, conventional war fighting capabilities could be seriously restricted (Deese, 1981/1982). U.S. and NATO war reserves of crude oil and petroleum products, in addition to other basics such as ammunition, are not capable of supporting major engagements beyond several weeks (perhaps less than two or three). Almost independent of the specific circumstances that developed, it would be essential to maintain access to Persian Gulf oil. If Japan and Western Europe could not count on these oil flows, the crisis or wartime bargaining balance would be shifted heavily toward the Soviet Union.

CONCLUSION

Generalization about comparative East–West vulnerability to economic diplomacy remains difficult while we are still trying to explain many past cases and understand current international markets. Little of the relevant past literature focuses on East–West relations or attempts to distinguish the multiple and changing objectives of nations involved in economic diplomacy. In at least a significant number of cases, it is clear that economic sanctions may have been more effective than early analyses indicated, especially when objectives included international markets and domestic politics beyond the target nation and focused on punishment or embarrassment rather than changing the target nation's policy. Yet we do know that as diplomatic tools these sanctions are frequently both difficult to use for specific purposes and potentially counterproductive. Although they may substitute for military force when applied carefully, they may well accelerate the use of military force and the outbreak of conflict when used without careful planning, timing, and execution.

We can discern certain vulnerabilities and opportunities for economic sanctions used by the Eastern or Western blocs in the 1980s. Allies are crucial to the power positions of both superpowers in economic diplomacy. For the United States, most Soviet vulnerabilities can be effectively exploited only with the concurrence, if not active cooperation, of at least the major nations of Western Europe. U.S.

global responsibilities and capabilities mandate different policies on some key issues, but without greater convergence on the perception of the nature of Soviet threats and appropriate responses, the West will not be able to convert this potential power to actual leverage.

The most important direct Soviet vulnerabilities to the Western business cycle, the weather, and the international prices of petroleum and gold may sometimes be helpful to Western purposes, but these are difficult to manipulate. They can, however, increase the effectiveness of indirect action taken by the West against Soviet needs for international liquidity, high technology, food grains, phosphates, and energy both domestically and in Eastern Europe. At the same time that the importance of inward looking domestic objectives of economic sanctions is increasing, especially in the West, the state of conditions in international markets is crucial to the outcomes. Poor harvests, slow economic growth rates, or depressed prices for gold and petroleum exports make the Soviet Union considerably more vulnerable to economic punishment, regardless of the probability of any shift in Soviet policy as a result of economic hardship.

Soviet allies are also central to the effectiveness of Western economic diplomacy. If U.S. or Western intent is to compel, deter, punish, or even reward the Soviet Union, there must be careful prior assessment of how effects will be distributed across Eastern Europe. Depending on conditions in international and regional markets, and in the Soviet Union, the effects of Western action may fall heavily, either directly or indirectly, on nations in Eastern Europe. Citizens of Poland or Romania may applaud the use of such measures against the Soviet Union, but if the effects fall elsewhere, Western effort is misplaced or even counterproductive. If the effects fall more heavily on Eastern European nations than on the Soviet Union, Western allies will be even more reticent than usual to support U.S. leadership in economic diplomacy. Given the state of the Polish economy, at least Western European nations will be extremely reluctant to take further action that might raise new political problems and Soviet counteractions.

Sanctions often seem to serve as the only apparently practical policy choice, yet they also seem frequently to be used without careful planning and execution. If they do substitute for a foreign policy of inaction, which signals weakness, or of overreaction, which leads to conflict, it is important to understand better how to minimize associated costs and maximize effects. Decision-makers should expect a greater probability of effectiveness (or counterproductive damage, if the effects turn against the initiating nation) where: political will is strong in the initiating state and weak in the target state; conditions escalate to crises or conflict; the initiating state capitalizes on short–term effects; finance and investment are used as well, or instead of, trade, aid, and high technology; selected use is made of secret as well as publicized bargaining. The ultimate test of statesmanship lies in finding a delicate balance between use of dramatic public diplomacy to rally public support against an external enemy and caution in not announcing unattainable objectives that may come back to haunt the initiating government. Often, positive sanctions will be more effective than negative ones for influencing target state behavior.

There are several other important considerations at a more detailed implementation level. It is increasingly necessary for even the United States to consult with at least key allies early in the process of evaluating sanctions. Whenever possible, sanctions should not be imposed retroactively, on an extraterritorial basis, or on goods or finance that can be obtained easily elsewhere. Finally, the costs of imposing sanctions should be distributed as equitably as possible, including all possible government to government measures before the private sector is asked to absorb serious losses. In the final stages of decision, leaders should, above all else, remember that the costs and dilemmas of economic coercion must be judged over a time span of years as well as weeks and months.

TABLE 6.1

Total East-West Trade 1978–1980

Eastern Imports (millions $)

	1978			1979			1980		
	U.S.	Total	U.S. as % of total	U.S.	Total	U.S. as % of total	U.S.	Total	U.S. as % of total
Poland	439	3,849	11	427	4,475	10	417	5,029	8
USSR	254	11,347	2	324	16,184	2	453	20,027	2
Soviet Bloc	1,256	24,583	5	1,355	32,975	4	1,424	39,298	4

Western Exports (millions $)

	1978			1979			1980		
	U.S.	Total	U.S. as % of total	U.S.	Total	U.S. as % of total	U.S.	Total	U.S. as % of total
Poland	677	5,251	13	786	5,669	14	710	6,012	12
USSR	2,249	13,331	17	3,604	16,528	22	1,510	16,902	9
Soviet Bloc	3,698	28,505	13	5,731	37,027	15	3,975	39,928	10

Sources: UN, OECD, U.S. Census Bureau, F.R.G.—Statistical Office 1977–1981.

TABLE 6.2

Trade of NATO Countries with European CMEA Countries,* 1979 and 1980 Exports (million $, f.o.b.)

Country/Area of Origin	Exports to European CMEA Countries		Exports to European CMEA as percent of total exports	
	1979	1980	1979	1980
Belgium-Luxembourg	1,059	1,308	1.9	2.0
Denmark	377	391	2.6	2.3
France	4,027	4,646	4.1	4.0
F.R.G.	11,270	12,671	6.5	6.5
Greece	361	525	9.3	10.1
Iceland	64	83	8.1	8.9
Italy	2,633	2,736	3.7	3.5
Netherlands	1,144	1,420	1.8	1.9
Norway	246	266	1.8	1.4
Portugal	100	92	2.9	2.0
Turkey	325	463	13.1	16.8
UK	2,058	2,628	2.3	2.3
Total European NATO	23,663	27,228	4.0	4.0
Canada	991	1,776	1.8	2.7
U.S.	5,674	3,853	3.1	1.7
Total NATO	30,328	32,857	3.6	3.4

*Bulgaria, Czechoslovakia, G.D.R., Hungary, Poland, Romania and USSR.
Source: U.S. Department of State, Special Report No. 92, November 30, 1981.

TABLE 6.3

Soviet Bloc Dependence on Western Loans and Credits (millions $)
(Annual Service Payments)

	1972	1973	1975	1977	1979
Soviet Union	476	729	1773	3115	4754
Bulgaria	182	217	313	572	885
Czechoslovakia	134	202	324	458	785
GDR	301	435	775	1,302	2,475
Hungary	140	224	324	548	1,236
Poland	274	487	1,219	2,887	5,800
Romania	337	447	667	699	1,174
Total	1,844	2,012	3,622	6,466	12,355
Total Pact	2,320	2,741	5,395	9,581	17,109

Source: Adapted from NFAC *Estimating Soviet & East European Hard Currency Debt.*

TABLE 6.4

Patterns in East European Oil Imports: 1971–1978 (Thousand B/D)[1]

Year	Total Oil Consumption	Oil Imports as a Percent of Total	Oil Imports from the USSR	Oil Imports from the USSR as a Percent Consumption	Oil Imports from Non-Communist	Oil Imports from Non-Communist States as Percent of Total Consumption	Equivalent Cost of E. European Oil Imports from Non-Communist States at OPEC Price ($ Million)
1971[2]	1217	71	895	74	– 25	– 20	$ – 27
1973	1539	77	1100	71	83	5.4	$ 155
1975	1676	79	1269	75	63	3.8	$ 278
1977	1943	81	1420	73	159	8.2	$ 747
1978	2063	83	1490	72	228	11.0	$1076
1979	2125	89	1559	73	235	11.0	$1601[3]

[1]Adapted from CIA ER IESR 81–004 (U) 28 April, 1981 pp. 25,27, and 28, and DOE International Energy Indicators. Excludes Yugoslavia.

[2]There is a discrepancy in data involving Oil Imports and Oil Imports from the U.S.S.R.

[3]If East European oil imports from non-Communist countries were maintained at the 1979 levels, the import cost would be $2.6 billion in 1980, and $3.0 billion plus in 1981.

TABLE 6.5

U.S.S.R. Sources of High Technology Products from the Western Industrialized Nations

(Millions of Dollars)

Source	1972 High Tech. Exports To USSR	1972 As Percent of Total	1977 High Tech. Exports To USSR	1977 As Percent of Total	1979 High Tech. Exports To USSR	1979 As Percent of Total	1979 As Percent of I.W. Country's Exports to USSR
Canada	0.7	0.2	7.2	0.3	11.3	0.5	1.7
U.S.A.	26.8	8.1	184.3	8.8	154.7	6.5	4.4
Japan	41.8	12.7	343.5	16.5	398.9	16.8	16.2
Bel–Lux	4.3	1.3	18.6	0.9	21.1	0.9	4.5
Denmark	4.6	1.4	14.6	0.7	17.1	0.7	18.1
France	38.0	11.5	232.9	11.2	376.8	15.9	18.8
West Ger.	79.4	24.1	677.0	32.5	668.3	28.2	18.5
Ireland	–	–	1.2	0.1	1.3	0.1	2.9
Italy	51.1	15.5	233.1	10.7	257.2	10.8	21.1
Netherlands	3.2	1.0	19.1	0.9	16.7	0.7	5.5
U.K.	43.4	13.2	46.1	2.2	94.0	4.0	10.5
Austria	4.8	1.5	73.0	3.5	43.7	1.8	8.5
Finland	5.4	1.7	67.0	3.2	70.9	3.0	4.6
Norway	0.2	0.1	1.4	0.1	8.2	0.3	9.4
Sweden	9.0	2.7	76.6	3.7	119.9	5.1	35.3
Switzerland	16.3	5.0	99.8	4.8	111.3	4.7	41.9
Total	329.2	100.0	2085.4	100.1	2371.3	100.0	13.1

Source: Adapted from John A. Martens, "Quantification of Western Exports of High Technology Products to Communist Countries, ITA, Project D–41, Dept. of Commerce, January, 1981

TABLE 6.6

Soviet Dependence on Grain Imports (Total Grain Inc. Wheat, Coarse Grains and Misc.)

	1971	1972	1973	1974	1975	1976	1977	1978	1979
A. Domestic Production									
1. Actual (Million Tons)	171.4	158.4	210.7	181.6	132.0	211.8	184.7	226.1	171.3
B. Imports									
1. Total (Million Tons)	7.8	22.5	10.9	5.2	25.6	10.1	18.4	15.0	30.5
2. From U.S. (Million Tons)	2.9	13.6	7.9	2.3	13.9	7.5	12.5	11.1	15.3
3. U.S. as % of Total	37%	60%	72%	44%	54%	73%	68%	74%	50%
C. Total Consumption (Million Tons)	169.5	177.1	201.8	193.9	171.1	208.1	215.0	219.7	217.3
D. Imports as Percent of Total Consumption	5%	13%	5%	3%	15%	5%	9%	7%	14%
E. Cost of Grain Imports									
1. Estimated $ Cost of Imports (Millions $)	72.5	652.5	1264.0	676.0	2073.3	1977.6	1232.8	1965.0	4483.5
2. $ Cost of Imports as A & Total Soviet Imports*	.7%	4%	6%	3%	6%	5%	3%	4%	

*Dollar cost of grain imports from U.S. as a % of total costs of grain imports is the same as B.3 above.

Adapted From: USDA Agricultural Situation: USSR: Review of 1979 and Outlook for 1980, and USDA: Statistical Report USSR, and CIA: Handbook of Economics Statistics.

1971 MT Grain = $ 9.3
1972 MT Grain = $ 29
1973 MT Grain = $ 116
1974 MT Grain = $ 130
1975 MT Grain = $ 81
1976 MT Grain = $ 192
1977 MT Grain = $ 67
1978 MT Grain = $ 131
1979 MT Grain = $ 147

BIBLIOGRAPHY

Adler–Karlsson, Gunnar. *Western Economic Warfare 1947-1967: A Case Study in Foreign Economic Policy.* Stockholm: Almquist and Wiskell, 1968.

Baldwin, David. "The Power of Positive Sanctions." *World Politics* 24 (October 1971): 19–38.

Barber, James. "Economic Sanctions as a Policy Instrument." *International Affairs* 55 (July 1979): 367–84.

Blechman, Barry M., and Kaplan, Stephen S., eds. *Force Without War: U.S. Armed Forces as a Political Instrument.* Washington, D.C.: Brookings Institution, 1978.

Brodie, Bernard. *Strategy in the Missile Age.* Princeton: Princeton University Press, 1959, pp. 131–44.

E. W. Colglazier, D. A. Deese, M. Lynch, T. Neff. *Energy & Security Working Papers.* Cambridge, Massachusetts: Energy Lab, M.I.T., 1983.

Dahrendorf, Ralf. *Europe's Economy in Crisis.* New York: Holmes & Meier, 1983.

Deese, David A. "Oil, War, and Grand Strategy." *ORBIS*, Fall 1981, pp. 525–55.

Deese, David A. and Nye, Joseph S. *Energy and Security.* Cambridge, Massachusetts: Ballinger Publishing Company, with Harper and Row, 1981.

Destler, I. M. *Making Foreign Economic Policy.* Washington, D.C.: Brookings Institution, 1981.

Diesing, Paul, and Snyder, Glenn H. *Conflict Among Nations: Bargaining, Decisionmaking and System Structure in International Crises.* Princeton: Princeton University Press, 1977.

Doxey, Margaret. *Economic Sanctions and International Enforcement.* London: Oxford University Press, 1971.

Finlayson, Jock and Marantz, Paul. "Interdependence and East–West Relations." *ORBIS*, Spring 1982, pp. 173–94.

Galtung, Johan. "On the Effects of International Economic Sanctions, with Examples from the Case of Rhodesia." *World Politics* 19 (April 1967): 378–416.

George, Alexander L., Hall, David K., and Simons, William E. *The Limits of Coercive Diplomacy.* Boston: Little, Brown, and Co., 1971.

Goldman, Marshal I. *Detente and Dollars: Doing Business with the Soviets.* New York: Basic Books, 1975.

_____. "Will the Soviet Union be an Autarky in 1984." *International Security,* Spring 1979, pp. 18–36.

Green, Jerrold D. "An Analysis of Galtung's General Theory of Economic Sanctions." For the Annual Convention of the International Studies Convention, 1982.

Grieve, Muriel J. "Economic Sanctions, Theory and Practice." *International Relations* 3 (October 1968): 431–43.

Hoffmann, Frederick. "The Function of Economic Sanctions: A Comparative Analysis." *Journal of Peace Research* 2 (1967): 141–59.

Howard, Michael. "The Forgotten Dimensions of Strategy." *Foreign Affairs,* Summer 1979, pp. 975–86.

Jervis, Robert. *Perception and Misperception in International Relations.* Princeton: Princeton University Press, 1976.

Katzenstein, Peter J., ed. "Between Power and Plenty." *International Organization,* Fall 1977.

Kissinger, Henry A. *A World Restored: Metternich, Castlereagh and the Problems of Peace 1812-22.* Boston: Houghton and Mifflin, 1972.

Knorr, Klaus. *The Power of Nations: The Political Economy of International Relations.* New York: Basic Books, 1975.

_____. "International Economic Leverage and Its Uses." In *Economic Is-*

sues and National Security, eds. Klaus Knorr and Frank N. Trager, pp. 99–126. Lawrence, Kans.: University Press of Kansas, 1977.

Kohl, Wilfrid L. *Economic Foreign Policies of Industrial States*. Lexington, Mass.: Lexington Books, 1977.

Krasner, Stephen D. "Domestic Constraints in International Economic Leverage." In *Economic Issues and National Security*, op. cit.

Licklider, Roy E. "The Failure of the Arab Oil Embargo of 1973–74." *Comparative Strategy* (forthcoming).

Losman, Donald. "International Boycotts: An Appraisal." *Politics* 37 (Spring 1973): 648–71.

Milward, Alan. *War, Economy, and Society*. Berkeley: University of California Press, 1977.

Olson, Richard S. "Economic Coercion in World Politics, with a Focus on North–South Relations." *World Politics* 31(July 1979): 471–94.

Paarlberg, Robert L. "Using Food Power: Opportunities, Appearances, and Damage Control." For the Annual Convention of the International Studies Association, 1982; Chapter 5, this volume.

Portes, Richard. "East Europe's Debt to the West: Interdependence is a Two-Way Street." *Foreign Affairs*, 1976/77, pp. 749–82.

Schelling, Thomas C. *Arms and Influence*. New Haven, Conn.: Yale University Press, 1966.

_____. *The Strategy of Conflict*. London: Oxford University Press, 1961.

Stern, Jonathan. *East European Energy & East–West Trade in Energy*. London: Policy Studies Institute, 1982.

Thies, Wallace. *When Governments Collide: Coercion and Diplomacy in the Vietnam Conflict 1964–1968*. Berkeley: University of California Press, 1981.

van Creveld, Martin. *Supplying War*. New York: Cambridge University Press, 1977.

Vernon, Raymond. "International Trade Policy in the 1980s." *Int'l Studies Quarterly* 26 (1982) 483–510.

Vienna Institute for Comparative Economic Studies. *Comecon Foreign Trade Data 1981*. Westport, Conn.: Greenwood Press, 1981.

Wallensteen, Peter. "Characteristics of Economic Sanctions." *Journal of Peace* 3 (1968): 243–67.

Weintraub, Sidney, ed. *Economic Coercion and U.S. Foreign Policy*. Boulder, Colorado: Westview Press, 1982.

Wu, Yuan-Li. *Economic Warfare*. New York: Prentice-Hall, 1952.

Young, Oran R. *The Politics of Force*. Princeton: Princeton University Press, 1968.

7

THE POLITICS OF
INTERNATIONAL SANCTIONS:
A CASE STUDY OF SOUTH AFRICA

David F. Gordon

INTRODUCTION

In recent years, and with ever increasing frequency, critics of South Africa's apartheid system of legally–enforced racial discrimination and oppression have looked to comprehensive international economic sanctions as the lever by which the global community might effect a change in South Africa's racial policies.[1] A range of international sanctions have been instituted: the United Nations Security Council adopted a voluntary arms embargo as early as 1963; in 1977, following the death of Black Consciousness leader Steven Biko and the government's crackdown on its opponents in October, the Security Council voted to make the arms embargo mandatory. In 1973, Arab members of OPEC placed an embargo on oil sales to South Africa. The United States, Canada, Sweden, and other Western countries have all taken measures in the past five years to limit some forms of economic exchanges with South Africa. Ever since independence, Black African countries have sought to cut their economic ties to Pretoria, with varying degrees of success.

There is a growing international consensus that fundamentally changing the racial structure of South Africa is a proper and legitimate concern of the international community. At the same time, there is a growing belief that international sanctions can contribute to this change. Within the United Nations, Black African states have followed a strategy of slowly building a legal basis for international sanctions against South Africa under Article 39 of Chapter VII of the United Nations Charter. While they have not succeeded in convincing the Western powers to support a program of comprehensive sanctions, they have succeeded in both legitimating international concern and action on South Africa's domestic situation and in placing the issue of sanctions on the agenda of the United Nations and its agencies. Deon Geldenhuys has written that, "South Africa is today the only candidate of UN enforcement action directed at changing its domestic status quo."[2]

In this chapter I am concerned as much with sanctions as a political process as I am with the potential impact of sanctions on the domestic order of South Africa. The South Africa sanctions issue is engendering an expanding academic literature.[3] The issue may be approached from a number of different directions, all of which are legitimate and offer important insights. These include historical, moral–legal, economic, and technical approaches. Although my analysis will touch on all of these themes, I have chosen an explicitly political approach to the issue. I am concerned with the political forces that have put the sanctions question on the international agenda, the factors affecting the ways that governments respond to the issue, the impact—both economic and political—of possible sanctions on the target state of South Africa, and the policy dilemmas that are generated for governments whose participation in sanctions are crucial for their success, i.e., the Western nations and in particular the United States.

That South Africa should be the target of international sanctions is in some sense ironic. In the interwar period, when the question of sanctions as an international political instrument was first raised, South Africa was on the side of the sanctionists. The South African Prime Minister, Jan C. Smuts, in his study of the League of Nations, made an impassioned plea for the utility of international sanctions as a means by which the global community could punish delinquent states.[4] The South African commitment was not merely rhetorical. When, in 1935, the League of Nations moved to terminate its sanctions against Italy—which had been imposed as a response to the Italian invasion of Ethiopia—South Africa was one of only two nations voting for their continuation.

Sanctions are economic measures directed to gain political objectives. The causal link proposed here—imposing sanctions generates hardships that lead to reducing persistence—has been the subject of a good deal of empirical research, the bulk of which is skeptical about the validity of the theory.[5] Nevertheless, sanctions continue to be undertaken as a policy response by governments to the actions of other governments in the international arena, a recent example being the United States sanctions against Poland in response to the repression of the independent trade union, Solidarity.

THE GOALS OF SANCTIONS

But although the meaning of sanctions and the theory of sanctions is straightforward, the reasons that governments initiate economic sanctions are not. Governments undertake sanctions for a variety of reasons, only some of which have to do with directly imposing hardships on a target country in order to force it to change its policies (see Chapter 1, this volume).[6] Liberal supporters of sanctions, especially in Western foreign policy circles, seek to utilize economic sanctions to force the Pretoria regime to dismantle the apartheid system and seek accommodation with its Black majority population.[7] Radical supporters of sanctions, including the anti-apartheid movement in Western countries and the Third World bloc in the U.N. and especially its Black African members, support sanctions as a means of undermining the Pretoria government by weakening its economic base and boosting the legitimacy and morale of its opponents.[8]

But, while the goal of changing South Africa's racial policy is the stated (or direct) goal of sanctions against South Africa, to the extent that governments, in particular Western governments, have undertaken sanctions they have been more a response to political pressures and imperatives emanating from both their domestic and international political environments than a seriously–conceived and well–planned effort to put pressure on the Pretoria government. That is, goals other than the direct goal of pressuring Pretoria to dismantle apartheid have been the dominant influence on Western governments in formulating their response to the South African dilemma. Participation in sanctions against South Africa have been primarily efforts to create the image of active opposition to apartheid in order to deflect opposition and maintain credibility and political support among Black African states and in response to growing domestic pressures on these governments to take active steps against South Africa. Western participation in sanctions have also been intended to send a signal to South Africa about the willingness of these governments to act, while at the same time avoiding the harsh trade-offs that either decisively opposing economic sanctions or fully supporting a comprehensive sanctions scheme such as the mandatory, universal sanctions suggested by African states in the U.N. General Assembly, would imply.

The predominance of these secondary goals derives both from the uncertain impact of sanctions on South Africa and from the economic interdependence between Western countries and South Africa that would generate high costs and risks to the sanctionists themselves.[9] The importance of secondary aims also derives from the fact that the racial conflicts generated by the apartheid system in South Africa have ramifications for both relations among the governments of the Western alliance and for domestic politics within a number of these countries, most importantly the United States. Robert McNamara discussed these factors in an address at the University of Witwatersrand in Johannesburg in October, 1982. "If South Africa fails to deal justly and effectively with its own internal racial problem," McNamara told his audience, "that failure will not only result in immense damage to its own society, but it will impose heavy economic, military and political penalties on other countries in the Western world as well, and particularly on the United States."[10]

The economic and political interdependence between South Africa and the Western world has generated diametrically opposed political pressures for Western governments. Conservatives cite economic and strategic interdependence to argue for a policy of greater tolerance toward South Africa,[11] whereas liberals argue that economic and political interdependence gives Western governments both an imperative interest and the means to actively effect change in South Africa.[12] Thus, the question of sanctions has increasingly been bound up in the domestic politics of several key Western countries, the most important of which is the United States.

THE PRESSURES FAVORING SANCTIONS

As a result of the growing international consensus concerning apartheid in South Africa, Black African states and the anti-apartheid movements in Western countries have effectively put the issue of sanctions both on the international agenda and the domestic agendas of Western governments. In international organizations and nongovernmental organizations, African countries have proposed sanctions modeled on those imposed by the United Nations on Rhodesia after the white minority's Unilateral Declaration of Independence in 1965 as the most effective way that the international community can both express its abhorrence of apartheid and undermine its existence. Public campaigns in Great Britain and the United States against apartheid have also emphasized the need for effective economic pressures against South Africa and have proposed various forms of economic sanctions. These have included universities selling stock in companies doing business in South Africa, ending bank loans and Export–Import bank services to South Africa, and boycotts of South African–produced goods, especially the Krugerrand gold coins.

The height of the pressure favoring sanctions was in the late 1970s when there were liberal governments vocally opposed to apartheid in both the United States and Great Britain, the two most important Western countries as far as South African sanctions are concerned. But, the election of much more conservative governments, under President Reagan and Prime Minister Thatcher, brought to power in Britain and the United States policy-makers unsympathetic to sanctions-style instruments for use against South Africa. In both countries the sanctions question was taken off the immediate political agenda because even supporters of sanctions decided to make their political weight felt in different ways. It would be naive, however, to believe that the question of sanctions against South Africa will not again emerge in a more direct fashion to confront Western policy-makers.

Sanctions, then, appear to have become a permanent part of the international politics of the racial conflicts in Southern Africa. The sanctions debate is likely to continue as long as the existence of apartheid itself. Advocates of sanctions have to face the problem that the history of prior attempts at internationally-enforced sanctions have not been very effective in their goals of bringing the target country to heel.[13] All of the major studies of the impact of the U.N.–sponsored mandatory sanctions imposed against Rhodesia agree that the sanctions failed in their direct goal of forcing the Smith regime to enter into negotiations with the British government for an internationally acceptable political arrangement within which decolonization could ensue.[14] Several analysts of the Rhodesian sanctions have gone so far as to conclude that in fact the impact of sanctions was the opposite of what was intended. Rather than weakening the capacity of the Rhodesian regime through weakening its economy, sanctions strengthened the economy. Thus, J. K. Moyana wrote in 1977 that, "in forced relative isolation, the Rhodesian economy under sanctions has improved in size and structure."[15] Why, we might ask, given the past history of sanctions efforts, should South Africa be different?

ARGUMENTS SUPPORTING SANCTIONS

Supporters of sanctions against South Africa present several arguments to support their contention that sanctions against Pretoria are more likely to be effective than previous sanctions have been. Sanctions supporters argue that the main reason for the failure of the Rhodesian sanctions was that South Africa and Portugal undermined the sanctions by providing Rhodesia with access routes to the outside world via Mozambican and South African ports. South Africa, despite her nonrecognition of Ian Smith's government in Salisbury, had an important stake in the failure of Rhodesian sanctions since it was already clear that South Africa would be a potential future target. To what extent this motivated South African material assistance to sanctioned Rhodesia is not known, but the fact of that support is well-documented. Perhaps the most important aspect of this was the role that South Africa played in maintaining a steady supply of petroleum to Rhodesia.[16] Thus, supporters of sanctions against South Africa argue, a crucial element needed for the success of comprehensive sanctions—unanimity of support—was missing in the Rhodesian case.

Sanctions supporters argue that the universal consensus that has been generated against the apartheid system would provide the international context for effective implementation of sanctions. Supporters also argue that despite the many incentives that will be generated for governments and businesses to evade economic sanctions, South Africa's geographical location—surrounded by oceans and hostile countries that will be committed to the success of the sanctions program—will make evasion difficult and monitoring relatively easy. Finally, supporters of sanctions argue that because of its advanced and complex nature, its wide range of ties to the international economy, and its reliance on imported oil, South Africa is especially vulnerable to sanctions.

ARGUMENTS AGAINST SANCTIONS

Opponents of sanctions against South Africa fall into two broad groups. On the one hand there are those who, for one reason or another, reject the notion that international action to change South Africa's domestic policies is either called for and/or legitimate. On the other hand, there are those who claim that international sanctions are not the best way to promote change in South Africa. The latter group includes an odd coalition of major transnational corporations with South African investments, Western governments, the Zulu leader Chief Gatsha Buthelezi, the Rev. Leon Sullivan and at least two of South Africa's Black-ruled neighbors—Lesotho and Swaziland. In this section I will concentrate on the arguments of this second group, while realizing that part of their argument owes to the reality and power of the first group.

Those who are skeptical of sanctions have made a number of counterarguments to support their contention that comprehensive sanctions against South Africa are unlikely to be an effective strategy for change. Skeptics argue that the international consensus is more apparent than real, that even if there is general agreement that apartheid is abhorrent, there is little agreement on what the actual objectives of sanctions should be or on what response by the South African government might be sufficient for sanctions to be lifted.[17] Skeptics further argue that Western countries, those whose support would be most critical to any program of comprehensive sanctions, are unlikely to ever exhibit enthusiasm over sanctions because of their dependence upon South Africa for a number of essential raw materials and their fear that the fall of the present South African government might lead to the emergence of a radical regime wishing to deny access to those raw materials to the West.[18]

Skeptics also argue that the South African economy, far from being vulnerable to comprehensive sanctions, is quite well-placed to resist sanctions as a result of both its diversified structure and the fact that South Africa's exports—gold and other minerals—are eminently marketable and would be able to enter into international markets without distinguishing their place of origin. Finally, skeptics argue that supporters of sanctions partake in what Galtung has described as the "naive assumption" that there is a direct relationship between economic hardship and undermining the political will of a regime to resist international pressure.[19] The Afrikaners, skeptics argue, will if anything be hardened in their inflexibility as a result of sanctions.

Although it is difficult to definitively evaluate these claims and counterclaims, it is useful to attempt such an evaluative exercise. For the purpose of this evaluation, the differences between those who see comprehensive international sanctions as a viable strategy (whom I call enthusiasts) and those who oppose sanctions or feel they are not a viable approach (whom I call skeptics) can be examined in four general areas: 1) the vulnerability of the South African economy to sanctions; 2) sources of support for sanctions; 3) the enforceability of sanctions; and 4) the political impact of sanctions within South Africa. I will discuss each of these in turn.

VULNERABILITY OF THE SOUTH AFRICAN ECONOMY

Even liberal Western governments who have been quite hostile to South Africa, such as the United States under the Carter Administration, have opposed comprehensive sanctions. One stated reason that these governments have given for their opposition is that South Africa would be able to survive any impact of sanctions. For example, President Carter's United Nations Representative, Andrew Young, declared in 1977 that South Africa was "amazingly in- dependent" and could withstand comprehensive sanctions for at least a decade.[20] British Labor Prime Minister Callaghan's U.N. Representative, Ivor Richard, made similar comments in explaining his country's opposition to a sanctions strategy. These liberal policy-makers' opinions have tended to reinforce a long–standing conservative argument about South Africa's economic autonomy and invulnerability. The South African government, for their own obvious reasons, have also stressed this point. But, scientific studies of the South African economy suggest that this image of economic independence and invulnerability is a myth.

There have been three serious efforts to evaluate the potential impact of sanctions on the South African economy. Two of these, by Arnt Spandau of the University of Witwatersrand and by Richard C. Porter of the University of Michigan, have dealt with general economic sanctions. The third, prepared by British economists Martin Bailey and Bernard Rivers for the United Nations Center Against Apartheid, dealt specifically with oil sanctions.

Bailey and Rivers conclude that an oil embargo is "the most effective form of economic pressure that could be put on South Africa," that it is both technically feasible and would be politically practical if implemented under the authority of the United Nations Security Council.[21] The potential success of an oil embargo has been significantly enhanced by the fall of the Shah of Iran. Before the creation of Ayatollah Khomeini's Islamic Republic, Iran supplied an estimated 90 percent of South Africa's imported petroleum. Despite pressure to stem the flow, the Shah persistently refused to take any action. Iran sold only about 5 percent of her total exports to South Africa; thus, there was no imperative economic interest behind the Shah's action. South Africa had given political asylum to the Shah's father during World War II, so the Shah must have felt especially indebted to the South Africans for this.

Offsetting the Shah's fall has been the relative collapse of the international petroleum market in the early 1980s that increases the incentives for both countries and companies to cheat on any oil sanctions that may be imposed on South Africa, making enforcement more difficult. In addition, the South African government is speeding up its own efforts to minimize the impact of an oil embargo through stockpiling, limitations on consumption, and the development of synthetic fuels. Two coal–to–oil conversion plants have already been put into operation and a third is expected to be completed by 1983 or 1984. At that time, these plants will be able to supply about 30 percent to 40 percent of South Africa's petroleum needs, according to analysts. Nonetheless, oil is still the Achilles Heel of South Africa's economy.

Spandau and Porter both attempt to predict, through computer–based simulations of the South African economy, the consequences of sanctions on the Republic's economic life. The impact of sanctions, of course, depends upon the form and extent of the sanctions. Spandau focuses his analysis on the impact of investment sanctions while Porter investigates the impact of import sanctions. Because of the different focus of the two efforts, and also because the models that the two economists derive have important differences, Spandau and Porter come to different conclusions. Spandau foresees any loss of foreign investment as having a substantial negative short–term effect on the South African economy. But, he also sees sanctions of this sort as opening up substantial opportunities for import–substituting industrialization. Thus, Spandau's analysis in some ways parallels those analysts of Rhodesian sanctions who saw those sanctions as having long–term benefits for the Rhodesian economy. Spandau does admit, however, that South Africa's technological dependence will set limits to import–substitution opportunities within her domestic economy.[22]

Porter casts his analysis somewhat differently. Although a full discussion of his analysis is beyond the scope of this chapter, the assumptions of Porter's simulation appear more realistic than those of Spandau. Porter criticizes sanctions enthusiasts who focus on investment limitations, emphasizing South Africa's capacity to take short–term retaliatory steps to counter such limitations. These steps would include the banning of capital outflows and remission of interest and dividends on foreign assets as well as the ultimate threat of the nationalization of foreign assets. His conclusion is that even in the short run investment sanctions are not likely to have a major negative impact on the South African economy.[23] Porter, however, stresses the high level dependence of South Africa on imported capital goods. "South Africa imports almost all of its capital equipment—with domestic industry essentially providing only the plant in which it is housed."[24]

Porter is concerned with examining in a precise way how limits on these imports might affect the economy. He simulates the loss of imports at 10 percent intervals of the total import amount. He finds that the impact of an up to 20 percent loss of imports would be relatively negligible, both in terms of effect on total output, exports, and employment. But, "at somewhere between 20 percent and 30 percent effectiveness, sanctions begin to 'bite'."[25] With 60 percent of imports cut off, Porter's model predicts a 50 percent drop in Gross Domestic Product, 10 percent white unemployment, one million fewer non-whites employed, and a cut of nearly one–half in available consumer goods. Porter's analysis also calls into question Spandau's conclusion about the South African economy's capacity to undertake large–scale import–substituting industrialization under the impact of sanctions. For import–substitution to occur, the South Africans essentially would have to create a capital goods sector. Although economies under externally-enforced stress tend to fare better than might be expected,[26] this would still be a very tall order. Thus, the available evidence and analysis seems to support the argument of sanctions enthusiasts that the South African economy is indeed vulnerable to economic sanctions.

SOURCES OF SUPPORT FOR SANCTIONS

On the issue of the sources of support for sanctions against South Africa the skeptics appear to have a much stronger argument. While the Western governments, whose participation in a comprehensive sanctions program would be a necessary condition for its success, share the broad concerns of African countries and other supporters of sanctions about the need for substantial change in South Africa's racial policies, they have at the same time consistently opposed comprehensive economic sanctions against South Africa and are unlikely to change their position in the future. This opposition lies, in the last analysis, on the dependence by the United States, Western Europe, and Japan on South Africa for a range of raw materials and minerals, the most important of which is chromite.[27] In addition, South Africa is becoming increasingly significant as a supplier of coal to the Western European countries. Given the importance to the West of developing nonpetroleum based energy sources, South Africa's substantial coal reserves and technological capacity in coal-to-oil conversion enhances its economic importance to the West. In addition to this raw material dependence, South Africa is an important economic partner—in terms of percentage of trade and investment—for several European countries, in particular Great Britain. The application of economic sanctions on South Africa would have serious repercussions for these economies.[28] Given the already precarious position of the British economy and the interdependence of all Western economies, this is a powerful factor working against any change in Western policy toward comprehensive universal sanctions against South Africa.

It is important to note that these factors affect Western governments of all political shades. France's socialist government, for example, has shown no signs of shifting from Giscard d'Estaing's opposition to sanctions. In the United States, the Carter Administration—clearly the American government most vocal in its criticism of South Africa—was firm in its opposition to sanctions, especially comprehensive international sanctions, as a policy instrument. In testimony before Congress in 1978, Assistant Treasury Secretary for International Affairs, C. Fred Bergsten, stated the Carter Administration opposition to bills that would have severely restricted trade with and investment in South Africa. Passage of the legislation, Bergsten argued, "could provoke retaliatory actions by the government of South Africa that could be harmful to U.S. economic interests."[29]

Western opposition to sanctions, however, should not be interpreted to imply that Western governments share a fundamental interest in the preservation of the status quo in South Africa. This argument has been raised both by conservative Western supporters of the South African government and by radical opponents of Western ties to South Africa. Conservatives argue that Western access to South Africa's vital raw materials would be threatened by the replacement of the present Pretoria government by a revolutionary Black regime which, they argue, is likely to be the only viable alternative.[30] Robert Price, however, has persuasively argued that any South African regime would need the revenues earned by the export of their raw materials and that the only viable market for these exports are the Western powers. In fact, a revolutionary Black government, because of its likely commitment to radically expanding services to the majority population of South Africa, would be even more dependent on these revenues (and on other economic resources that only the West could offer) than is the present regime.[31] The overriding Western economic interest in South Africa is access to raw materials, not support for a particular regime. Just like their conservative counterparts, radical critics similarly overstate the convergence of interests between Pretoria and the West. This leads them to view any criticism of South Africa or pressures on Pretoria by Western governments to be merely cynical gestures. It is, however, the *lack* of converging interests that has led Western governments to respond to the demands for action against South Africa, despite the reality of the constraints imposed by mineral dependence. How Western countries are likely to respond to this policy dilemma will be addressed later in this chapter.

ENFORCEABILITY OF SANCTIONS

Will a sanctions program against South Africa be capable of being effectively enforced? Enthusiasts argue 'yes', basing their opinion on both the international consensus against South Africa and South Africa's geographical location surrounded by oceans and enemies. In the last section, I concluded that the implications of the international consensus were more than counterbalanced by the mineral dependence of Western countries upon South Africa. The nature of a competitive international economy, the complicated issues of sharing the costs of a comprehensive sanctions program, and the tremendous cost of a blockade–type enforcement exercise further reinforce the limited base of support for sanctions. As was the case in the question of support for sanctions, skeptics appear to have a better case in arguing that the chances for effective enforcement of sanctions is not high.

The very factors that make South Africa vulnerable to sanctions create severe problems of enforcement. South Africa is highly integrated into the international economic system. Especially in periods of international economic downturn, states are reluctant to upset market and trading patterns since one state's retreat creates a void for another state to fill. So many states and firms have significant interests in South Africa that there would be tremendous opportunities and incentives for evasion of sanctions. South Africa's international experience and network of ties has already significantly minimized the impact of the international arms embargo and the long–standing Organization of African Unity sanctions policy.[32]

The costs of any sanctions program against South Africa will be highly uneven both within countries and between countries. This will create extremely complicated political problems that will further limit the likelihood of successful enforcement. Within countries, the groups having to pay the largest costs for sanctions will generally oppose them. Unless governments are able to devise ways to spread the costs of sanctions—not an easy task—these groups will both retain a strong incentive to attempt to evade sanctions and are likely to mobilize politically against the sanctions–imposing government. For a country with extensive economic links to South Africa, such as Britain, this could create substantial political problems.[33]

Similarly, sanctions will affect different countries unequally. Individual countries are unlikely to accept the necessity of unduly bearing the burdens of sanctions against South Africa. But the international political instruments that might resolve these problems—specifically the United Nations and its agencies—do not have the authority or the organizational and financial capacity to undertake these tasks. In the absence of this capacity, the likelihood of effective enforcement is further diminished.

Finally, South Africa's extensive coastline would mean that measures short of a naval blockade would greatly limit the effect of any trade sanctions. The costs of such a blockade would be tremendous. Moreover, to be effective, it would demand high levels of commitment from the very governments—the Western powers—who are least enthusiastic about sanctions. In 1965, Amelia Leiss calculated that it would take 50 to 60 warships and 300 aircraft to enforce such a blockade.[34] Given the strengthening of the South African naval capacity since that time, these estimates are probably on the conservative side today. Nor would the sea necessarily be the only outlet for South African trade. Unless an effective international mechanism was developed to compensate regional Black African countries for the costs of sanctions to them, the possibility of these countries cutting their economic and infrastructural links to South Africa is very slim. This would offer additional routes through which sanctions could be evaded and add substantially to the cost and political complexity of enforcement. For all of these reasons, then, those skeptical of sanctions appear to have a more convincing argument on the issue of enforcement.

POLITICAL IMPACT OF SANCTIONS

What will be the political impact of sanctions on South Africa? Sanctions enthusiasts contend that South Africa's international economic ties—investment and trade—are an important source of both the capacity and the will of the white minority regime to maintain the system of racial domination.[35] They often stress the symbolic importance to the white community of the presence of dozens of major Western firms and banks in South Africa, contributing to the incapacity of the whites to consider fundamental changes in the domestic social order. The implementation of internationally-supported comprehensive sanctions, they argue, might open the way for a substantial rethinking by the white community, putting new policy options on the South African political agenda. South Africa has not responded positively to other, more diplomatic, forms of persuasion, nor has rapid economic development had the liberalizing effect that some analysts hoped for. The experiences of decolonization elsewhere in Africa have demonstrated that white minorities need to be jarred into rethinking their position and forced into giving up racially–based privileges. Sanctions, enthusiasts maintain, is the best means available for exerting the necessary push.

While the above rationale is presented by liberal supporters of sanctions, a somewhat different argument is offered by radical enthusiasts. Liberals stress the role of sanctions in lessening the South African government's capacity to maintain apartheid which will in turn weaken its will (or, alternatively, the will of the white community) to 'stay the course', and set the stage for constructive change through a process of interracial bargaining and mutual accommodation. Radicals, while agreeing with the role of sanctions in limiting the capacity of the South African regime, view the political scenario somewhat differently. They are pessimistic about the possibility that any change in government policy generated from sanctions might lead to a negotiated resolution of South Africa's conflicts.

Rather, they feel, the impact of sanctions will be two–fold: on the one hand weakening the capacity of the government and exacerbating political cleavages and conflicts in the white community, and on the other hand generating political legitimacy and support, both among Black South Africans and in the international arena, for the revolutionary opponents of the regime.[36]

Skeptics view both of these scenarios as naive. They argue that the political impact of sanctions do not flow directly from their economic effects; rather, they are the outcome of cultural, ethnic and other social factors. The Afrikaners, skeptics argue, are more likely to become even more resistant to change than before under the impact of sanctions. The "larger mentality" and the powerful defensive ethnic consciousness with which the Afrikaners are imbued will lead them to turn inward and become even more fearful of change. The specific political result of sanctions, skeptics argue, would be the strengthening of the more conservative elements in Afrikanerdom—the *verkramptes* and the Conservative Party/Herstigte Nasionale Party rightist opposition—at the expense of the reformers in the ruling National Party.

Skeptics are also dubious about the capacity of sanctions to weaken, in any fundamental way, the South African government since the likelihood of effective enforcement of sanctions is so slim. On the other hand, skeptics feel that the marginal impact of sanctions could be to limit the very resources that might have been used to implement reforms while weakening the social forces in South Africa—foreign corporations and the domestic entrepreneurial and technocratic classes—that favor reform. Finally, they argue, that far from exacerbating conflicts in the white community, sanctions are more likely to generate political unity among the whites, pointing to Rhodesia as an example of precisely that outcome.

Of the four categories of issues dividing the enthusiasts from the skeptics, the question of political impact is clearly the most difficult one from the point of view of attempting to reach even tentative conclusions. Differences between skeptics and enthusiasts derive largely from fundamentally divergent perceptions about the nature of political forces within contemporary South Africa. Rather than directly evaluating the question of potential political impact of sanctions, we will now shift our analysis to South Africa itself in order to investigate how it has responded to the threat of sanctions and what that might tell about the political forces involved and what future responses might be.

Before moving on, however, one irony should be noted. Generally, within Western countries, political conservatives have given more credence than have political liberals to the South African government's claim that they have begun to embark upon a serious effort to reform their domestic society. Conservatives have also tended to be very skeptical about taking up sanctions as a policy approach on the South Africa issue while many liberals have supported the use of sanctions. But, if the South African government is indeed serious about reform this would lend credence to the liberals' enthusiastic view of the political effectiveness of sanctions since this reform inclination has emerged substantially in response to the threat of potential economic sanctions. Prime Minister Botha, setting the stage for his reform initiative, said in 1978, "I am always concerned when people threaten us because I believe that by deliberation you can avoid the application of sanctions."[37] If, on the other hand, the reforms are mere window-dressing, as liberal observers usually assert, this could lend credence to the conservatives' skeptical view of the political impact of sanctions.

SOUTH AFRICA'S REACTION

How has South Africa responded to the economic sanctions that have already been exerted against her and to the threat of more comprehensive sanctions being enforced by the international community? I will discuss the political response, the policy dilemmas that the threat of sanctions generates for the leaders of South Africa, and their economic efforts to undermine the potential effectiveness of sanctions. The external pressures on South Africa to change its internal arrangements have ebbed and flowed since they were first raised in the United Nations early in the postwar era. The two periods when the sanctions instrument was most alive as a policy option and when international pressures against South Africa were greatest were 1963–1965, the high tide of decolonization in Africa, and 1976–1978, the period of the Soweto uprising, the flowering of the Black Consciousness Movement, and the death of Steven Biko and the subsequent crackdown on opponents of the regime.

During the first of these periods, the response of the South African government to external pressure and threat of sanctions was purely defensive and hostile to any reform. The Prime Minister, Verwoerd, tightened both the apartheid laws and the legal controls over government opponents. Significantly, white confidence that had been shaken by decolonization elsewhere in Africa and by the Sharpeville Massacre of 1960 was also restored during this period.

South Africa's response to the second period of intensified external pressure and threat of more comprehensive sanctions has been less clear–cut and more ambiguous. On the one hand, there are important elements of similarity. As was the case in the earlier period, South Africa tightened its security laws, became further militarized and sought to utilize the external threat as a means of generating white political unity. In the 1977 election, the National Party won its greatest electoral victory, garnering 135 of 165 seats on a platform that stressed South Africa's capacity and will to stand up to the outside world and especially to the new American President, Jimmy Carter. But, there are also differences between the recent South African response and that of the mid–1960s. In the late 1970s, the leaders of South Africa verbally committed themselves to initiating basic reforms in their domestic order. While the reality of the efforts undertaken so far clearly makes a mockery of the promise, the reform movement is significant if for nothing more than the fact that it reflects a perceived need on the part of South Africa's rulers to make their domestic system more viable, both internally and in the eyes of the outside world.[38] Recent experience, then, gives some credence to the view that South Africa must be sensitive to pressures exerted by economic sanctions or the threat of more substantial uses of sanctions instruments.

But, although international pressures may have induced the present South African government to articulate a strategy of domestic reform (I leave aside here the question of the goals of the government's reform), continued international pressures and threats to force the government to make more significant reforms may very well undermine what reform efforts have been undertaken and perhaps even lead to the removal of the "verligte" (enlightened) Botha regime. Continued and increasing international threats gives to Botha's rightwing opponents a platform to mobilize for a more decisively hard–line response similar to that undertaken by Verwoerd in the mid–1960s. The constitutional reforms proposed by Botha in 1982 that would create separate parliamentary assemblies for whites, Indians, and Coloureds with an Executive President and a cabinet drawn from all three racial groups, were the trigger in the split of the National Party. The Transvaal leader, Andries Treurnicht and a core of his extreme right-wing followers resigned in protest from the National Party to form the new Conservative Party. Whether the Conservatives emerge as a viable opposition to the National Party remains to be seen, but there is little doubt that their ability to do so will be enhanced by an international environment that is increasingly hostile and in which international support for sanctions is growing.

This produces a harsh dilemma for Prime Minister Botha. While the very emergence of a right-wing challenge serves to limit his capacity to move ahead of the white electorate on the reform issue, the specter of the sanctions issue again rearing its head in the West if he does not move ahead on reforms poses an equal threat. This is not the threat of sanctions themselves. Our analysis has indicated that there is only a remote possibility that they will be comprehensively and effectively employed. The threat to Botha is that his right–wing opponents will utilize the reemergence of international interest in sanctions to mobilize opposition to reform and to Botha in particular in favor of a Verwoerdian approach that is more in keeping with the historical traditions of Afrikaner nationalism. The means by which P.W. Botha seeks to escape being stuck on the horns of this dilemma will be one of the important features of the South African political scene in the immediate future.

Analysts skeptical of the viability of sanctions as an instrument to modify the behavior of governments have stressed that potential target states do not simply sit back and wait for the hardships that sanctions will bring; rather, they take active steps to mitigate their effects.[39] South Africa has been under the threat of sanctions for over two decades and provides a classic case of this process at work.

While the public response of South African officials to the possibility of sanctions has been to deny their potential effectiveness and to stress any potential benefits they might bring to South Africa (i.e., impetus for import–substituting industrialization), South Africa has concurrently moved to preempt the sanctionists by protecting their economy as much as possible. Several measures have been undertaken in this regard. The most important of these has been the development, under the auspices of SASOL—the government-owned coal, oil and gas corporation—of a major capacity to synthesize oil from South Africa's large reserves of coal.[40] Two of these plants are currently in operation with a third to come on-line in 1983. Combined, these plants will be able to supply perhaps as much as 40 percent of South Africa's petroleum needs. A second measure undertaken by the South African government to protect itself against potential sanctions has been the stockpiling of essential goods. It is believed that the South Africans have at least several years of petroleum supplies stockpiled in abandoned mines. Under the National Supplies Procurement Act, the Department of Industry has set aside increasing funds to assist companies stockpiling key goods such as chemicals, machine parts, and aircraft spares.

Even before the threat of sanctions was raised, the South African government had been following an economic strategy emphasizing the expansion of local manufacturing and increasing self–sufficiency.[41] The threat of sanctions gave added impetus to these trends. South Africa has increased its local–content stipulations in the manufacture of motor vehicles. The government has also supported a program to urge South African consumers to buy locally–produced goods rather than imports. These preemptive initiatives, however, are not without possible costs. Some South African economists have expressed fears that these steps, if taken too far, could misallocate resources creating inefficiencies detrimental to the overall growth of the economy.[42]

Finally, the South Africans have warned that they would take retaliatory measures in the face of any comprehensive sanctions efforts. These might include both withdrawing certain strategic raw materials from the international market and efforts to drastically undercut world market prices for major raw materials. This poses a potential threat both to the strategic needs of South Africa's trading partners—the Western powers—and to the ongoing international efforts to stabilize the world market prices for primary commodities. Although South Africa depends on mineral exports for a large proportion of government revenue and would thus be limited in her capacity to withhold minerals from the world market, she does retain some scope of action particularly for certain key minerals, such as chromite, for which alternative sources are not available and which do not account for a large percentage of export earnings. Ironically, South Africa under a white minority regime probably has more flexibility in this area than would any majority–based government, no matter how radical in outlook or pro–Soviet in international political orientation.

POLICY DILEMMAS FOR THE WEST

The South African government's initiatives to preempt the adverse affects of sanctions and the uncertainties surrounding the political impact of sanctions on South Africa provide a good point to refocus the discussion on the policy issues generated for the major Western powers. The central policy dilemma facing Western nations is how to reconcile the perceived need for fundamental change in the domestic order of South Africa—and growing international pressures to actively participate in generating that change—with the constraints posed by mineral dependence and other Western interests in the region. Larry Bowman has summarized the problem as follows:

> There is no ignoring certain facts: African countries are committed to the liberation of South African blacks; weapons and training will be made available to all who are prepared to commit themselves to the struggle; and there is little indication that South Africa's white rulers are prepared to compromise in any substantial way in their determination to retain power and resist African majority rule. This is a recipe that can only lead to disastrous conflict.[43]

But the real policy crunch for the West in Southern Africa still lies in the future. Black African states and their allies, in formulating their strategy for liberation in Southern Africa, have clearly separated the issues of independence for Zimbabwe and Namibia from the issue of apartheid in South Africa, concentrating on resolving the former before tackling the latter. In this, their strategy has focused on working closely with Western governments to achieve internationally–recognized transitions to majority rule through negotiations. They have realized that South Africa's cooperation is needed for a resolution of these conflicts. This has served to postpone the time when real pressure is put on the Western powers to act more decisively against apartheid within South Africa.

After the Namibia dispute is resolved, the much more difficult issue of internal relations in South Africa will dominate Black Africa's diplomatic agenda, and pressures on Western governments will increase. South Africa's apparent adoption of a regional strategy of destabilization against her Black–ruled neighbors will facilitate the African states' task of preparing a legal case for U.N. enforcement action against South Africa on the basis of the U.N. Charter. South Africa's regional destabilization will make it easier for African states to persuade the Security Council to declare either 1) "a threat to the peace," 2) "a breach of the peace," or 3) "an act of aggression," the three actions in Article 39 of the Charter that would call for international enforcement action by the world body. Thus, the dilemmas facing Western governments are almost certain to get harsher in the future.

At the broadest level, there is agreement among Western governments and within Western foreign-policy-making circles that they should seek a way in which to promote peaceful change in South Africa through improving the social and political situation of the Black majority. This outlook flows from both the direct goal of encouraging reform in South Africa and the indirect goals of responding to what Black African states increasingly see as a matter of utmost principle and domestic political pressures to undertake actions against apartheid. But this does not easily translate into policy. There are important disagreements within Western policy–making circles on the best means to achieve these ends.

There are three broad approaches to the issue of change in South Africa that are current in these policy–making circles. Each includes some notion of sanctions, but these notions differ among themselves and all three differ from the concept of universal comprehensive sanctions. None of the three approaches leads in a straightforward way to specific policies; rather, they function as conceptual maps for guiding thinking about policy options.[44]

The first of these approaches is "communication," of which the Reagan Administration's policy of "constructive engagement" is a variant. The 'communication' approach emphasizes the use of contacts and positive incentives (carrots) as a means of influencing change in South Africa. Although not necessarily opposed to all sanctions measures, this approach stresses the point that South Africa is more likely to be influenced by those it perceives as friends rather than by those it perceives as enemies. The notion of sanctions involved here is that of positive sanctions.[45] The "communication" approach is based upon the perception that government–led reform is on the agenda in South Africa. Chester Crocker, the architect of the Reagan Administration policy, has written that South African politics are now "rooted in pragmatism" that is capable of generating meaningful political change.[46]

The second approach is that of "graduated pressure." This view argues that fundamental change is bound to occur in South Africa in the foreseeable future and that Western pressure can both influence the form of this change, can limit the amount of violence that will be involved, and can retain good relations with African and other Third World governments and thus limit Soviet influence that might emerge out of political upheaval in South Africa. Robert Price, a proponent of this approach, argues that while the South African regime itself is not committed nor by itself capable of generating fundamental reforms, "Pretoria is highly sensitive to leverage applied through the international economic system, and may modify its policies in response."[47] Advocates of this approach argue that only active Western pressure against South Africa will be able to derail the movement within the United Nations for universal, mandatory sanctions which, due to mineral dependence, would be against the national interests of the Western powers. The notion of sanctions here is a more delicate tactical instrument than those of comprehensive sanctions. The degree of economic pressure could be increased or decreased depending upon the actions of the South Africans.

The third approach is "disengagement." Advocates of "disengagement" argue that South Africa is destined to become a snakepit in international politics. They feel that both the "communication" and "graduated pressure" approaches place the West in too much of a high-profile position in an environment that is fundamentally unstable and unpredictable. They argue that the West's capacity to influence the course of events in South Africa is extremely limited. Active, public involvement—no matter what the approach—is likely to have far greater costs than benefits to Western governments. This view emphasizes both the domestic political problems and potential conflicts within the Western alliance that might be generated by too great an involvement through either "communication" or "graduated pressure." The precise policies that "disengagement" would follow would depend primarily on the political pressures from both the international and domestic environments but would involve a general minimizing of ties to South Africa without involving a break in essential trade relations. The "disengagement" notion of sanctions views them explicitly as flowing out of secondary goals; they have no instrumental value. The recent Rockefeller Study Commission Report is somewhat based on "disengagement" style analysis, although its policy recommendations have much in common with those that might emerge from the "graduated pressure" approach.[48]

Although the differences between these policy approaches to South Africa are important, it needs to be noted that, thus far, the range of policies undertaken by Western governments has actually been quite narrow. A comparison of the Carter and Reagan Administrations offers a case in point. The differences between these administrations' policies is very often overstated. Both put the resolution of the Namibia conflict through negotiation at the top of their agenda; both emphasized the need for peaceful change in South Africa; both support the arms embargo; both oppose comprehensive trade or investment sanctions; both have denied the legitimacy of South Africa's policy of granting "independence" to the so-called Black Homelands. This is not to say that there aren't differences but that the broad lines of policy are not so dissimilar. The question is whether the range of *future policies* will continue to be so narrow. My feeling is that chances are that it will, though one can never be certain in predicting future trends.

CONCLUSION—THE FUTURE OF SANCTIONS

Beyond pure speculation, what can be said about the future of sanctions against South Africa? Certain conditioning factors appear to be certain: the international pressures in favor of comprehensive sanctions will remain strong, if anything becoming stronger in the wake of South Africa's regional destabilization activities; with the eventual settlement of the Namibia conflict, the focus of Black African states will shift decisively to the issue of apartheid in South Africa; South Africa will not, on its own, undertake reform initiatives that come close to satisfying even moderate elements within the international system; Western governments will continue to be dependent upon South Africa for strategic raw materials, limiting their scope of action.

Given the uncertainty surrounding the impact of sanctions, the difficulty of enforcing comprehensive universal sanctions, and the mineral dependence of Western countries and extensive dependence of African states in Southern Africa, the likelihood of universal mandatory sanctions against South Africa in the foreseeable future is slim. But, given the certainty that the international and domestic pressures for sanctions will intensify, the most likely future scenario is what might be called "creeping sanctions." These would take the form of policies such as restrictions on loans, restrictions on export guarantees and tax credits, termination of preferential trade agreements, discouragement of new investments, and embargoes on an ever–widening range of goods. These "salami sanctions" will be a response more to the secondary goals discussed earlier in the chapter than a serious instrumental effort to generate change in South Africa. As Margaret Doxey has written, "The pressures governments exert behind the scenes to impel others to adopt sanctions may be more persuasive than the sanctions themselves."[49]

Why should this be the case? A fundamental reason, it seems to me, is that despite recent remarks about the impending upheaval in South Africa by observers such as Robert McNamara, more serious (and knowledgeable) analysts are much more pessimistic about the likelihood for change in South Africa. R. W. Johnson, in his book *How Long Can South Africa Survive?*, answers his question—a very long time.[50] Simon Jenkins of the *Economist*, one of the most astute observers of South Africa, writes that, "the clock of South Africa's history might be at five minutes to midnight, but it seems resolutely stuck there."[51] Lawrence Schlemmer and David Welsh, South African social scientists, similarly conclude that the balance of political forces within South Africa simply do not offer the possibility for fundamental change in the near future.[52] In a context where the internal pressures for change are still weakly developed, the secondary objectives of sanctions are more likely to be dominant.

The problem of "creeping sanctions," of course, is that they are unlikely to work as a means of bringing about change in South Africa, at least in the short term. It is not unlikely that they would serve to further enhance the political power of ultraconservative forces in South Africa by generating a foreign devil who is also a paper tiger and can be taken on without having to pay high costs. Nor would "creeping sanctions" be likely to deter the supporters of more comprehensive sanctions from pressing forward with their case. Thus, I am pessimistic about the capacity of sanctions in any likely near-term scenario to effectively work to fundamentally change the political direction of the South African government—the liberal argument favoring sanctions. Whether or not they might materially weaken the South African government and assist the political capacity and will of the opponents of the regime—the radical argument in favor of sanctions—is another question that at this point is impossible to assess.

NOTES

1. For a well–argued example of this position see Abdul S. Minty, *The Case for Economic Sanctions* (New York, U.N. Center Against Apartheid, 1976).
2. Deon Geldenhuys, "The Political Prospects for Sanctions–Interaction of International Pressures and Domestic Developments," in *South Africa and Sanctions: Genesis and Prospects* (Johannesburg, South African Institute for International Affairs and South African Institute of Race Relations, 1979).
3. See, for example, Margaret Doxey, *Economic Sanctions and International Enforcement* (New York, Oxford University Press, 1980); R. James, ed., *Foreign Investment in South Africa: The Policy Debate* (London, Africa Publications Trust, 1975); Richard C. Porter, "International Trade and Investment Sanctions: Potential Impact on the South African Economy, *Journal of Conflict Resolution* (Vol. 23, No. 4, 1979).
4. J. C. Smuts, *The League of Nations: A Practical Suggestion* (London, Hodder and Stoughton, 1918), pp. 60–63.
5. See Doxey, *Economic Sanctions*, and C. L. Brown–John, *Multilateral Sanctions in International Law: A Comparative Analysis* (New York, Praeger, 1975) for comparative case studies.
6. See James Barber, "Economic Sanctions as a Policy Instrument," *International Affairs* (Vol. 55, No. 3, 1979) for a discussion of the multifaceted rationale for sanctions.
7. See, for example, the essays in R. Segal, *Sanctions Against South Africa* (Harmondsworth, Penguin Books, 1964).

8. See Martin Legassick and David Hemson, *Foreign Investment and the Repro-duction of Racial Capitalism in South Africa* (London, Anti–Apartheid Movement, 1976).

9. See C. R. Hill, "The Western European States and Southern Africa" in G. Carter and P. O'Meara, *International Politics in Southern Africa* (Bloomington, Indiana University Press, 1982).

10. Quoted in *The New York Times*, October 24, 1982, p. 22.

11. See K. Adelman, "Conflict in Southern Africa," in *International Security* (Vol. 3, Fall, 1978).

12. See L. Bowman, "The Strategic Importance of South Africa to the United States: An Appraisal and Policy Analysis," *African Affairs* (Vol. 81, No. 323, 1982).

13. Doxey, *Economic Sanctions*, p. 143.

14. See L. Kapungu, *The United Nations and Economic Sanctions Against Rho-desia* (Lexington, MA., D.C. Heath, 1973); H. Strack, *Sanctions: The Case of Rhodesia* (Syracuse, Syracuse University Press, 1978).

15. J. K. Moyana, "The Political Economy of Sanctions and Implications for Future Economic Policy," *Journal of Southern African Affairs* (October, 1977).

16. T. Bingham and S. Gray, *Report on Supply of Petroleum and Petroleum Products to Rhodesia* (London, Foreign Office, H.M.S.O., 1978).

17. Doxey, *Economic Sanctions*, p. 86.

18. See R. J. Hanks, *The Cape Route: Imperiled Western Lifeline* (Cambridge, Institute for Foreign Policy Analysis, 1981) for an argument on the strategic need for the West to support the Pretoria government.

19. Johan Galtung, "On the Effects of International Economic Sanctions with Examples from the Case of Rhodesia," *World Politics* (Vol. 19, No. 3, 1967).

20. Quoted in the Johannesburg *Star*, November 8, 1977, p. 1.

21. M. Bailey and B. Rivers, *Oil Sanctions Against South Africa* (New York, U. N. Center Against Apartheid, 1978), pp. 7, 8, 87.

22. Arnt Spandau, *Economic Boycott Against South Africa: Normative and Factual Issues* (Wynberg, Juta and Co., 1979).

23. Porter, "International Trade and Investment Sanctions," p. 186.

24. *Ibid.*, pp. 589–90.

25. *Ibid.*, p. 604.

26. I thank Professor Porter for referring me to J. Hirshliefer, "Disaster and Recovery: a Historical Survey" (Rand Corporation, 1963) which discusses this theme.

27. The best analysis of Western mineral dependence on South Africa is Congressional Research Service, *Imports of Minerals from South Africa by the United States and the OECD Countries* (Washington, Government Printing Office, 1980).

28. Hill, "The Western European States and Southern Africa," p. 42.

29. "United States Private Investment in South Africa," hearings before the House of Representatives Committees (Washington, Government Printing Office, 1978).

30. Hanks, "The Cape Route," p. 20.

31. R. Price, "U.S. Policy Towards Southern Africa" in G. Carter and P.

O'Meara, *International Politics in Southern Africa* (Bloomington, Indiana University Press, 1982).

32. C. Cannizzo, ed., *The Gun Merchants: Politics and Policies of the Major Arms Suppliers* (New York, Pergamon Press, 1980).

33. This is one of the arguments used by the Rockefeller Foundation Study Commission in opposing comprehensive sanctions as a U.S. policy. See *South Africa: Time Running Out* (Berkeley, University of California Press, 1981), p. 422.

34. Amelia Leiss, ed., *Apartheid and United Nations Collective Measures* (New York, Carnegie Endowment, 1965).

35. L. Litvak *et al.*, *South Africa: Foreign Investment and Apartheid* (Washington, Institute for Policy Studies, 1978).

36. Abdul Minty, *The Case for Economic Disengagement*, p. 3.

37. Quoted in the *Rand Daily Mail*, October 20, 1978, p. 1.

38. See the analysis by Robert Price, "Apartheid and White Supremacy: The Meaning of Government–Led Reform in the South African Context," in R. Price and C. Rosberg, *The Apartheid Regime* (Berkeley, University of California Press, 1980).

39. Doxey, *Economic Sanctions*, p. 141.

40. Desaix Myers *et al.*, *U.S. Business in South Africa: The Economic, Political and Moral Issues* (Bloomington, Indiana University Press, 1980), pp. 138–42.

41. H. Adam and H. Giliomee, *Ethnic Power Mobilized* (New Haven, Yale University Press, 1979).

42. Personal discussions at the University of the Witwatersrand, September, 1982.

43. L. Bowman, "The Strategic Importance of South Africa," op. cit. p. 186.

44. This part of the analysis relies heavily on James Barber and Michael Spicer, "Sanctions Against South Africa: Options for the West," *International Affairs* (Vol. 55, No. 3, 1979).

45. See David Baldwin, "The Power of Positive Sanctions," *World Politics* (Vol. 24, No. 1, 1972).

46. Chester Crocker, "South Africa: Strategy for Change," *Foreign Affairs* (Vol. 59, 1980–81), p. 324.

47. Robert Price, "U.S. Policy Towards South Africa," in Carter and O'Meara p. 209.

48. Rockefeller Study Commission, *South Africa: Time Running Out*, pp. 410–55.

49. Margaret Doxey, *Economic Sanctions*, p. 128.

50. R. W. Johnson, *How Long Will South Africa Survive* (New York, Oxford University Press, 1977), p. 305.

51. Simon Jenkins, "South Africa: Survey," *The Economist* (June 21, 1980).

52. Lawrence Schlemmer and David Welsh, "South Africa's Constitutional and Political Prospects," *Optima* (Vol. 30, No. 4, 1982).

8

IDEOLOGY AND THE CONCEPT
OF ECONOMIC SECURITY

David J. Sylvan

"Let the punishment fit the crime"—W. S. Gilbert

International crimes frequently provoke calls for punishment by economic sanctions. Just as frequently, opponents of sanctions argue vehemently that such policies are at best useless and at worst self–defeating. Both sides in the debate have been able to call upon studies by social scientists; thus, the likelihood that any new piece of research can be counted upon to break the logjam must be counted as miniscule at best. What *can* be useful is a new perspective on these issues, and that is what this chapter attempts to provide.

Specifically, I begin by setting out and criticizing two standard approaches to the sanctions question. I then relate the issue to a larger topic and put forward a conceptual framework for addressing the latter. In the third part of this chapter, I illustrate both the framework and an appropriate methodology for studying it by an analysis of several empirical cases. Finally, I conclude with a discussion of some implications for future study of these issues.

STANDARD APPROACHES

There are two fairly common approaches to the study of economic sanctions. One we could term "psychological"; the other, "economic." A good example of the psychological approach is

Galtung's well–known article (1967) on sanctions in Rhodesia (see Chapter 2, this volume). Galtung argues that sanctions can, and in most cases will, provoke psychological mobilization processes; these rouse people out of their accustomed behavior and galvanize them into creative responses. As a result, the economy is transformed to meet the challenge of sanctions, the public rallies around its political leaders, and leaders of admired sanctioning countries come to be viewed negatively.

The economic approach comes to fairly similar conclusions about the aggregate consequences of sanctions but does so in a different way. Its primary focus is on the completeness of sanctions (how much trade is actually cut off) and the flexibility of "production structure and consumption requirements" (Porter 1978, p. 107). Depending on the extent of these phenomena, losses in aggregate welfare (defined through a community utility function) may range from large to negligible. In the actual case of Rhodesia, most studies find little negative effect.

Although the two perspectives appear quite distinct, they do share several problematic assumptions.[1] The first has to do with the concept of flexibility, a crucial contextual variable that helps determine the success or failure of sanctions. Regrettably, neither approach says much about *why* flexibility exists: Galtung links it to "crisis" and Porter to a "mature" economy, but neither author provides any explanation. Thus, instead of serving as a useful concept, "flexibility" is merely a label for "successful" responses to external sanctions.

The second difficulty in both the psychological and economic approaches resides in the way they treat the target of the sanctions. The economic perspective's assumption that it is meaningful to treat communities as having "community indifference curves"[2] (Porter 1978, p. 95) mirrors the psychological perspective's analysis of the "target society . . . as an organism with a certain self–maintaining potential" (Galtung 1967, p. 409). This holistic view is at best unjustified (to be fair, both authors briefly discuss a few specific sectors or groups, but that is not their primary emphasis; at worst, it flies in the face of what we know to be profound cleavages within Rhodesian society—and a good many other places as well.

The holism issue leads in turn to a final common problem. Not only do both approaches pass over differences among types of people who live in polities against which sanctions are aimed, but neither approach bothers to discuss in more than a cursory fashion *anyone's* concerns. Both authors assume, of course, that whites wanted to keep political power and maintain a high standard of living, but this hardly helps explain why sanctions were tackled head–on, and why a Muzorewa–type puppet solution was resisted so strenuously for so long. As a result, critical *decisions* are treated as routine background assumptions. Hence, in spite of their accurate predictions, the standard approaches to the study of economic sanctions are more obfuscatory than enlightening. A different approach would seem to be called for.

CONCEPTUAL FRAMEWORK

The preceding section points to three questions that need to be addressed when analyzing economic sanctions: *who* is threatened by sanctions; *what* are their concerns; and *why* do or do they not exhibit flexibility in their responses? As phrased, these questions are pertinent to threats beyond economic sanctions; given that sanctions are imposed for political reasons and, by all accounts, reacted against as such, it seems useful to address the three questions as they bear on the issue of broader threats to political regimes. Specifically, I propose to examine the *logic* of regime responses to political threats in general, albeit with particular attention to economic sanctions. (No claim is made here that economic sanctions are exactly like other kinds of political dangers. But sanctions do share certain features with other threats, and there are also explicit relationships between sanctions and policies such as internal subversion—e.g., the U.S. destabilization campaign against Allende.)

How then should one study this issue? First, it is important to analyze the political *base* of whatever political regime is under investigation. No government, no group of political leaders can maintain itself in power without some sort of support. That support may come from certain classes or class fractions (e.g., peasants; big industrialists), or it may come from certain cultural groupings (e.g., religious or language groups; "tribes"). Whatever base of support a regime has can then be studied to adduce the general contours of its concerns (material or otherwise). Those concerns are important constraints on regimes' freedom of maneuver when responding to threats; more importantly, they help to define just what the threats are.

The various relationships among elements of a regime's base and between those elements and other groups in society are patterned according to certain *constitutive rules* (Searle 1969, chapter 2). Properly speaking, these rules constitute relationships between social actors. For example, one rule that helped constitute relations between moneylenders and Qashqa'i nomads in prerevolutionary Iran was that "[t]he merchant paid low market prices for pastoral products—often buying them at low prices months before they were delivered—and charged high market prices for his goods" (Beck 1981, p. 114). This rule—springing from the nomads' increasing need for cash—had as its consequence that "nomads were forced to trade on increasingly unfavorable terms *all* their products with their creditor and borrow money *only* from him" (Beck 1982, p. 114). Clearly, this dependence of the Qashqa'i on the moneylenders was only possible as a result of the rule governing nomad–moneylender relations.[3] Put differently, the specific relationship between nomads and moneylenders in the Fars area of prerevolutionary Iran was constituted (in part—there were other rules) by the pricing rule described above. The second step in studying economic sanctions or other types of political threats, then, is to uncover the constitutive rules of the relevant political and economic relations involving a regime's political bases.

People do not engage blindly in rule–governed activities. They participate in those activities on the basis of a certain kind of understanding about the way in which they relate to other groups. This kind of understanding encompasses several kinds of rules that enable individuals to exist as specific types of people (e.g., moneylenders, nomads, army officers):

- What sorts of activities do I (or we) engage in?
- How do I understand those activities?
- What am I trying to accomplish?
- How can I reconcile my activities with my goals?

Enabling rules give people identity and help them function in that identity as members of society. Enabling rules also serve as tools by which people understand (to some degree) the constitutive rules relevant to their lives. Without enabling rules, James's description of the world as "bloomin', buzzin' confusion" would be correct (cf. Cicourel 1964).[4]

Enabling rules tend to come in interrelated sets. Although it is certainly possible for an individual's enabling rules to be eclectically chosen and basically unrelated to each other, this does not happen very often. Instead, the rules cohere; knowing some rules, we could deduce others. Similarly, there are not infinitely many sets of rules extant; rather, certain sets tend to be associated with certain types of people.[5] Thus, for example, a survey of Nicaragua National Guardsmen in the early 1970s found considerable coherence among their attitudes, with the vast majority exhibiting a "monomaniacal concern with internal security" (Ropp 1972, p. 111). Examination of documents from other members of the Somoza coalition (e.g., the family newspaper *Novedades*) does not reveal this concern, nor, for that matter, was it evident in the attitudes of army cadets from Nicaragua's neighbor, Honduras.[6]

Many sets of enabling rules are tacit and nonverbal, observable only through ethnographic–type techniques. Some sets, though, are explicit and verbalized (though not necessarily in written form). Among the latter are sets pertaining to dominance relationships; these are ideologies.[7] As with other enabling rules, ideologies, too, cluster by social groupings (although there are individual exceptions). The third step in studying economic sanctions or other types of political threats, then, is to detail the ideologies of the groups constituting a regime's political base. Note, by the way, that the dominance relations to which ideologies pertain are not restricted solely to fealty toward the very top. In Pahlevi Iran, for example, one important component of the Shah's base—the bureaucracy—was

> . . . represented by the great flatterers and sycophants. They relate in the political system as opportunistic reflections of the Monarch and their subservience, humility, and obsequiousness in his presence is a sight to behold. In their own formal posts, however, they suddenly become "little Shahanshahs" and relate to their subordinates in a similar network. This time, however, they see others as extensions of their own personalities and expect them to act as such. Thus, the same man who considered himself the Shah's "slave," expected all his subordinates to view him in the

same way when he became Managing Director of the National
Iranian Oil Company (Bill 1972, p. 127).

As this passage illustrates, ideologies appear particularly important
to study since they act (to borrow a metaphor from Foucault) as cap-
illaries through which power circulates.

A SIMPLE MODEL

We are now in a position to construct a simple model of the way
in which economic sanctions—as a particular type of political
threat—succeed or fail in affecting a regime's hold on power. Let us
start with a few definitions. *Economic sanctions* are policies aimed at
changing conditions of production in order to be a political threat to
a foreign regime. *Political threats* risk the loss of support (conditional or absolute) of vital elements of a regime's political base. An
extreme political threat involves the irreversible loss of vital elements
of a regime's political base. Rules are *disrupted* by making difficult
or impossible the practices by which they are acted upon.[8] Finally, a
group's *world* is a coherent combination of constitutive and enabling
rules involving that group.

Hypotheses

Clearly, not all sanctions succeed in becoming political threats,
much less extreme threats. What follows are some hypotheses
about the conditions sanctions must satisfy in order to pose significant dangers to regimes. Several things about these hypotheses
should be noted. First, they are static in character. It is a difficult
task to trace the path by which sanctions may move from incommo-
dities, to serious inconveniences, to absolute hamperances, and, finally, to positive dangers of a loss of liberty.[9] Processes of this sort
can, in fact, be modeled (see, e.g., Bennett and Alker 1977), but they
are beyond the ambit of this chapter. Second, the hypotheses
sketched below pertain to necessary, not sufficient conditions for the
transformation of sanctions into extreme political threats. Regimes
usually rely on the backing of several political elements so that even
if one becomes disaffected, things can still be held together. A com-

plete model of economic sanctions would have to specify the decisional criteria by which a regime assessed the backing of various members of its political base. Third and last, the model is cast in the form of categorical statements: rules are or are not put in jeopardy by specific policies. This simplification is not problematic because of the *measurement* fact that policies vary in the intensity of their effects, since most assessment heuristics are compatible with bivariate higher–order coding. The real problem here is the univariate quality of characterization, since policies may in fact be simultaneously hazardous and nonhazardous with respect to constitutive or enabling rules. Regrettably, no rigorous method exists for dialectical analysis of the sort implied here.

HYPOTHESIS ONE. For any given element of a regime's political base, if economic sanctions disrupt either the group's constitutive rules or its ideology (but not both), then the sanctions will result in a nonextreme political threat to the regime.

HYPOTHESIS TWO. For any given element of a regime's political base, if economic sanctions disrupt both the group's constitutive rules and its ideology, then the sanctions will result in an extreme political threat to the regime.

HYPOTHESIS THREE. Economic sanctions will only be effective in their goals to the extent that they result in disintegration of a regime's domestic political base.

The thrust of the hypotheses is that only when sanctions work domestically to attack both the constitutive rules and ideologies of a regime's political base can they be parried successfully. I will give first a heuristic justification for this claim and then a more detailed formal argument for each of the hypotheses.

Rationale

Under ordinary circumstances, the world of any group involves a fit between its constitutive rules and ideology (Sylvan 1981). There are several ways in which this fit can be destroyed. First, the constitutive rules can be disrupted but not the ideology. In that case, the group's definition of itself would no longer correspond to the activities in which it is engaged. This could provide a challenge for the group to reconstitute its activities along similar lines as before, albeit with modifications to take account of changed circumstances. Ideology would serve as a guide in this reconstitutive effort. (Understandably, in individuals analogous processes are said to provide evidence of "strength of character.") Both Galtung's and Porter's accounts of Ian Smith's Rhodesia sketch this sort of scenario.

Second, sanctions may succeed in disrupting a group's ideology, but not its constitutive rules. In that case, confusion or befuddlement might result, but the social relations that constituted the regime's political power would continue. After a while, a similar ideology could be reestablished. A good example of this process is the United States boycott of the 1980 Olympic Games in Moscow as a "punishment" for the Soviet Union's invasion of Afghanistan. Press reports at the time suggested that the boycott did succeed in bewildering and annoying a number of Soviet citizens, including governmental and party leaders.[10] Still, the ideology was eventually reconstructed, with net consequences well–known.

Now consider what would happen if a group's world were to be destroyed by dint of disrupting both its constitutive rules and its ideology. Neither set of rules would be available to help reconstruct the other, and the group likely would disintegrate as a cohesive political force with which to back the regime. If the group were a vital element in the regime's political base, this clearly would constitute an extreme political threat. To put it another way, attacks on either constitutive rules or ideology, but not both, can be fended off because of their incompleteness. Only a simultaneous attack on both sets of rules leaves no escape hatches for rebuilding.

It is for this reason that "successful" sanctions must involve *domestic* political threats. For a regime to be in danger of toppling, vital elements of its political base need to disintegrate through attacks on their ideology and constitutive rules. Although it is certainly conceivable that important parts of a regime's base may be foreign (e.g., the U.S. government plays this role for a number of countries), those parts are, almost by definition, large enough that changes in production conditions are extremely unlikely to be capable of disrupting their constitutive and enabling rules. In addition, almost all external political backing for a regime is transmitted through domestic groupings (e.g., the armed forces, the Finance Ministry, or business executives) who will feel the brunt of economic sanctions only when *their* ideology and constitutive rules are under attack. On heuristic grounds, then, the model's hypotheses appear justified.

Formalization

I turn now to a more formal argument. The crux of the claims made above concerns the conditions for both the *possibility* of a regime's political base reconstructing its world and the *necessity* for its collapse. A formal technique well–suited for the analysis of such questions is modal logic, the logic of the necessary and possible existence of certain worlds.[11]

As hinted at above, it is a reasonable simplification to treat a group's worlds as falling into two categories: success and failure. The former comprises constitutive rules and ideologies that fit together coherently; the latter comprises constitutive rules and ideologies which, because of their disruption, fail to fit together coherently. The critical question for the study of economic sanctions, then, is whether any failures they induce in the elements of a regime's political base are permanent or only temporary. From the standpoint of the model's hypotheses, this question can be rephrased as follows: is it true that disruptions of either constitutive rules or ideologies create temporary failures, whereas disruptions of both create permanent ones? Here is where modal logic comes in. A temporary failure is one in which eventual success is not necessarily possible. Thus, the foregoing question can again be rephrased, this time to facilitate an answer by means of modal logic:

- Do economic sanctions that disrupt either a group's constitutive rules or its ideology, but not both, create failures from which eventual success is necessarily possible?
- Do economic sanctions that disrupt both a group's constitutive rules and its ideology create failures from which eventual success is not necessarily possible; and
- Can economic sanctions that do not act on a regime's domestic political base create failures from which eventual success is not necessarily possible?

Here is the terminology I will be employing.[12] The standard model $M = \langle W,R,P \rangle$, where W is a set of possible worlds and P an assignment of sets of possible worlds to atomic sentences. (An atomic sentence is a statement about conditions obtaining in a world.) R is a relation between possible worlds of the type $\alpha R\omega$, which may be interpreted to mean that the world ω is possible relative to the world α. If α is the world of failure for a vital element of a regime's political base, then our interest is in whether there exists another world of success, ω, accessible from α, in which the survival of that element (and thus, in this model, of the regime), has to be possible. Symbolically, we want to know if the schema $S \rightarrow \Box \Diamond S$ is valid in various classes of standard models, where S is the sentence "The regime's base element—and hence the regime—survives"; $\rightarrow$ is the conditionality sign; $\Box$ is the necessity sign; and $\Diamond$ the possibility sign.

In the arguments that follow, I will start by assuming the truth of that which we wish to find out: whether success is indeed possible after failure. I will then proceed to look for consistent or contradictory implications of the assumption as a basis for accepting or rejecting it. Consider first the initial hypothesis. Say that there have been attacks on a group's constitutive rules, though not its ideology, and that after some early failures, the group's world has been reconstituted. Since, in order to fit the enabling rules, the new constitutive rules will have to be essentially similar to the old ones (Sylvan 1981),[13] they will be vulnerable to similar disruptions in the future. This means that failure is again possible even after success has been achieved. A similar conclusion applies to the case of ideology being under attack, but not constitutive rules.

The import of the preceding argument is that if either a group's constitutive rules or its ideology is attacked, but not both, then the world of failure is just as reachable from the world of success as I have assumed that the world of success is from the world of failure. Using the terminology introduced above, a situation of partial attack on a group's rules is one in which symmetry relations hold. That is to say, if $\alpha R\omega$, where α is a world of failure and ω a world of success, then $\omega R\alpha$ as well. We can now ask whether, in this symmetric standard model, $S \rightarrow \Box \Diamond S$.

The answer is straightforward. Let α be a world of failure in a symmetric standard model M and assume that $| = M\alpha A$, i.e., that A is true in α in M. Our goal is to show that $| = M\alpha[\Diamond A$, and therefore we must demonstrate that for every ω in M such that $\alpha R\omega$ there is another world λ (not the same as ω) in M such that $\omega R\lambda$ and $| =$

$M\lambda A$. Now, remember that I have assumed ω to be a world in M such that $\alpha R\omega$. By R's symmetry, $\omega R\alpha$, which means that there is a λ in M (that is, α) such that $\omega R\alpha$ and $| = M\lambda A$. Thus, the schema under investigation (i.e., sucess necessarily being possible after failure) is indeed valid in the class of symmetric standard models; moreover, the schema is clearly consistent with the assumption made initially of success being possible after failure. Such consistency is a strong argument in favor of the assumption under conditions of the first hypothesis, and hence (since the assumption essentially restates it) is a justification of that hypothesis.[14]

Let us turn now to the second hypothesis and say that in this case, there have been attacks on both a group's constitutive rules and its ideology. In addition, assume as before that, after a period of failure, the group is once again in a world of success; i.e., that both new constitutive and new enabling rules have been cobbled together coherently. It is important to realize that in this case, the group would bear little resemblance to its former self: it would behave differently toward other groups and think of itself and its activities in a different way from before. (This is, to put it mildly, a rather steep price for survival.) Consequently, any of the earlier types of attacks on the group's constitutive rules or ideology would be unlikely to be successful since the target rules would (by necessity, for defensive purposes) have changed sufficiently so that no easy fit would obtain between them and the attack. New types of attacks could of course be effective, but these would produce a different world of failure from the first go around. Moreover, since any new attacks would of necessity be considerably different from the old ones, the attacker would have to change its modus operandi considerably. This minimizes the chance of effective new attacks any time in the short– or medium–term. What this all means is that if both a group's constitutive rules and its ideology are attacked, the original world of failure is not reachable from the newly constructed world of success. When coupled with my assumption that the world of success *is* reachable from the original world of failure, the situation becomes one of asymmetrical relationships. Symbolically, $\alpha R\omega$ (where α and ω are, as before, worlds of failure and success, respectively), but it is not the case that $\omega R\alpha$. The question is now whether, in the class of asymmetric standard models, the schema $S \rightarrow \Box \Diamond S$ holds as it does in the class of symmetric standard models.

As it turns out, the schema is invalid. For example, take the schema $J \rightarrow \Box \Diamond J$ and an asymmetric standard model $M = <W,R,P>$, in which $W = [\alpha,\omega]$ (where α and ω are distinct), $R = [<\alpha,\omega>]$, and Pn $= [\alpha]$, $n \geq 0$. Because of the assignment condition Pn, J is true in α. However, because of the asymmetric quality of the model (as depicted in the relation condition R), there are no alternative worlds of ω,[15] and thus $\Diamond J$ is false in ω. Consequently, $\Box \Diamond J$ is false in α since, as I assumed earlier, ω can be reached from α. As a result, the example of the schema is false in α, and this means that the schema itself is invalid. In this case, then, the schema's vision of necessarily possible success following failure does not obtain—a result that contradicts the assumption that success is possible after failure. Such contradiction of the assumption constitutes grounds for rejecting it under conditions of the second hypothesis. That hypothesis, remember, claims that if both constitutive and enabling rules are under attack, success is impossible after failure, which is precisely what we have just found. Thus, the second hypothesis, too, appears justified.

Let us finally consider the last hypothesis. I will assume, as before, that a group whose world has been disrupted by economic sanctions can reconstitute its world successfully. The question then becomes whether the conditions associated with disruption of domestic groups' worlds are incompatible with that assumption. Conversely, it is also important to know if the assumption is consistent with disruption restricted primarily to foreign groups' worlds. I will begin with an examination of the latter case and then look at the former.

If a threat came primarily from attacks on the rules of a regime's foreign base, then the immediate source of those attacks would probably lie outside the country. (An example here would be U.S. sanctions against the Soviet Union to punish martial law in Poland.) In that case, it would be almost impossible for the regime to prevent future disruptions even if it were to succeed (per assumption) in countering the first wave of problems. Thus, the world of failure would be as reachable from the world of success as I have assumed that the latter is from the former. Here we have our old friend the symmetric standard model which, as demonstrated above, has logical implications concordant with the assumption of success being possible after failure. What that means, of course, is that if economic sanctions affect primarily a regime's foreign political base, they are not likely to be very effective since the regime can indeed pull itself back together after an initial failure.

As one might expect, the story is different for domestic political bases. If attacks disrupt primarily the domestic elements of a regime's political base, the immediate source of those attacks would likely be internal and thus open to strong and direct counter-measures by the regime. This is true even though the origin may be external. For example, U.S. economic pressure on the Allende regime in Chile contributed to the significant erosion of middle–class living standards. The resulting disaffection of this group was manifested quite graphically, and the ensuing "chaos" seriously weakened the hand of the constitutionalist segments of the armed forces. Assuming for the sake of argument that the regime's counter-measures were effective, they would likely have succeeded by eliminating as important political actors those internal groups that served as the immediate sources of attack on the regime's domestic base. One should also keep in mind that crackdowns of this sort would be likely to result in "lessons" being learned about keeping a watchful eye on other potentially disruptive groupings. Consequently, if elements of a regime's domestic base were to pull themselves back together after undergoing disintegrative attacks, they would not be likely to face serious threats for quite some time to come. Hence, although I have assumed that success is possible after failure, the reverse would not be true. In modal logic terms, this means an asymmetric standard model which, it will be recalled, logically implies that success is not a necessary possibility after failure. That conclusion contradicts the assumption of success being possible after failure and warrants the assumption's rejection. What we have, then, is the finding that when economic sanctions lead to the disintegration of a regime's domestic political base, recovery is for all practical purposes impossible. When this observation is coupled with the demonstrated ineffectiveness of attacks focused on a regime's foreign political base (see above), the third hypothesis appears fairly well justified.

To sum up, the three hypotheses of the model appear reasonable on both heuristic and more rigorous criteria. The proof of the pudding is in the eating, though, and for this reason, I turn now to an empirical investigation of the model.

EVIDENCE AND ILLUSTRATIONS

I will focus my examination on three countries: Iran, Nicaragua, and Cuba.[16] In the first two cases, I will concentrate on the prerevolutionary regimes; in the last, I will examine the first few years after the fall of Batista. In all three countries, of course, the regimes (at least at one point) had a base of support spread across several different groups, both at home and abroad. (This is not to deny that the bases differed both in identity and scope.) For simplicity's sake, since this is only an illustration, I will focus on just one element in each regime's base. A comprehensive study, of course, would deal with all vital elements and their interaction. Finally, although my primary emphasis is on economic sanctions, I will also deal with other types of political threats; for the cases I am dealing with, information pertaining solely to sanctions is somewhat scarce.

Background

Before proceeding to a schematic analysis of each case, I will begin with a more discursive look. Consider first the "central" element in the Shah's political base: the armed forces (Abrahamian 1982, p. 435). The officer corps were of "relatively unprivileged background" (Halliday 1979, p. 73)—clerks, farmers, etc.—and thus had an incentive to try and enrich themselves. Lower ranks were filled to a great extent by conscription: illiterate peasants made up a large part of this group. The military's primary task was to safeguard the nation, defined operationally as the dynasty. Since the Shah's father had come to power via the military, he impressed on his son the importance of keeping tight control over the armed forces. Consequently, the Shah intervened actively in military affairs, repeatedly shuffling officers around so that they developed the ethos of being a technical tool.

It was difficult to reconcile dynasty protection—an inherently political task—with an ideal of professionalism and technology. The Shah recognized the strains resulting from this conflict and tacitly cut a deal with the officers. He would provide them with advanced weapons and training (this satisfied his own technological and expansionist urges), thus helping them to be technical and professional; simultaneously, the more favored officers would receive

sinecures or other posts that were licenses to steal. This latter benefit would, of course, only come to those who served the monarch
loyally: a payoff for protecting the dynasty. However, if too many
soldiers were corrupt on a large scale, popular resentment would
rise. This potential problem necessitated restricting opportunities
for graft, and that could most easily be done by making literacy a
criterion for large-scale corruption. Thus, a preference emerged for
illiterate peasants among the lower ranks, and they gained through
the social mobility the army provided. For both officers and rank
and file, then, an ideology of professional service to the Shah existed, an ideology that tied together social background, social environment, and goals and interests.

This halcyon state of affairs did not last forever. When pro-
longed popular unrest began, the privates and NCOs, being so close
to the "masses" in the urban slums (newly arrived from the countryside), began to waver in their repressive zeal. Similarly, to the extent
the officers were lured by avariciousness for either weapons or
money, they began to see a long dry spell ahead, as the urban protests and oil field strikes dried up export revenues, threatened lower
defense budgets, and made graft more difficult. Additionally, certain high-ranking officers had become so rich from years of thievery
that they were able to leave the country and settle into comfortable
exile abroad. Thus, as the protests of 1978 spread, the military
found it increasingly difficult to achieve its goals by going down the
line with the Shah. By the end of the year, army units began to
disintegrate.

As the process unfolded, it soon appeared that there was no way
for the military to put things together again. The war against the
protesters could not be won by force, since the lower ranks either
refused to fire against the public or in some cases actually turned on
their officers. This meant that the only solution short of capitulation
was negotiation with the protesters, but that policy would have almost surely had as one outcome an enforced prohibition on officer
corruption *and* a drastically reduced weapons budget. Consequently, once the situation deteriorated for the army, no alternative
was perceived to be available that would have restored its privileges. The road led from power to weakness but not back again.
Since a strong and loyal military was the backbone of the Shah's
support, the army's dilemma meant that no possible world existed in

which he could maintain himself in power. The Shah therefore could not avoid the collapse of his regime: whatever he did, he would end up losing the throne.

The situation in Nicaragua was similar in important respects. The National Guard (clearly the most vital element in Somoza's political base) was smaller than its Iranian counterpart; there was no conscription; and sophisticated military equipment was unavailable. But the soldiers—officers and enlisted men—came from the same type of social backgrounds as their Iranian counterparts; they had the same institutional role, goals, and interests (e.g., corruption); and their ideologies operated in much the same way (as guardians, rather than professionals—see below). The National Guard did face somewhat different problems than the Iranian Army. For one, its opponent was armed and, since the peasants were all volunteers, problems of queasiness in regard to firing on a civilian population were not present. But on the other hand, it lacked its customary near-monopoly on violence, since the Sandinistas had sparked large numbers of people to acquire arms (albeit rudimentary ones). As the conflict wore on, the Guard found itself with shortages of ammunition and spare parts (in part, this was because of U.S. pressure in the last few months of the fighting),[17] a problem exacerbated by economic problems (sabotage; drying up of foreign credit) that led to severe foreign exchange shortages. Thus, the enlisted men were facing growing enemy forces with insufficient supplies and insufficient manpower. And, as in Iran, when the National Guard's situation began falling apart, there was no way to put it back together. Like the Shah, Somoza had no alternative to losing power. (Indeed, since Somoza relied on the National Guard even more heavily than the Shah relied on the army, one might say that he was "more doomed.")

Finally, consider the role of lower class groups (e.g., factory workers and slum dwellers) in postrevolutionary Cuba. After its assumption of power in 1959, the Castro regime faced (and still faces) extensive United States threats. The best known of these, of course, are the Bay of Pigs invasion and various C.I.A. and Mafia assassination plots against Castro, but there were a number of sabotage attempts against economic and other installations as part of Operation Mongoose. (In addition, the United States instituted a trade embargo, along with a number of overt forms of economic pressure.) These activities were rebuffed by revolutionary militia (often comprised of factory members protecting their workplace), local armed committees (such as the Committees for the Defense of the Revolution), and other forms of armed action.

The interesting thing about this type of "revolutionary defense" is that it sprang up largely spontaneously (especially in the early 1960s) in reaction to threatened or actual sabotage. By all accounts, workers showed considerable enthusiasm since it was *their* factories and neighborhoods being saved. As such, citizen spontaneity was a successful organizational response to danger or actual (if temporary) defeat. This kind of vigilance in the first decade after 1959 served as an important basis of the regime's survival in the face of external aggression. Thus (as with other issues) the regime could fail for a time when confronted with economic sabotage and yet still have the possibility (often realized) of later (and ultimate) success. In other words, the Castro regime could go from success to failure and back again.

A Closer Look

With the background information sketched above, we are now in a position to analyze the three cases according to the schema set out in the model. Let us begin with the relevant constitutive and enabling rules. The general convention I will follow in the presentation of these rules is to employ two syntactical formulas. For constitutive rules, I will write sentences of the form, "In order to deal with . . . , do . . . ." This formulation nicely highlights the social relational quality of constitutive rules and at the same time points to their defining nature. For enabling rules, I will write sentences of the form, "We are . . . trying to . . . by doing . . . ." This formulation encompasses all of the various tasks that enabling rules comprehend, particularly their quality of distinguishing some groups from others.

In Iran before the revolution, army officers' (and officers in other services as well) social relations were characterized by the following constitutive rules:

- To deal with superiors (other officers, the Shah), act with obedience and near–servility.

- To deal with other army personnel, command.
- To deal with outsiders, be corrupt and repressive.

For all of the groups mentioned, the constitutive rule governing their relations with army officers was the mirror image of that specified above (e.g., the Shah commanded officers; merchants acquiesced in corruption with the army, etc.) It is important to realize that these rules really did constitute social relations. For example, if there was a group toward whom army officers were neither corrupt nor repressive, then they could not have been dealing with outsiders.

Army officers' ideology was as follows. Officers are professionals whose job it is to maintain public safety against open threats; to do this, they

- need the right tools (i.e., weapons) to do their work; and
- deserve monetary rewards (e.g., payoffs) as a condition of their work.

(Notice that the ideology specifies maintenance of public safety against *open* threats; it was SAVAK'S job to protect against covert ones.) This ideology clearly fit the constitutive rules quite nicely. It accounted for corruption (a reward for a tough job) and servility (professionals don't care about surface appearances); it had internal coherence (notice the parallelism of need and desert); and it provided simultaneously a way of looking at the world and a method of self–understanding.

The Iranian case fits the model's hypotheses quite nicely. Mass demonstrations led draftees to waver in their duties, a violation of the mirror image of the second constitutive rule. Oil worker strikes and bazaari militancy cut into opportunities for corruption, thereby attacking the third constitutive rule. Continued waves of demonstrations, 40 days apart, slowly began to ritualize (without, of course, reducing the brutalization of) the use of repression; this weakened further the third constitutive rule. As a result of the strikes (not only in the oil fields, but also among civil servants), monetary flows were seriously reduced, thereby disrupting the second enabling rule (and, foreseeably, the first). A combination of peaceful demonstrations (peaceful, that is, on the demonstrators' side) and lightning guerrilla raids on military posts led to a growing realization on the part of many officers that their weapons—fighter planes, howitzers, and so forth—were for the most part inappropriate (and certainly inadequate) for combating the threats they currently faced. This meant that the tools the army had were not what they needed, which was a violation of the first enabling rule. Thus, both the constitutive rules and the ideology of army officers were attacked by the protests against the Shah. This tends to substantiate the model's second hypothesis. In addition, the army was clearly an element of the Shah's domestic base, and this lends partial support to the third hypothesis.

In Nicaragua, the constitutive rules pertaining to National Guard officers were basically the same as in Iran. The ideology, though, was different in important respects. Consider the following. National Guard officers are guardians whose job it is to maintain the Somoza family in power against all threats; to do this, they

- need to have a near–monopoly of violence in Nicaragua; and
- deserve monetary rewards (i.e., payoffs) as a condition of their work.

As with the Iranian case, National Guard ideology fit their enabling rules. The smallness of the National Guard compared with the Iranian army, and their even more intimate relation with Somoza than the army had with the Shah, account for the guardian motif in the ideology. This element of the enabling rules was quite compatible with the need to have a near–monopoly of violence, since guardianship presupposes a more comprehensive view of role (for example, not being restricted merely to open threats) than the maintenance of safety. If one is to prevent threats from even surfacing, there needs to be a great disproportion between one's available force and that of any opponent (particularly if, as an elite guardian, one does not have many companions in arms). Still, even though the Guard officers' ideology was different in this important respect from their Iranian counterparts', they fitted onto the same constitutive rules because the core element of the ideology's first element—the notion of a hierarchy of violence—was the same.

In Nicaragua, as in Iran, both the constitutive rules and ideology of the Guard officers came under attack. As the fighting continued, more and more poorly–trained peasants were shanghaied into the Guard, and the officers found it impossible to command them to perform all but the most rudimentary activities. This violated the second constitutive rule. The strikes and opposition of businessmen made corruption far less rewarding, thus disrupting part of the third constitutive rule. The widespread and, after a time, coordinated urban revolts spread the Guard thin and weakened somewhat the degree to which they could be repressive toward all opposition simultaneously (again, this is not to deny the terrible violence that the Guard perpetrated), thus cutting further into the third constitutive rule. Strikes and economic sabotage seriously attacked the second enabling rule. Finally and most importantly, the continued and broad–based armed opposition shown by the people absolutely destroyed the first element of the Guard's ideology: never again would the Guard enjoy a near–monopoly of violence. Serious fighting could conceivably go on for years to come—that, and not the Guard's unquestioned superiority in most tactical engagements, was the real lesson of the renewed fighting in the spring of 1979 (following savage repression in the fall of 1978). Thus, as with Iran, both the second hypothesis and a portion of the third appear to be substantiated.

Let us finally consider Cuba. Lower classes' relations with the regime were constituted by the following rules:

- In order to deal with the regime, lower classes provided support in the form of militias and revolutionary defense committees.
- In order to deal with lower classes, the regime provided economic assistance (including jobs) and a sense of national dignity.
- In order to deal with other groups in (and out of) society, both lower classes and the regime acted in a wary or oppositional fashion.

Lower class ideology was of the following sort. Lower classes are defenders of the revolution whose job it is to safeguard the revolution's achievements against threats; to do this, they

- value spontaneity to guard against sabotage or rebuild sabotaged facilities; and

- have an ethos of sacrifice if needed to help assure the long–term success of the revolution.

Clearly, this ideology fit the constitutive rules. Spontaneous safeguarding activity was of great help to an embattled regime, both in and of itself and against any opponents. Economic assistance was most easily distributed through organizations. Dignity made sacrifices worth bearing. And, as with the other countries, both sets of rules were internally coherent. The constitutive relations between regime and lower classes, for instance, were ones of reciprocity and complementarity. Sacrifice and rebuilding went hand in hand.

With these rules in mind, we can understand better just why United States' anti–Castro activities were unsuccessful. C.I.A.–sponsored sabotage against economic and other installations certainly succeeded in reducing severely the economic benefits the regime could bestow on its supporters. Although such travails were made somewhat more palatable by the ethos of sacrifice, there was no denying that for groups far down on the economic ladder (e.g., landless laborers who came close to starving in the "dead time" between harvests), a squeeze on benefits was quite painful and not altogether understandable.[18] However, the first enabling rule set people to work rebuilding, which carried with it the promise of eventual prosperity. And, to the extent that the first enabling rule involved foregoing other economic benefits through long hours of guard work or rebuilding, the ideology of sacrifice served as justification. Thus, the Cuba case is an example of the way in which ideology can be used to reinstitute previously disrupted constitutive rules (in this case, the second one). Here, then, is an example in accord with the model's first hypothesis.

Trade sanctions posed a problem different from economic sabotage. No number of armed patrols or Sunday working days could bring U.S. equipment, technology, or spare parts into Cuba. Unquestionably, the embargo hurt. Yet, the harm suffered was not fatal. In part, this was because the Soviet Union picked up some of the slack, providing the Cubans with large quantities of economic aid. In part, it was because the Castro regime used United States hostility and subversion as a justification for further expropriations and redistribution of income from wealthier to poorer groups. The burden that remained was one that could be borne by the lower classes as a reasonable revolutionary sacrifice. Trade sanctions, then, proved to be ineffective because they disrupted the regime's foreign political base (the Soviets) and its political opponents (the wealthy) far more (at least at first) than its domestic base. This is additional partial support for the model's third hypothesis; in combination with the cases of Iran and Nicaragua, it provides a reasonably complete justification of the hypothesis. Overall, then, the three cases appear to support each of the model's hypotheses.

Historical Lessons and Counterfactual Deductions

The utility of the model put forward in this chapter is not restricted to a straightforward rereading of the recent history in Iran, Nicaragua, and Cuba. We can also use the model to deduce some more pointed conclusions about economic and other sorts of sanctions—both real and conceivable.

One conclusion concerns the finding that attacks on a regime's political base are effective insofar as they affect domestic rather than foreign elements of that base. Thus in Iran, for example, we would not expect that Carter's economic sanctions would have had much effect on the Islamic Republican Party (IRP) regime. Even if the sanctions had been rigorously applied with no opportunity for circumvention (cf. Shehadi 1981), they would at first have hurt primarily industrialists, factory workers, and professionals, who were not part of the IRP domestic base (Clawson 1981). Only after several years would the sanctions have bit into reserves far enough to force the IRP to begin hurting its base. Thus, whatever led the IRP to release the U.S. hostages, it was not economic sanctions.

Similar conclusions attend Reagan's economic and military warfare against the Sandinista regime in Nicaragua. The United States has drastically reduced economic aid (only the private sector continues as a recipient), lobbied with some success against foreign loans, and cut down on certain types of trade. In addition, of course, the C.I.A. is actively working with former National Guardsmen and disaffected Miskito Indians to harass (and perhaps, depending on the news source, overthrow) the regime. The first of these strategies affects primarily the middle class, small traders, and factory workers—none of whom are vital elements of the regime's political base.[19] The second strategy relies on groups who have at most miniscule proportions of the population inside the country who would back them in the event of intense fighting. As a result, the exile armies are restricted to rape, pillage, and looting: gruesome and repulsive activities that attract no one to their side. As in Iran, sanctions and other threats simply cannot succeed as long as they fail to affect the regime's domestic political base. Indeed, in both countries, the regimes control the state sufficiently so that they can channel the negative effects of sanctions toward their enemies and away from their base.

Finally, consider Cuba. U.S. policy toward what it considers Cuban "imperialism" (sending troops to Angola and Ethiopia) has proceeded by attempting to "punish" the Soviet Union. (I will leave aside the logic of punishing an adversary by scaring one's allies.) Regardless of whether the Soviet's leaders really have begun to feel contrite, it is patently obvious that the Soviet Union can only influence the Cubans by persuasion, inducement, or threats. The first of these requires working through the regime, whereas the latter involve some sticks or carrots applied or extended to the regime's political base. Since that base appears strongly loyal to the regime (see the enabling rules listed above), the possibility of proceeding other than by persuasion appears slight. Again, lack of direct United States access to the Cubans' domestic political base strongly reduces whatever threat U.S. policy (short of an invasion) might pose to the Castro regime.

A second conclusion from the model concerns the finding that attacks on a regime's political base must include disruption of the base's constitutive rules in order to pose an extreme political threat to the regime. That finding sheds some light on Kirkpatrick's charge that human rights policies pushed by the Carter Administration weakened the Shah in Iran and led to his downfall (Kirkpatrick 1982). To put it mildly, this claim is erroneous. While it is indisputable that easing press restrictions helped lead to fiercer verbal attacks on the Shah, one would be hard-pressed to say that those verbal attacks helped provoke the large demonstrations or the oilfield strikes that eventually toppled him. Even during the harshest censorship by SAVAK, mullahs were free to preach inflammatory sermons in their mosques, and that is what sparked the massive demonstrations. As for the strikes, a critical factor in their genesis was the role of leftist organizations, most of which remained banned until the day of the Shah's departure. Human rights qualms did not hold back the armed forces from vicious and brutal repression nor did U.S.-inspired concern over freedom of speech finally lead recruits to refuse to obey orders to shoot their compatriots. The armed forces disintegrated because their constitutive rules were disrupted (along with their ideology), a condition that cannot be pinned on Jimmy Carter, Amnesty International, or an insufficiently tough Shah.

Kirkpatrick has also claimed that human rights pressure from Washington led Somoza to grant too much freedom to his opponents in Nicaragua, with disastrous results for his tenure in office. This claim, too, is primarily fiction. To be sure, when Somoza lifted the state of siege in 1977, organizing against the regime could be done more overtly and *La Prensa* could thunder a bit more loudly. But organizing had occurred clandestinely for several years on a widespread basis—including the distribution of arms—and *La Prensa* had not exactly been silent before. None of this "liberalization" affected the repressive zeal of the National Guard in any way. As for the Sandinistas, the *Tercerista* (insurrectional) faction had been planning attacks for some time and, by all accounts, their first move (assault in several places the same day in October, 1977) had nothing to do with the lifting of the state of siege (Black 1981, chapter 7). That move, along with the assassination of Pedro Joaquin Chamorro, was what sparked the Monimbo fighting in February, 1978, and the example of that fighting, along with subsequent National Guard repression, unleashed a flood of recruits for the subsequent uprising in September. Human rights pressure from Washington did not to any significant degree weaken the National Guard's constitutive rules; popular pressure, arising from years of dictatorship and discontent, did.

Finally, consider the case of Cuba. A virulent opponent of the Castro regime might say that the discussion in the previous section merely points to the need for a far more widespread sabotage campaign. In that way, the argument might go, the damage from sabotage might have been so great that rebuilding would have been impossible. As with Kirkpatrick's arguments, this kind of thinking falls into the realm of fantasy. For in order to conduct a massive sabotage campaign of the sort envisioned, the C.I.A. would have had to infiltrate and disrupt the various spontaneous popular organizations in which lower classes were organized. Needless to say, such an effort would have been practically impossible: how does one infiltrate a spontaneous organization that did not exist the day before? Of course, *if* this sort of infiltration could have been accomplished successfully, then a serious blow would have been struck at several constitutive rules (those pertaining to support and the receipt of assistance) and, potentially, at the ideology as well (spontaneous organization might have become suspect after a while). Thus, the Cuban example points up the lesson drawn from Nicaragua and Iran: that only if constitutive rules are disrupted can a regime's base, and hence the regime, be in serious danger.

Consider last a third conclusion that could be drawn from the findings in the previous sections: in order for political threats to be extreme, they must disrupt the ideology of a regime's base. We have seen that in Iran, U.S. human rights policy was not the Shah's undoing. If, however, Carter had wished to depose the Shah, he could have done so fairly readily by halting arms shipments. A move of that sort would have attacked army officers' ideology, while at the same time giving them less reason to obey the Shah. In terms of political impact on the army, only drastic policies (such as an arms embargo) with effects functionally equivalent to oil strikes could have resulted in disintegration. Similar conclusions hold in Nicaragua. (Of course, to entertain such thoughts is to realize just how supportive the United States was of Somoza and the Shah—a fact often forgotten amid fulminations about selling our friends down the drain, and so forth.) U.S. policy simply did not disrupt the ideology of its clients' political base.

By the same token, only measures of an extreme sort would have succeeded in weakening the Castro regime. On the one hand, a massive invasion by United States troops probably would have succeeded in deposing Castro—although it would have meant a guerrilla war for years to come. On the other hand, if the United States had offered massive economic aid (say for "reconstruction"), it could have weakened the enabling rules of sacrifice and organization against the Yanqui menace. Severe disruption of the ideology would have resulted (who, after all, would be the enemy?) and this might well have forced a change in constitutive rules. Instead of becoming opponents of the regime, bourgeois elements might have been seen as valuable "moderate" links to U.S. largesse and been given a place in the government. Certainly this would have changed the regime's character—quite possibly in a way far more drastic than envisaged by the White House. Of course, such a scenario is speculative and unrecoverable but, like the might–have–beens explored for Nicaragua and Iran, it does point to the importance of political threats involving attacks on the ideology of a regime's base (and just how far from that U.S. policy actually was).

Thus, the model appears useful in understanding not only why certain regimes fell and others survived (and the relation of those events to economic sanctions), but also why certain events *failed* to happen, and what might have resulted if other events *had* occurred. If these findings are combined with the internal coherence of the model, it appears that the model has some claim to be correct.

CAVEATS AND CONCLUSIONS

In spite of its virtues, the model is still too sketchy to be of use for understanding all the complexities of economic sanctions and political threats. Among other things, one would have to include the other elements of a regime's political base along with the corresponding elements of opposition forces. Each of these would have a set of constitutive rules and ideology that would have to be elucidated. Then the interaction of different elements would have to be modeled, along with the changes in various rules over time. Often, groups quite consciously alter their ideology to be consistent, or to adapt to changing constitutive rules. A more complete model would have to take into account those strategic moves, and that would necessitate careful attention to subtle differences in ideology. In a sense, this chapter merely opens the gate to a vast landscape of possibilities.

Equally interesting, though, are the ramifications of this type of research design for the pure study of economic sanctions. What they point to, I think, is the importance of both ideologies and constitutive rules in explaining the success or failure of various sanction campaigns. Economic security is not simply a function of some unspecified "flexibility" or psychological rallying; it is a result in large part to people's feelings that the future holds hope for *them* to protect *their* own goals and interests. Those feelings, in turn, are often related to the breadth and ubiquity of the threat posed by sanctions.

If we are to believe Galtung, white Rhodesians focused on Harold Wilson as archvillain after the Unilateral Declaration of Independence. This was certainly much easier to do then than in the latter part of the 1970s when towns and farms across the country were under attack. Indeed, it may be this degree of ubiquity—attacks from large numbers of forces within the country—that made the C.I.A.'s campaign against Allende so effective.

Finally, this perspective clearly points to the importance of combining the study of external sanctions and internal activities. Subversion has been linked to sanctions in a number of covert operations over the years; revolutions are habitually the target of foreign intervention aimed at strangling them. To persist at this late date in separating economic sanctions from the gamut of other punitive activities carried out in international relations is to be not only scholarly insensitive, but politically naive and morally obtuse.

NOTES

1. My arguments here are not based on hindsight; the *fact* that the Rhodesian economy finally collapsed under the strain of the war does not in and of itself prove Galtung or Porter wrong as far as *external* sanctions go. (Although note the political naiveté of Galtung's contention that "territorial integrity makes [internal sanctions] impossible unless they are combined with a military presence" [1967, p. 383].) Rather, my points have to do with the *logic* of the two perspectives.

2. I here pass over the logical difficulties in the blithe assertion of equivalence between aggregated individual utilities and communal utility.

3. As one might expect, this rule changed for a while after the advent of the Islamic Republic, which outlawed interest on loans (Beck 1981, p. 115). Recent evidence, though, indicates that the moneylenders have managed, in part, to reestablish their old relationship with the nomads because of the government's failure to provide a continuing source of credit for the Qashqa'i (Clawson 1981).

4. Searle distinguishes between constitutive rules and regulative rules, with the latter governing behavior in a "don't do that" sense. In terms of the concepts laid out in this chapter, regulative rules are a subset of enabling rules, concerned with the relation between other constitutive and other enabling rules. I will discuss this relation at greater length in the next section.

5. This is understandable given that enabling rules help make sense of constitutive rules. People who are placed by constitutive rules in a determinate position vis-à-vis others will tend to be socialized in a certain way or to prefer certain things, and this leads them to enabling rules that reflect or idealize that socialization or those preferences. Indoctrination, of course, also plays a role.

6. See Ropp (1972); and Ropp and Pearson (1974) for evidence on the attitudes. The evidence on *Novedades* comes from my own research.

7. This concept of ideology is drawn from the classic discussion in Marx and Engels's *The German Ideology*, although it differs from their usage in important respects. In particular, I do not claim that ideology is merely a reflection of existing power relations, even though justification and mystification are among its functions. Furthermore, as I will discuss below, changes in ideology can and do lead to changes in constitutive relations; this notion is, to put it charitably, underemphasized in Marxist theory. Then, too, my anchoring of ideology within a conceptual framework based on constitutive and enabling rules finds no explicit echo in classic Marxist writing.

8. Although rules are "in people's heads" they have no existence apart from the actions by which they are carried out and given meaning.

9. The wording of this sequence is taken from Professor Moriarty's complaint to Sherlock Holmes in "The Final Problem."

10. Contrast this with the vaunted Rapid Deployment Force, whose principal effect appears to have been the spurring of Marine Corps to invest in desert camouflage.

11. See von Wright (1974, part 1) and Elster (1978) for good conceptual introductions to the ideas underlying modal logic.

12. The argument will be made with a class of models possessing intuitively reasonable characteristics; they are known as Kripke models. The terminology and proofs are drawn from Chellas (1980, chapter 3).

13. This is because there is only deep structure for any given set of rules. See Munkres (1975, chapter 8) for a mathematical proof on this point concerning the fundamental group of a topological space.

14. Indeed, the argument is a *proof* of the hypothesis. I am wary of using this term, though, because it is strictly applicable only to a formal system. The model I have advanced does not fall into that category, since there are implicit measurement rules (e.g., the semantic link between temporary failure and necessarily possible success) as well as purely formal elements. (In passing, it should be noted that most supposedly formal systems in social science make use of such semantic suppositions and are, therefore, properly speaking, not amenable to logical demonstration or disproof. Cf. Cicourel [1964].)

15. In fact, there could be an alternative world of ω—say some novel world of failure—but, as indicated above, this would require a totally new strategy of attack and therefore can be de facto ruled out for all but time periods so lengthy as to be politically irrelevant.

16. Material for this section comes from a larger study on U.S. foreign policy and revolutions in Third World countries. Among studies particularly useful in this section were Zonis (1971); Halliday (1979); Keddie (1981); Abrahamian (1982); Millett (1977); Bendana (1978); Lopez C. et al. (1980); Somoza (1980); Black (1981); Bray and Harding (1974); Halperin et al. (1976); Thomas (1977); and Petras (1981).

17. It is difficult to find out just how severe the shortages were. In his apologia, Somoza claims that they were one of the two principal reasons for his downfall (1980, chapter 16), along with Carter's "treachery." In a notably sympathetic ac-

count of the revolution, Black also makes mention of arms shortages (1981, pp. 160, 178–79). However, the National Guard was receiving extensive deliveries of *Israeli* ammunition and other weapons as late as May of 1979, only two months before the end of the fighting, and the evidence is that the shortages were not as important in the Guard's defeat as the widespread and continuing armed opposition of the populace.

18. Cf. Oscar Lewis's findings along these lines (1977), particularly those relating to the potential for disaffection on the part of destitute groups. Not surprisingly, this evidence hastened Lewis's involuntary departure from Cuba.

19. The core elements of the base are small peasants, urban slumdwellers, and certain student groups. Landless laborers and factory workers are regime allies but are not part of the base. Other groups in Nicaragua are important for economic or other reasons, but are neither base elements nor allies of the Sandinistas.

BIBLIOGRAPHY

Abrahamian, Ervand. 1982. *Iran Between Two Revolutions*. Princeton: Princeton University Press.

Beck, Lois. 1981. "Economic Transformations Among Qashqa'i Nomads, 1962–1978." In *Modern Iran*, edited by Michael E. Bonine and Nikki R. Keddie. Albany: State University of New York Press.

Bendana, Alejandro. 1978. "Crisis in Nicaragua," *NACLA Report on the Americas*, Nov.–Dec.:2–42.

Bennett, James P. and Hayward R. Alker, Jr. 1977. "When National Security Policies Bred Collective Insecurity: The War of the Pacific in a World Politics Simulation." In *Problems of World Modeling*, edited by Karl W. Deutsch et al. Cambridge, Ma.: Ballinger.

Bill, James A. 1972. *The Politics of Iran*. Columbus, Oh: Charles E. Merrill.

Black, George, 1981. *Triumph of the People*. London: Zed Press.

Bray, Donald W. and Timothy F. Harding. 1974. "Cuba." In *Latin America: The Struggle with Dependency and Beyond*, edited by Ronald H. Chilcote and Joel C. Edelstein. New York: John Wiley & Sons.

Chellas, Brian F. 1980. *Modal Logic: An Introduction*. Cambridge: Cambridge University Press.

Cicourel, Aaron. 1964. *Method and Measurement in Sociology.* New York: Free Press.

Clawson, Patrick. 1981. "Iran's Economy: Between Crisis and Collapse," *MERIP Reports* 98 (July–Aug.):11–15.

Elster, Jon. 1978. *Logic and Society.* Chichester: John Wiley & Sons.

Galtung, Johan. 1967. "On the Effects of International Economic Sanctions, with Examples from the Case of Rhodesia," *World Politics* 9(3).

Halliday, Fred. 1979. *Iran: Dictatorship and Development.* Harmondsworth, U.K.: Penguin.

Halperin, Morton H. et al. 1976. *The Lawless State: The Crimes of the U.S. Intelligence Agencies.* Harmondsworth, U.K.: Penguin.

Keddie, Nikki R. 1981. *Roots of Revolution: An Interpretive History of Modern Iran.* New Haven: Yale University Press.

Kirkpatrick, Jeane. 1982. *Dictatorships and Double Standards.* New York: Simon and Schuster.

Lewis, Oscar. 1977. *Living the Revolution: An Oral History of Contemporary Cuba.* Urbana: University of Illinois Press.

Lopez C., Julio et al. 1980. *La Caida del Somocismo y la lucha Sandinista en Nicaragua.* Ciudad Universitaria Rodrigo Facio, Costa Rica: Editorial Universitaria Centroamericana.

Millett, Richard. 1977. *Guardians of the Dynasty: A History of the U.S. Created Guardia Nacional de Nicaragua and the Somoza Family.* Maryknoll, N.Y.: Orbis Books.

Munkres, James R. 1975. *Topology: A First Course.* Englewood Cliffs, N.J.: Prentice–Hall.

Petras, James F. 1981. "The Working Class and the Cuban Revolution." In *Class, State and Power in the Third World.* Montclair, N.J.: Allanheld, Osmun.

Porter, Richard C. 1978. "Economic Sanctions: The Theory and the Evidence from Rhodesia," *Journal of Peace Science* 3(2):93–110.

Ropp, Steve C. 1972. "Goal Orientations of Nicaraguan Cadets," *Journal of Comparative Administration* 4 (May).

Ropp, Steve C. and Neale J. Pearson. 1974. "Attitudes of Honduran and Nicaraguan Junior Officers Toward the Role of the Military in Latin America." Paper presented to the Annual Meeting of the Southwest Political Science Association, March.

Searle, John R. 1969. *Speech Acts*. Cambridge: Cambridge University Press.

Shehadi, Philip. 1981. "Economic Sanctions and Iranian Trade," *MERIP Reports* 98 (July–Aug.):15–16.

Somoza, Anastasio. 1980. *Nicaragua Betrayed*. Boston: Western Islands.

Sylvan, David J. 1981. "Structural Analysis of State Policy. I: Static Connection." Paper presented to the International Studies Association, Philadelphia, March 18–21.

Thomas, Hugh. 1977. *The Cuban Revolution*. New York: Harper & Row.

von Wright, George Henrik. 1974. *Causality and Determinism*. New York: Columbia University Press.

Zonis, Marvin. 1971. *The Political Elite of Iran*. Princeton: Princeton University Press.

INDEX

ABOUT THE EDITORS AND CONTRIBUTORS

MIROSLAV NINCIC

Miroslav Nincic is Associate Professor of Politics at New York University. At the time this volume was edited, he taught at The University of Michigan where he was also Co-Director of the Office of International Peace and Security Research. He is author of *The Arms Race: The Political Economy of Military Growth* (1982) as well as of numerous articles.

PETER WALLENSTEEN

Peter Wallensteen is Associate Professor of Peace and Conflict Research and Director of the Department of Peace and Conflict Research at Uppsala University in Sweden. He has also been Associate Professor of Political Science at The University of Michigan. Professor Wallensteen is author of *Ekonomiska Sanktoner* (1971), *Structure and War: On International Relations 1920–1968* (1973), as well as of numerous articles.

DAVID A. DEESE: Associate Professor of Political Science, Boston College.

JOHAN GALTUNG: Professor, Institut Universitaire d'Etudes du Développement, Geneva.

DAVID F. GORDON: Assistant Professor of International Relations, Michigan State University; Assistant Research Scientist, Center for Research on Economic Development, University of Michigan.

JERROLD D. GREEN: Assistant Professor of Political Science, University of Michigan.

ROBERT L. PAARLBERG: Assistant Professor of Political Science, Wellesley College.

DAVID J. SYLVAN: Assistant Professor of Political Science, Syracuse University.